All you need to know about
Personal Computers

All you need to know about **Personal Computers**

Geoff Oakshott

Future Business Books
Future Publishing Limited
Beauford Court
30 Monmouth Street
Bath BA1 2BW

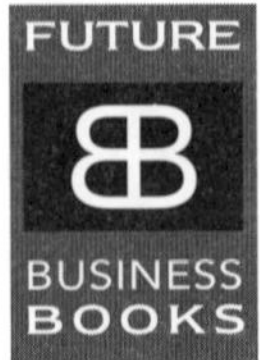

Future Business Books
Future Publishing Limited
Beauford Court
30 Monmouth Street
Bath BA1 2BW

ISBN 1 85870 055 8

British Library Cataloguing in Publication Data

A CIP catalogue record for this book is available from the British Library

Books Editor Ian Jones

Cover Design by M4 Marketing Communications Ltd, Newbury, Berkshire
Design and layout by The Cool Type Foundry, Ashburton, Devon
Printed in Great Britain by Redwood Books, Trowbridge, Wiltshire

About the author

Geoff Oakshott has always enjoyed explaining how things work. He started his writing career with articles on such diverse subjects as inertial navigation, automatic control, aeronautical and marine autopilots. This was long before the PC era, though one 'story' was the magnetic storage drum, forerunner of today's hard disk.

Geoff worked in Fleet Street as a copywriter before starting his own industrial advertising agency. He earned his living from graphic design for many years, doing it the hard way with scalpel and rubber solution. He entered the world of personal computing before the advent of desktop publishing, which changed his life.

He spent a couple of years as Editor of *C Magazine*, but always considered the C language too cryptic for ordinary mortals. Relieved to find that *QuickBASIC* was quite fast enough and gave more immediate results, including the ability to develop a suite of programs to make life simpler for users of numerically controlled machines in real time.

Now settled in Devon, his aim is to continue writing, to keep looking at the world of computing through fresh eyes, to make light of the jargon and generally to de-mystify the fascinating new world that surrounds us.

Acknowledgements

The Author wishes to express his gratitude to the following organisations for their co-operation and support in the preparation of this book:

FDS Graphics, Exeter
Grey Matter Ltd
The Lotus Corporation

Preface
How do we get there, please? xvii

Introduction
Getting into computing xix

It doesn't have to be difficult xxi

Taking it one step at a time xxi
This is for you xxii
The Glossary xxiii
How to use the book xxiii
Key to icons xxiv
All you *need* to know xxvi
All expense spared xxvi

Chapter 1
How do they do it? 1

The elements of a computing machine 3

Memory 3
Programmability 4
What a computer does with letters 4
Computers: thick as two short planks 5
Binary arithmetic 6

Combining the elements 9

Visual display 10
Storing information 10
Programs and data 12

Do you need a computer? 13
Who are you? 14
What is a personal computer? 16
The next step 18

Chapter 2
Hardware 19

What you need 21
Software is the deciding factor 21
The physical side 23
Peripherals 24
The extras you can't do without 24
Peripheral advice 28

Chapter 3
Windows 29

What is *Windows;* what are windows? 31
Looking in, getting on 32
What do you get with *Windows?* 34
File Manager 35
Control Panel 36
Print Manager 38
Clock 38
Write 40
Paintbrush 40

Character map 40
Terminal 41
Calculator 42
Calendar 42
Cardfile 43
Notepad 43
Macro recorder 43

Chapter 4
DOS: the operating system 45

All main services for the computer 47
Introduction to the operating system 47
A selection of **DOS** commands 48
Starting as you mean to go on 65
A little knowledge 65
CONFIG.SYS 66
AUTOEXEC.BAT 66
Batch files 67
Interrupts 70
Excuse me a tick, I'm pressing a key 70
RTFM (read the friendly manual!) 71

Chapter 5
Storing the information 73

Grin and bear it 75

Files and directories ... 75
The root directory ... 79

Chapter 6
Memory ... 81

Computer memory vs human memory ... 83

Thinking space ... 85

Conventional memory ... 85
RAM: Random access memory ... 86

Read-only memory ... 89

Stored information ... 89

How memory is organised ... 89

Taking the 'random' out of random access memory ... 89
Extended memory (**XMS**) ... 90
Expanded memory (**EMS**) ... 91

Chapter 7
The keyboard ... 93

The keys ... 95

Escape key ... 96
Function keys ... 96
Print Screen key ... 97
System Request key ... 97
Scroll Lock ... 98

Pause 98
Break 98
Indicator lights 99
Logical Not / Grave Accent / Bar 99
Circumflex key 100
Asterisk (Star) 100
Underline 101
Backspace (Delete right to left) key 102
Insert key 103
Home key 103
Page Up key 104
Num Lock key 104
Number key pad 105
Tab Key 106
Return (Enter) key 107
Delete key 108
End key 109
Page down key 109
Caps lock key 110
Shift keys 110
Pipe (broken bar) & Backslash key 111
Less Than key 112
Greater Than key 113
Ctrl (Control) keys 113
Alt (Alternative) keys 114
Cursor keys 114

UK, US and other keyboards 115

Getting the right keyboard in *Windows* 116
Getting the right keyboard for **DOS** 117

Using the keyboard for other languages 119

Using characters not on the keyboard 119
The Character Map 121
Writing occasional documents in foreign languages 124
Working mostly in foreign languages 124

Character sets (code pages) 125

Chapter 8
Word processing 129

Jumping into *Windows Write* 131

Beyond the typewriter 132
Selecting text to change 133
Changing the typeface 133
Short-cut keys 136
Saving your work 137
Editing text 139
Undo 144

Adding pictures to *Windows Write* 145

Three ways to import graphics 145
Moving a picture in **Windows Write** 149
Changing picture size in *Write* 150
Changing the look of a whole paragraph 152

Printing from *Windows Write* 156

Setting up the printer 156
Printing the document 161

Features of other word processors 163

Word processing beyond *Write* 163
Your next step in word processing 167

Chapter 9
Databases 169

What is a database? ... 171
Records and fields ... 171
A 'people' database ... 172
A 'things' database ... 172
Storing and retrieving information ... 173
Windows Cardfile ... 173
Records ... 174
Index field ... 174
Using *Cardfile* ... 175
Cardfile's facilities ... 175
Setting up a *Cardfile* ... 177
Extracting information from *Cardfile* ... 182
Using a real database ... 183
Fields ... 183
Queries ... 183
Working with *FoxPro* ... 184
First step to programming in *FoxPro* ... 192
You have done the groundwork ... 194

Chapter 10
Spreadsheets ... 195

What spreadsheets do ... 197
Applications ... 198
Viewing other areas of the worksheet ... 202
Changing the look of a worksheet ... 203
Adding pictures to worksheets ... 206
Summary ... 206

Chapter 11
Desktop publishing 207

The next step after word processing 209

The uses of **DTP** 210
The facilities 213
General features 217
Words & pictures from other programs 221

Chapter 12
Multimedia 225

Films and encyclopaedias on your screen 227

The interactive medium? 227
The equipment you need 228
What multimedia can do 229

Summary 232

Music 232
Presentations 233
Games 233
Reference works 233
Teaching aids 233
Multimedia for its own sake 233

Chapter 13
Programming 235

Writing cheap and cheerful programs 237

High and low level languages 237
'What's in a name':
a sample *QuickBASIC* program 238
The whys and wherefores of
'What's in a name' 240
Testing and running programs 250

Epilogue 253

Go forth, and let the computer
do the multiplying 253

Be sure that 'new' means 'better' 253
Check with the computer press 254
No-one will ever know it all 254

Glossary 255

Appendix A
ANSI Codes for use in Windows . 291

Appendix B
ASCII Codes for use in DOS 297

Using the ASCII code to draw boxes 303

Drawing the boxes with a batch file 303

Index 307

Preface

How do we get there, please?

When you need to ask the way, pray that you don't meet the oldest inhabitant. He knows the road like the bottom of his ale tankard. He'll tell you to turn left five furlongs before the old haunted oak tree down by Hogscrouch Acre. He might remember to add that it was blown three fields away by the hurricane of '87, or he might not.

Many software user manuals are originated by computing's equivalent of the oldest inhabitant: the programmers.

Now the programmers don't just know the road, they laid every stone *and* applied the finishing touches to the tarmac. In consequence they have lost the ability to see it from the newcomer's point of view.

Furthermore they have the habit of giving us great lists of all the tools supplied with their programs. This is all fine and dandy, but it would be far more helpful if they spent as much time telling us *why* and *on what occasion* one might need to use them in the first place.

Which is why so many first-timers spend half their pocket money on paracetamol, and why most tech support telephone lines are permanently engaged.

This book was conceived and written with that scenario in mind. The aim is to give you a useful small scale map, a route planner, which will help you find your way happily to your larger scale destinations.

INTRODUCTION

Getting into computing

This book is for absolute beginners and for existing computer users who would like to extend their knowledge beyond the routine jobs they do every day.

It doesn't pretend to contain the sum of all human wisdom on the subject, but it does give you the practical help and advice that many of us would have welcomed when we were faced with our first IBM PC all those years ago!

If you need to know how to type and print 25 copies of your cv before coffee break, turn to Chapter 8. If you need to know what *segmented hypergraphics* are, go to the Glossary. If you want a 'good read' on computing generally, start at Chapter 1.

Introduction

Getting into computing

It doesn't have to be difficult

In this book is all you need to know to live happily ever after with your personal computer.

There is actually *more* in here than you'll need to get started, but you don't have to absorb half the book before making your first move. In fact if you take a quick look now at Chapter 8 you'll see how to use a word processor, and how you could be typing your first letter within two minutes of sitting at the computer.

Taking it one step at a time

So where's the problem? Why do some people throw up their hands in horror at the very idea of using a computer? What is the mystery?

The situation is exactly the same as learning to drive a car. When you had your first driving lesson there were those unfamiliar controls: the clutch, the gear lever, the accelerator, the handbrake; all of them had to be adjusted so that you didn't roll backwards down the hill with the car in neutral and the engine roaring ineffectually. Just when you were going nicely other cars would get in the way, pedestrians would walk out in front of you, traffic lights would turn green before you were ready to move off. Life was hell.

But now driving is second nature. You took time to study it; now you can cope. Using computers is exactly the same: if you are prepared to take things a step at a time then you'll get there much sooner than you expect.

The beauty of it is that there is absolutely no risk to life or limb, even first time out.

You can choose how far you want to go. You can take the easy route and find out just enough to get by, or you can delve a bit deeper. You may even get hooked. You'll be introduced to the joys of programming, which may lead you further afield into more exotic languages. The choice is yours.

There are thousands of people who use computers every day without having the faintest idea of what's going on inside the big grey box that they put floppy disks into from time to time. So don't feel that you have to know all about everything before you can make a start.

Computing is like everything else in this world: as easy or as difficult as you want to make it.

This is for you

Yes. It really is for you. This book has been written for people who have never used a computer before. It will also come in handy if you have used one but are scared stiff in case an enquiring ten-year-old starts looking over your shoulder.

This is the first of a series of 'Need to Know' computer books. The others will go into much more detail in specific areas of computing. You'll find all the groundwork here. When you are ready to use a particular piece of software covered by a 'Need to Know' book, it will take you as far as you want to go.

Welcome to this new and exciting world. Don't be put off by the apparent abundance of super-brains in this field; they are the specialists. Their presence doesn't mean that computers are beyond the intellectual capacity of the rest of us!

The Glossary

There are bound to be unfamiliar words and phrases in this book; regrettable but inevitable in a world that is spawning new jargon every day.

If it is possible to explain them in the text without spoiling the flow, then it will be done. If not, they'll be ***written in bold italics like this*** and you'll find them in the glossary.

Everything in the glossary will also be listed in the index. This is so that you will only ever need to look in one place to find where the answer is.

There are also ideas, concepts, ways of doing things that are common to many of the chapters. For example scroll bars are used in most *Windows* applications: word processing, desktop publishing, drawing and painting programs. Similarly the principles of cut and paste are used almost universally.

So rather than repeating the same detailed explanation in each chapter, these will appear in the index with a bold page number. These bold page numbers take you to a fully detailed explanation of the subject.

Chapter 8 is exceptional in that you can read it straight through without referring to the glossary or the index.

How to use the book

You can read Chapter 1 straight away. Where other chapters show the Hands On icon you'll derive most benefit from having the book beside you while sitting at the computer.

When you are directed to information which runs on to following pages, we use the standard abbreviation 'ff'. For example, page 62ff means the information is on pages 62 and 63, possibly going on even further.

Key to icons

These symbols are used wherever there is something of special interest or significance. You'll find that they also serve as mental bookmarks reminding you, for example, that you read the explanation for a piece of jargon at the top of a right-hand page about halfway through the book. This will help you find it again more easily without having to resort to the index.

A generally useful piece of information. Any time you see the symbol it will be pointing at a less obvious, but perhaps more effective way of achieving your ends. Or it might offer to take you a step further. You can accept or ignore the advice. In any event, it will still be there if you need it later.

This shows you the way through the dense thickets of jargon you might meet in some 'instruction manuals' explaining the whys and wherefores as you go. Technical jargon can be irritating when you don't understand it, but it does save time when you can abbreviate half a dozen or more words into a single expression.

Most programs will offer you a quick way round many routine procedures. For example, the 'long' way of saving your work is to click on the File menu and from there select Save; many software houses have adopted Ctrl+S as the quick way. All you do is hold down the Control Key (marked Ctrl) and type S.

You've just learnt something really valuable! A typical 'don't forget' is to save your work often: every five minutes is a good idea. If you just typed a brilliant letter, capturing every nuance in exquisite prose, you don't want it all to disappear when somebody pulls your plug out of the socket to do a bit of hoovering.

Something to be avoided. It could lead to your having to do some of your work all over again. A typical example might be the warning not to fiddle with the set-up of your computer by, say, changing the selected printer or the screen driver.

There are certain things which you should not attempt unless completely sure of what you're doing. If you ignore this advice you won't damage your computer hardware, but you might upset the system temporarily. It would be a good idea to ask someone to help you over this stage.

This is where you find out how easy it can be if you take things one step at a time. You will be sitting in front of your computer with the book open, using the keyboard and the mouse. You'll find out what to do and why you do it. If this is the first time you've used a computer you will also discover that it won't explode if you make a mistake!

These will be presented in such a way that if you don't need, or want, to go into the explanation at the time, you can skip over it without breaking the sequence of your reading.

All you *need* to know

It should be obvious that a book of this size would not claim to contain the sum of all human knowledge on the philosophy and practice of personal computing and its hardware and software. What it *does* contain is all you *need* to know as a first-time computer user, as a manager, as someone whose job involves the use of a personal computer, or simply as an enquiring mind who wants to know what computing is all about.

With this book 'under your belt' and at your side you will be able to take on unfamiliar programs with an easy mind; you will have done all the essential groundwork.

If you find, as many do, that the subject is fascinating and that you want to go on to specialise in, say database programming or ***modem*** design, then there is of course much more to learn.

Take comfort from the fact that there is no-one in the world who has absorbed all there *is* to know.

All expense spared

Most of the examples use the facilities already provided by Microsoft *Windows*, which is 99% likely to be loaded on your machine. So you won't have to rush out and buy any more software before you can try the 'hands on' examples.

CHAPTER

1

How do they do it?

This chapter explains what computers do and how they do it. The emphasis is on the principles: the 'how and why'; the 'thinking processes'. At the end of the chapter is a brief description of the physical bits and pieces: the 'nuts and bolts'.

How do they do it?

The elements of a computing machine

A computer is a programmable electronic calculator with memory. The ordinary calculator will multiply 3 x 3 and show you the answer. It may have a 'memory' for storing this result so that you can then multiply 4 x 4 and add the two calculations together to make 25.

Memory

In the days before calculators you might have written the first result, 9, on a piece of paper so that you didn't forget it while you were multiplying four by four. Then you would have written 16 below the 9, and added them up to 25. The paper was your 'memory'.

Computers have phenomenal amounts of memory: 8Mbytes (8 million bytes) is normal. And that's just for their 'mental arithmetic'; they can 'write down' many times more than that, depending on the hard disk size.

To avoid confusion you should know that a calculator's 'memory' is a storage space that holds one number. Thus a calculator with eight 'memories' can store eight numbers. Computer memory (without getting too technical at this stage) is one gigantic store.

There's more on memory in Chapter 6.

Programmability

We are all programmed in one way or another. We respond to stimuli in a certain way: we eat when we are hungry; we fall asleep when we are tired.

The difference between us and computers is that they have no option but to carry out the instructions in their programs; we, at least, can override the program and skip a meal or stay up late.

Continuing the calculator analogy, a computer could be programmed to ask you for two numbers, multiply them together, ask you for two more, then add both products together and present you with the result. The computer would appear to be just as quick whether the numbers were 3 x 3 or 429383.85972 x 987547.251.

More on programming in Chapter 13.

What a computer does with letters

To a computer the letters of the alphabet are just some more numbers. When you type 'A' on the keyboard it goes away and thinks: someone just pressed a key to tell me they want ASCII code 64, I'd better activate the corresponding pattern of dots on the screen.

ASCII code

The ASCII code, from 0 to 255, is set out in Appendix B. ASCII stands for American Standard Code for Information Interchange. Every letter of the alphabet is given its own number.

Because the computer deals only with numbers, it thinks of anything we write in these terms, but then pumps it back out again in the form that we understand.

Fortunately, we can just type away at the keyboard, seeing the words appearing on the screen, and perhaps later on the printed page, without giving any of this a second thought.

As this all happens in millionths of a second, you could be typing away at 120 words per minute and the machine would still be wondering what was holding you up.

Well, it *would* be wondering if it were capable of thought but, of course, it isn't. Now is the time to clear away that popular misconception.

Computers: thick as two short planks

Computers are as quick as lightning, but they are only carrying out a series of predefined operations. At no time will a word processing program stop and say "Surely you don't mean that" or "Hold on a minute, who was this 'Attilla the Hen'?".

Yes, there are spelling checkers, but these too are moronic. 'Hen' is a perfectly good word in its own right and so will provoke no comment when used in the same context as the fearsome invader.

Similarly if you ask a database for information on 'John Brwon', nothing will show up. *You* know you mean 'John Brown' but unless you type it correctly you'll elicit no useful response. Which is why so much use is made of pick lists from which you have no option but to choose the correct spelling. Though there's still nothing to prevent you from choosing the wrong person!

Computers can *appear* to be bright, after all they can be programmed to provide artificial intelligence, but all they are doing is comparing the numbers correspon-ding to the question you asked with the numbers related to the data they have already been given.

Also you'll get no sensible reply to questions they haven't been programmed to answer. Neither are they considering the actual subject matter nor weighing up any pros and cons.

So by all means treat your computer politely, but there's no need to look upon it with awe. Any of us could do just as well, perhaps even better, if we could work at a rate of 66 million operations a second.

Now we'll have a look at the way computers handle all those numbers.

Binary arithmetic

Don't run away, it's as easy as 1 + 1 = 10!

(But if you find the whole idea horrendous, skip to the next bit on page 8. You'll still be able to drive your computer quite happily without knowing all this. Besides, nobody's looking.)

Binary arithmetic

Electrical and electronic devices are very well adapted to counting on one finger. They are either on or off. We make the most of this by saying that they are worth one when they're on and nought when they're off. Here we have the beginning of a very simple system; nothing as complicated as the ten fingers we use for our sums.

We don't, of course, switch the entire computer on and off each time, only the individual counters inside it.

It's called 'binary arithmetic' because there are two numbers, 0 and 1, as against the ten numbers, 0 to 9, used in the decimal, or 'denary', system. PCs are *digital computers*, which are concerned only with numbers and these numbers are binary digits.

Just for your interest, analogue computers *deal in quantities: distance, weight, time. The old slide rule was an analogue device because it made an analogy between numbers and distance The higher the number, the greater the distance from zero. When it multiplied two figures together, it was actually adding their lengths.*

The humble kitchen clock also uses analogue computing principles. It harnesses mains frequency to drive a motor at a constant speed. The motor drives a train of gears which drive the hands, thereby converting time into distance. We're not looking directly at time at all, only at the distance the hands have moved round the dial.

When a decimal counter has reached 9 and a further 1 is added, it carries one over to the next higher column and puts a nought where the nine used to be:

$$\begin{array}{r} 9 \\ \underline{1} \\ 10 \end{array}$$

so nine plus one becomes ten.

The binary counter uses the same principle but, as it only has two digits, the need to 'carry one' occurs rather more often. It gets to 1 and when a further 1 is added it carries one into the next higher column and puts a nought where the one used to be:

$$\begin{array}{r} 1 \\ \underline{1} \\ 10 \end{array}$$

and one plus one becomes 'one nought', which has exactly the same value as one plus one in the decimal system, only there we call it 'two'.

As the binary digits don't go as high as two we can't call them the same thing even though their value is identical.

The computer isn't concerned with giving names to its totals. It simply adds up each successive one:

one	1	(same value as decimal one)
plus one	1	
	10	(equals one nought) (same value as decimal two)
plus one	1	
	11	(equals one one) (same value as decimal three)
plus one	1	
	100	(equals one nought nought) (same value as decimal four)

You've probably noticed a pattern beginning to emerge. A number in a column in the decimal system is worth *ten* times the same number in the previous column, for example 1 becomes 10 if moved to the next higher column, and 100 if moved up another.

In the same way a number in a binary column is worth *twice* the same number in the previous column. '1' in a binary column is worth '10' when moved to the next higher column and '100' when moved up another.

So the values in the decimal columns increase in powers of 10:

$$397 = 300 + 90 + 7$$

or

$$3 \times 10^2 + 9 \times 10^1 + 7 \times 10^0$$

similarly the values in binary columns increase in powers of 2:

$$111 = 100 + 10 + 1$$

or

$$1 \times 2^2 + 1 \times 2^1 + 1 \times 2^0$$

(binary 111 has the same value as decimal 7).

Bits, bytes and nybbles

Now we can see where the Kilobyte and the Megabyte came from and exactly what they mean.

Bit

The words 'binary digit' have been compressed to 'bit'.

Byte

Byte is the name given to a group of eight bits.

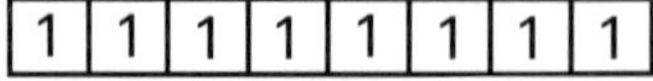

Eight bits are the exact number required to hold any character of the alphabet (there are 256 characters in a computer's alphabet). Binary 11111111 = decimal 255.

Nybble

A nybble is half a byte (honest, guv'), but the word is not in general use.

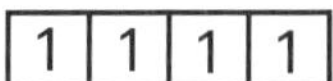

1	1	1	1

Kilobyte

A Kilobyte is 1024 bytes. This seems a bit eccentric when all the other kilos are a thousand times their basic unit: the kilometre is 1000 metres; the kilogram is 1000 grams.

The reason is that numbers of bytes are always powers of two, so you can have 0 bytes, 1 byte (2^0), 2 bytes (2^1), 4 bytes (2^2) and so on. The power of two that's nearest to a thousand is 1024.

Megabyte

A Megabyte is a1024 Kilobytes, which is 1,048,576 bytes. Generally thought of as a million bytes.

We shall be meeting Megabytes (Mbytes) and Kilobytes (K) again, especially in Chapter 6 which discusses memory.

Combining the elements

We have looked at the three basic essentials of a computer: memory, programmability and a form of arithmetic that it can cope with simply and quickly.

There are a couple of other things which will come in handy: (1) a screen to display the progress and results of our calculations and (2) some means of storing these results, and the programs that produced them, for future use.

Visual display

Computer screens are also known as 'monitors' and sometimes VDUs (Visual Display Units). However there's nothing wrong with calling a screen a screen.

The first were monochrome: either green or amber. Then came the colour screens which you will see everywhere in daily use.

Storing information

Temporary storage

Computer memory is volatile, which is to say that when the computer is switched off it forgets everything (know the feeling?). Though this may seem wildly impractical, there is sound reasoning behind it.

Consider your thought processes when asked to do the sums we looked at on page 3. If your mental arithmetic is up to scratch you would have said 'three threes are nine; four fours are sixteen; nine and sixteen are twenty-five'. This would have run through your head in a flash.

Just suppose that instead of doing it in your head you had to write down each stage of this process. Even if you were able to write very quickly, the whole thing would have taken a great deal longer.

The computer's calculations work on the same principle. If it can do its sums in its head (memory, see page 85) rather than write each stage to disk (permanent storage) then it too will be much quicker in presenting the answer. Since one of the main benefits of using a computer is its speed, and it may have to carry out a number of operations to arrive at the simplest of conclusions, it makes sense to take the risk of power failure rather than work at a snail's pace.

Permanent storage

The hard disk

This is where your programs and data are kept. When you switch the computer on in the morning everything is there ready for you to continue the work you were doing the previous day.

The hard disk is hidden away inside the computer, with a flashing light to tell you that it is either pumping information into memory, saving data from it or copying stuff from a floppy disk. There are other occasions when it will be working, but we'll come on to those later.

You may hear hard disks called 'Winchesters', or 'fixed disks'. It is true that they are 'fixed' in the sense that they can't be whipped in and out as readily as floppies, but there are now removable hard disks. The term is also misleading in that it implies lack of movement, whereas they are actually spinning at some 3000 rpm (7000 rpm or more for the bigger ones) all the time the computer is switched on.

Floppy disks

These are for moving information from one hard disk to another, whether between desks or across the Atlantic. In the days before hard disks the floppy disk was the only storage medium for a PC, and things moved along very slowly indeed!

The most common 'floppy' you'll meet is the 3½ inch disk, which doesn't appear to be floppy at all as the case is made of stiff plastic. However if you take one apart you'll find a circular piece of very floppy plastic, coated with magnetic oxide. The disk is rotated inside its case by the floppy drive and records information in a similar way to recording tape and cassettes.

When you buy computer programs they come on floppies which are copied to your hard disk. If the program is a small one you *could* run it from the floppy, but the speed of data transfer is very much slower than to and from a hard disk.

Programs and data

Let's look at an imaginary program and its data (we'll be writing programs in Chapter 13).

You're a chicken farmer, free range of course, and you want to know in simple terms how effective your enterprise is.

There are two main points that interest you: how much the feed costs and how much you are getting for the eggs. If you are not earning as much as you're spending then you might as well not bother getting up at the crack of dawn every morning to let the hens out.

The program, once written, will always stay the same (unless you decide to change it for a newer version). Some of the data, such as the cost of feed, will remain constant between price rises, other variables, such as Ermintrude's laying ability, may vary from one day to the next.

The program will ask you pertinent questions:

How much feed did you last buy?
What did it cost?
How much feed did you use this week?
Any other expenses, vet's bills etc?
How many eggs did they lay this week?
How much are you charging per dozen?
How many dozen have you sold this week?

and set up data files to record the conclusions it draws after processing your answers.

All this data will be saved, or 'written', automatically to the files which the program set up on the hard disk. This will happen a few thousandths of a second after you have answered the final question. When you switch off the computer and go to roost, all your data will be safe.

There are certain types of program, used for word processing (WP), drawing, desktop publishing (DTP) and some other subjects, where the end of your input is not so clear cut. The program has no indication of when you have finished. For these you have to start the saving process manually, usually by pressing one or two special keys; the chosen keys vary from one program to another, but a popular key combination is Ctrl + S.

Control Key

The Control Key, marked Ctrl, is at the bottom left of the keyboard. It is always used in conjunction with one or more other keys, especially for short-cuts to things that would take much longer if you used the standard way.

Do you need a computer?

We are living in a high tech age. Civil and military aircraft depend on specialised computers to tell them where they are now and where they're going to be in ten seconds time. Space flight would be utterly impossible without computer-aided navigation. Commerce and industry would grind to a halt without their mini and mainframe computers.

Who are you?

As to the personal computer, well, that depends on who you are and what you're doing.

The small business user

If you have a small business, a PC can look after your accounts, print invoices and statements and enable you to send out standard letters and mail shots. It can give a more businesslike look to your correspondence and it can keep a record of your stock.

That's the good news. The bad news is that you are going to have to find the money to pay for it, the time to learn how to use it and yet more time to feed it with all the information that you used to collate by hand.

The designer

If you're into graphic design then a PC is as essential as the drawing board which it outdates. The same applies to engineering design: a good CAD (computer-aided design) program will change your life.

Have a look at the cautionary tale 'Peripheral advice' in Chapter 2 before parting with your hard-earned pennies. You don't necessarily have to have a high resolution printer or plotter, you can do your proofs on a low-end device and then get a specialist filmsetting bureau to produce the final output.

The writer

Yes. Buy a computer with a word processing program. If you buy a dedicated word processor, which is a glorified typewriting device that can handle words and nothing else, you will have saved a few hundred pounds but wasted several hundred more which you could have invested in a proper PC. Suppose you want to put pictures in with your words? There are DTP programs for around the £50 mark which will do that job, and a great many more, superbly.

Suppose you want to send your publisher a manuscript through the post. A 3½ inch PC disk is a lot cheaper, and a whole lot easier to replace if it should get lost. Also you will be able to read other people's disks and play *Windows* solitaire (patience) when the ideas have stopped flowing.

The student

You will have access to a terminal, and will have to book in and take your turn in the computer room with everyone else. If a favourite uncle can be persuaded to part with the necessary, then you can get your own. Life will be much easier at work and you will be able to put some productive hours in at home out of term time.

The school teacher

From primary education onwards the computer is much used in schools. The problem is that the authorities have usually decided that their pupils should have any type of computer *but* the industry standard. In consequence both you, as a teacher, and they, as pupils, are living in a different world to the rest of us. If your education authority is enlightened, and is using PCs, then, of course, you should have one.

The retired person

If you have done the sensible thing and kept those little grey cells ticking over, and if your capital reserves can run to £1 500 or so, then go for the new lease of life that a PC and printer will give you.

For a start there will be innumerable clubs and societies near you who would welcome a computerised Secretary or Treasurer with open arms. They have probably been wanting to publish a club magazine for years but not been able to find anyone with the time to run it. As suggested for the writer above, lash out another £50 for a DTP program and you'll be able to play for hours, with really worthwhile end results for your community and yourself.

The professional

Yes, this does mean doctors, lawyers, accountants, not self-styled 'professionals'.

Your professional body will be able to direct you to programs, or suites of programs, written specifically for your purposes. Unless your secretaries are still men dressed in black, sitting up at high desks and using quill pens, you will undoubtedly be fully computerised already.

What is a personal computer?

The name 'Personal Computer' was given to the first IBM PC to distinguish it from the big mainframe machines and the many home computers that were about at the time.

It was primarily a business machine, though it could also be used at home and for games.

As so often happens in this world, other people saw it was a good idea and set about getting round the patents so they could profit from the originator's brainchild. There followed a rash of 'IBM compatibles', some of which were less compatible than others and wouldn't run programs designed for the IBM.

As also happens, most of the copies were cheaper so they were bought in large quantities in preference to the original.

The physical PC

A PC, then, is any computer which will run programs written for the IBM PC. It consists of two main parts: a screen to display what's happening and a box, usually known as the System Unit, which contains a chip called the ***CPU***(Central Processing Unit). This chip is so central to the performance of the PC that the whole kit is named after it. For example one of the faster PCs is a '486 DX2 66', which describes both the machine and the chip which drives it. Most computer manufacturers use chips from the same sources, so you will see the 'Molto-Cheapo 486 DX2 66', the 'Super 486 DX2 66' and so on.

CPU

The numbers 286, 386, 486 give an indication of the speed of the computer that uses them. This is shown in more detail under CPU in the glossary.

Within the system unit is the hard disk. It will also have one or more floppy drives with their slots facing the front so you can put disks into them.

Round the back are the connectors (or 'ports'). They're not called sockets because some of them are male connectors, with pins sticking out. These connectors are bolted to the ends of 'cards' (printed circuit boards with resistors, capacitors and yet more chips attached to them) which are tucked away out of sight inside the system unit, where they are plugged in to the 'Motherboard'.

Each of the peripheral devices: the screen, the printer and so on (see page 24), is attached to the computer via a connector on its own special card.

Most PCs have at least one serial port and one parallel port. The mouse will usually be plugged in to a serial port, the printer into a parallel port and the screen into the video port. However some of the more exotic peripherals have special needs and so will have their own cards, perhaps with extra memory chips on them, so that they can perform better than the standard devices while still being given the same information.

The next step

Have a break, then have a look at the chapter that deals with your main area of interest.

CHAPTER

Hardware

The first step in buying hardware is to consider the software.

How to save money by not buying the newest and fastest if you won't be using its full potential.

Brief descriptions of peripheral devices, their functions and why you may or may not need them.

2

Hardware

What you need

Software is the deciding factor

Before you can choose a computer you should know what programs you are going to run on it. We'll look at two extremes.

A step back in time

Suppose you needed a computer solely for writing letters. You could be using word processing software which would run easily on a relatively slow machine, such as a ***286***. This presupposes that you could take a few steps back in time, via the second-hand market, and find a combination that people were using quite happily a few years ago.

You wouldn't need *Windows* because there were some good word processors running in DOS, such as *WordPerfect 5.1*. You would need a printer.

A kit such as this could be picked up for a few hundred pounds. The drawback is that you would be entirely on your own. All the support contracts would have expired long ago and if anything went wrong, as with a second-hand car, it could cost as much to repair as it cost you to buy.

Marking time

While medium speed computers like the ***386SX*** are still available with a year's on-site warranty, you could achieve the same end with greater peace of mind, albeit at greater cost. There are plenty of word processors running in *Windows 3.1* (currently with 90 days free support) and low cost laser printers, also fully supported. 100Mbytes of hard disk space and 4Mbytes of RAM would be plenty.

RAM

RAM, random access memory, is fully explained on page 86.

Taking a step forward

The thing to bear in mind is that whatever system you go for, it is bound to be superseded within six months, probably even sooner. Staying at the forefront is an expensive game, so if you don't *have* to have the biggest and fastest, stick with the set-up that works for you.

Now we'll consider the 'power users'. These will have a serious need for fast processors (***486DX2 66*** and above) incorporating a ***maths coprocessor***, plenty of ***RAM*** and a generous amount of hard disk space.

Typical examples of demanding applications are computer-aided design (CAD), large scale desktop publishing (DTP) and the manipulation of large spreadsheets. Full-time CAD and DTP users will want acres of hard disk space, probably around the gigabyte mark (1000 megabytes) to accommodate their output. All power users need fast processors: the ***Pentium*** chip is the current leader in this field, with ***clock speeds*** up to 100MHz (to give you a comparison, the original IBM PC-XT ran at 4.7MHz). As for RAM, 16Mbyte is a workable minimum.

The 'Power PC', a joint IBM/Apple venture, promises to knock everything else into a cocked hat *eventually*. But until the programs you use have been rewritten especially for it, there is no threat to the present league leaders, the ***DX4***s and Pentiums.

Somewhere in between

Those are the two extremes. General office work should be sensibly fast, but needn't cost a fortune.

The physical side

The drive

Today's standard floppy drive is the 3½ inch 1.44Mbyte. No sensible manufacturer would offer a ***system unit*** (the box the computer lives in) without one. You can still take up the option of adding a 5¼ inch 1.2Mbyte drive, but unless you have a lot of stuff already on 5¼, or need to pass files to a machine with only a 5¼ inch drive, there is no point. Software suppliers now assume that everyone has a 3½ inch drive, and send out their distribution disks in this format by default. If you have only 5¼ inch drives, make sure you tell them when placing your order.

Tower or desktop

Desktop system units are short and wide, tower units are tall and thin. Having the system unit in front of you is useful because you can see where the disk slot is, instead of having to fumble for it. You can also see a desktop's drive lights which tell you when the hard and floppy drives are working.

Towers can go on the floor underneath or beside the desk. They can stand on top of the desk, but tend to dominate it; also they obstruct the view if anyone interesting walks by.

The monitor

Most new computers come with a 14 inch ***SVGA*** (Super Video Graphics Array) monitor. This is perfectly adequate for standard applications. However many manufacturers are now giving the option of paying a bit extra and choosing a 15 or 17 inch screen.

All of these should conform to current Swedish safety standards for the emission of radiation, just to be on the safe side.

As with all things there are benefits and drawbacks. The higher the ***resolution*** to which you set your monitor, the slower your machine will run. This is because the more ***pixels*** there are, the greater the processing power needed to put them in the right place on the screen.

Peripherals

The extras you can't do without

The printer

There is unlikely to be anyone who can do without a printer of some kind. The programmer will need an 80-column ***dot matrix printer*** for program listings; the spreadsheet user will want a 132-column dot matrix; the office manager will call for laser printers, ***ink-jets*** or ***bubble jets*** for their silent output; the creative person would like a colour printer; the printing firm that produces its ***typesetting*** in-house will use a 1200 ***dpi*** laser printer or a ***photosetter***.

There are plenty of low to medium output quality printers to choose from, as well as an ever-growing choice of colour printers. Ultra-high resolution laser printers and photosetters are produced by a few specialist manufacturers.

Equipment reviews

Your best course before buying a particular brand of printer, indeed before buying any computer equipment, is to watch the magazine reviews. Don't settle for one reviewer's opinion, try to get hold of several.

If you are in a hurry, ask the manufacturer or distributor for reviews of the equipment you are thinking of buying. If there are favourable ones about, they will have ordered reprints for just such an occasion.

The scanner

Scanners are used extensively in the graphics business. They look at text and illustrations in a similar way to the input side of a fax machine. The image is scanned in very thin strips across the paper; the resulting pattern of 'here's a bit of black' and 'here's a bit of white' is converted to bits (binary digits) and the whole picture is turned into a ***bitmapped*** file. Colour scanning works the same way, but there's more to look for and more information to store in the resulting colour bitmap file.

OCR (Optical character recognition)

If you have reams of typewritten or printed text that has to be put into your computer, either for subsequent word processing or DTP, then a scanner with OCR software is what you need.

The OCR software will recognise patterns of dots (bits) as letters of the alphabet and convert them into a text file which can then be passed to your word processor for editing. Although OCR software is now extremely sophisticated, it can't be expected to tell the difference between a full stop and the mark of an itinerant housefly. Even so, a bit of editing takes considerably less time than a mass of copy-typing which would in its turn have to be checked and edited.

The tape streamer

Although computers are extremely reliable, accidents do happen. Most of these are caused by human error, such as the unwitting deletion of valuable files.

There are ways of recovering lost information, but the determinedly accident-prone user will probably have over-written those files with new data and so rendered them unrecoverable anyway.

So how do you make a copy of what is on your hard disk? One way is to copy every single file onto floppies using the COPY command (page 52), which will take a very long time indeed. Alternatively you can use the BACKUP command (page 49).

BACKUP will not only save all the information from your hard disk and copy it to floppies, but it will compress it so that it takes up less space. The disadvantage of backing up onto floppies is that it is time-consuming. You have to feed in a new diskette every minute or so; 200Mbyte of information from a hard disk will need about 120 floppies and take at least two hours to complete.

The ideal way of backing up is to use a tape streamer. The data cartridges are quite expensive but well worth it for the convenience. As much information as you want from the hard disk will just stream out onto the tape. It is quite simple to restore any or all of the files when necessary.

The uninterruptible power supply (UPS)

If you are working in an area that is prone to unexpected power failures, temporary 'brown-outs' or 'spikes' from a nearby arc welder, you need an uninterruptible power supply. It will give you a clean and continuous supply of electric current.

This is a box with batteries in it, taking a charge from the mains when it needs to. When the mains voltage changes, however slightly, a sensor in the UPS switches the output to battery power. You hear a reassuring buzz that lets you know the UPS has taken over. You are 'fireproof' and everyone else is cursing because the last time they saved their work was half an hour ago.

The amount of time you have to save your work and make an orderly exit depends on the capacity of the UPS and the amount of equipment you are running from it; consult the manufacturer if possible or find someone knowledgeable to tell you the size you need.

For maximum benefit and lowest cost it is necessary only to connect your system unit and monitor to the UPS. Printers and other peripherals can drain the juice out of the batteries quite quickly, and it is less crucial to complete a print job than it is to save data.

The modem

We can transmit words by telephone, words and pictures by fax, and computer files by modem.

The modem sits in between the computer and the telephone socket. When you are sending information it modulates binary digits, translating them into sound that can travel down the telephone lines. When you are receiving information it demodulates the sound signals, converting them back into the original binary digit form that your computer can understand. This *mod*ulating and *dem*odulating process gave rise to the name 'modem', now pronounced 'mowdem'.

You need software to control the modem, and once again *Windows* provides something that will at least get you started. This is the Terminal program whose icon is in the Accessories window.

A modem will give you access to all the ***Bulletin Boards*** in the world. Anywhere that can be reached by telephone can be reached by modem. There are small bulletin boards that manufacturers and distributors often have so that you can find the latest product developments and ***download***(receive) new drivers. There are large groups, such as CIX and COMPUSERVE over which you can take part in slow moving and protracted conferences and 'talk-ins', and there is the gigantic INTERNET via which you can consult global sources of reference. However, the telephone meter is ticking away all the time you're on!

Peripheral advice

Unless you are going to be using your PC for Computer-Aided Design (CAD) or Desktop Publishing (DTP) or in some other area which demands extra-high resolution, stick with industry standard peripherals. Not only are high resolution screens and printers very much more expensive in the first place, but their requirements are usually totally ignored by the major software houses.

When a new version of *Windows* comes out, or the latest update to your favourite DTP program, you are more than likely to find yourself out in the cold. You will have a screen and/or printer that is not compatible with the new way the software house has chosen to present its information. They take good care, of course, to talk to the manufacturers of the biggest selling screens and printers first, so their users won't raise a storm of protest.

You may be able to get new ***drivers***, or you may find that your equipment manufacturer has made a 'commercial decision' not to support you any more.

So don't fall into the trap.

CHAPTER 3

Windows

What is Windows*; what are windows? What do you do with* Windows*?*

The answers are here, together with explanations and descriptions of all the accessories that come with *Windows*.

3

Windows

The only unfortunate thing about *Windows* is that it killed off the earlier GEM ***environment***.

Environment

A set of programs designed to work together, ideally giving seamless and transparent access to many interlinked facilities. Windows is an environment, as is DOS and as was GEM.

GEM also had a graphical user interface (GUI) and its applications included two lovely drawing programs: GEM Draw and GEM Artline, which were gradually caught up and then overtaken by various other *Windows* applications after their demise.

That note of nostalgia aside, *Windows* has a great deal going for it. Everybody has converted their programs, or written new ones, to run in *Windows*.

What is *Windows;* what are windows?

Windows is the name of the product created by Microsoft that allows other programs to run within it. The advantage of this is that all the applications can share the same facilities and have text, pictures and numbers passed between them.

These programs are viewed through 'windows' just as you might look into the different rooms of a brightly lit house from the outside. The *Windows* manual suggests that you think of all these windows as being on a desktop, but most desktops are horizontal while the screen on which you're looking at the windows is vertical. As you're looking *through* the windows to see what's going on *inside* them, the house analogy might be helpful.

The main difference between these windows and house windows is that they can be moved about, resized, added to or removed without calling in the builders.

Looking in, getting on

For anything to happen in a window, we've got to open it and get in there. Program Manager, the picture that comes up when you start *Windows*, shows a series of ***icons***, usually collected together in like-minded groups in separate windows. You can drag the icons out of one group and into another if you wish, but they come pretty well arranged in their group windows.

When you install a new program, such as *CorelDRAW!* shown below, it creates its own group window and puts the application icons in there, ready to go.

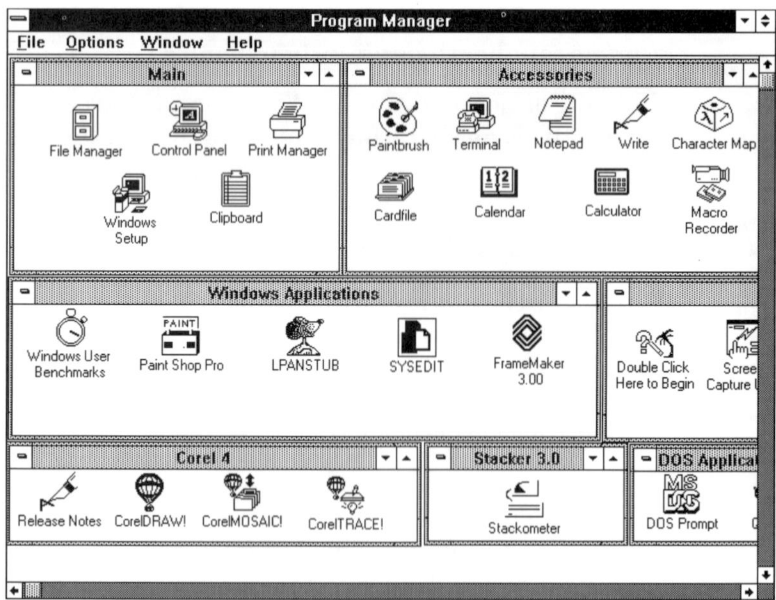

When you double-click the mouse with the cursor on your chosen icon, that window opens. We'll open the *CorelDRAW!* window and put something in it.

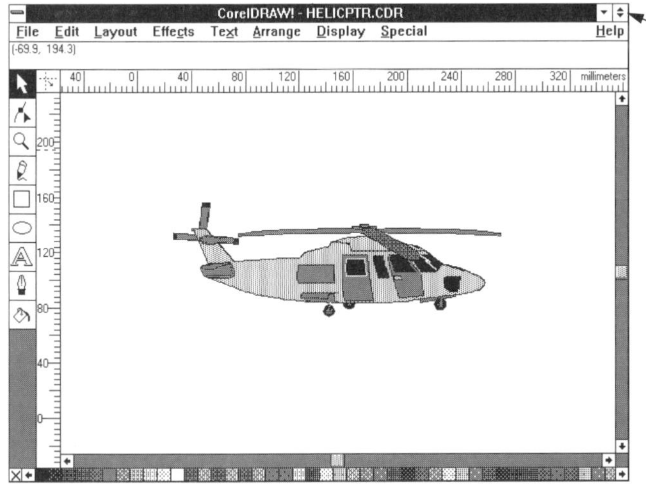

The restore button, used to restore the window to its former size. The maximise button, previously in the same place, has been clicked on to open the window as far as it will go, for maximum visibility.

While working on something it is usually best to view it with the window wide open for maximum visibility. If it is not already filling the screen, click on the button marked with an upward pointing arrowhead at the top right of the window; that is the 'maximise' button.

When the maximise button has been clicked on, it changes to a 'restore' button with a pair of upward and downward pointing arrowheads. Clicking on that restores the window to its previous size.

Suppose you wanted to use this drawing as part of a letter, you could now open a word processing or desktop publishing program, and paste in the drawing.

We'll use *FrameMaker* (which isn't one of the standard parts of *Windows*) as its graphics handling capabilities are rather better than *Write*. You'll notice the *FrameMaker 3.00* icon in the *Windows* Applications group of Program Manager on the facing page.

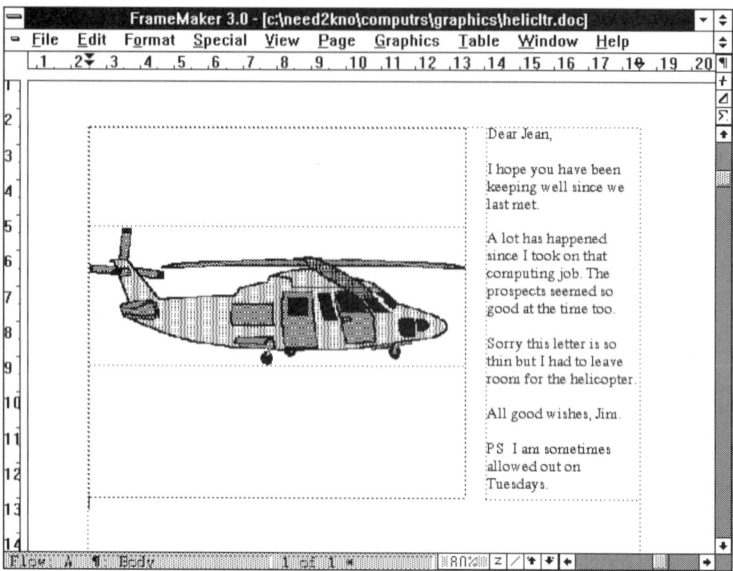

The various dotted rectangles in this screen shot are just guides, by the way; they don't show on the paper when the document is printed.

What do you get with *Windows?*

The short answer is a great deal, in both senses. Do read the *Windows* manual for the full story on each one, but here's a list followed by brief summaries.

File Manager, page 35
Control Panel, page 36
Print Manager, page 38
Write, page 131
Paintbrush, page 40
Terminal, page 41
Calculator, page 42
Calendar, page 42
Cardfile, page 43
Character map, page 121
Clock, page 38
Notepad, page 43
Macro recorder, page 43

File Manager

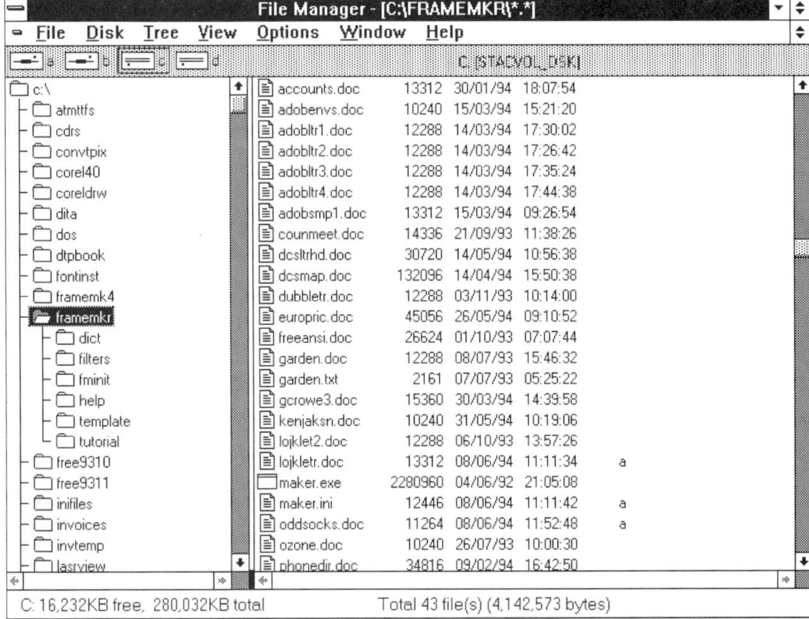

The main display shows a list of directories on the left, with as many files as can be displayed from the selected directory (use the ***scroll bar*** on the right to see more). All file details are shown, as selected from the View menu. You can choose to view only the file names.

The File menu is the one you will be using most often:

Control Panel

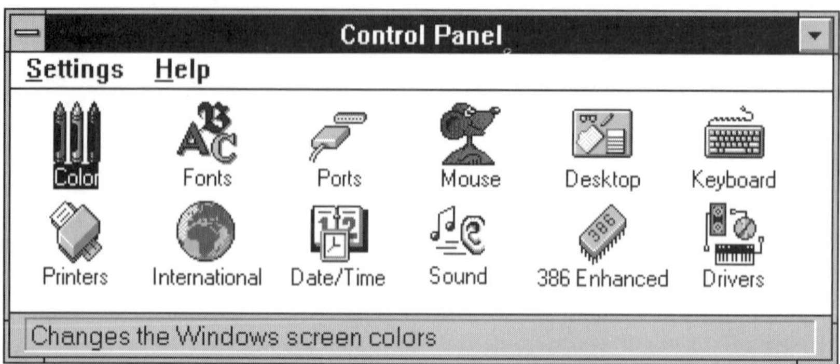

This is an Aladdin's cave of facilities for setting up your *Windows* ***environment***.

The **Colour** icon is shown selected, for setting up the screen colours to suit the mood, from soft pastel to vivid plasma.

A double click on the **Fonts** icon enables you to see samples of each of your fonts in turn, to remove fonts or to add them.

From **Ports** you can set up communication parameters to talk to serial devices. This sounds a bit 'techie' but the manual that comes with the device will always give you the correct settings to copy in.

Mouse gives you tracking speed, double-click speed and the opportunity to change over the left and right buttons.

Explanations for jargon in the following text are on page 39 to save you turning to the glossary. Just flip the page over.

The **Desktop** icon contains settings for background patterns, cursor blink rate, ***screen saver***, windows and icon spacing.

Keyboard contains a slider for changing the speed at which any character will be repeated while you hold its key down, and another slider which determines the length of time a key has to be held down before it will start repeating.

The **Printers** icon lets you set up as many printers as you have connected to the computer (as well as some you haven't, for example you can choose here to ***print to a file*** for onward transmission to a ***photosetter***).

International lets you set up the country, language, keyboard, measurement system, date and time, currency and number formats.

Date/Time shows you the current setting of your system clock/calendar and allows you to change them.

Sound enables you to 'personalize' the warning sounds from your computer speaker for different events.

386 Enhanced allows you to change the size of your ***swap file*** and generally optimises *Windows* for running in ***enhanced mode***.

The **Drivers** icon is for use when installing ***expansion cards***, such as SoundBlaster, ***MIDI*** cards and ***graphics tablets***.

Print Manager

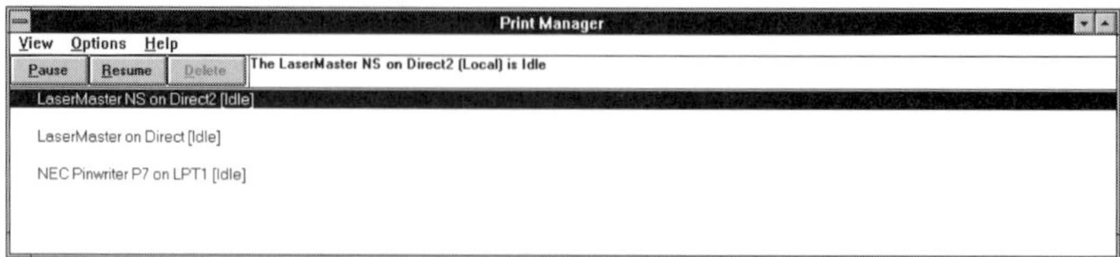

Print Manager is switched on or off within the Printers window of Control Panel, and not, as you might expect, from its own window. Occasionally you may come across a printer that doesn't like working with Print Manager; if odd things happen, check with the printer manufacturer's tech support people.

Its main task is to manage a queue of print jobs while you get on with other work. Without Print Manager activated, a long print job monopolises the computer and you just have to wait until the printing is finished.

You can open Print Manager at any time and see how the job is progressing. It also tells you which printer is being used for which job.

Clock

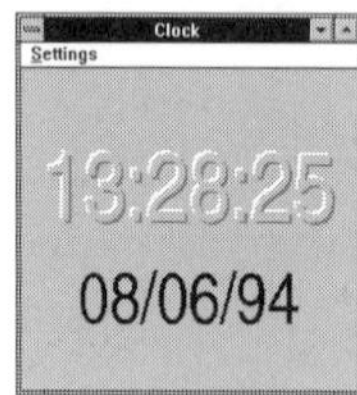

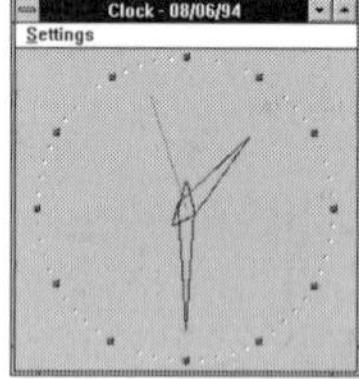

You have a choice of digital or analogue. Either of them can be reduced in size and left ticking away in a corner of the screen. Seeing the seconds going by can be a distraction if you're working to a deadline!

Screen saver

The facility is built into *Windows* (accessed via the Control Panel icon, then the DeskTop icon) to switch the screen off if nobody's used the keyboard or mouse for a while. This is to prevent the current picture from being burnt into the screen if it is left on for an extended period.

Print to a file

Instead of printing on to paper in the usual way, it sometimes happens that you need your work to be printed by a type of printer that you yourself don't possess, for example a PostScript printer or a photosetter. In this case you prepare the page(s) as normal, but use the *Windows* Printers setup to choose the required printer and, instead of connecting it to a port, use 'print to file'. Either print directly to a floppy disk or copy the file on to a floppy. The information on this disk can now be used on another printer.

Photosetting

Also known as filmsetting. Producing printed material of a very high quality for subsequent reproduction in quantity. Photosetting machines produce their output on film or bromide, to resolutions of 1270, 2540 and more lines per inch.

Swap file

An area of the hard disk to and from which information in memory is swapped, to free that memory for more immediate use. Also known as virtual memory. You can choose to have a permanent swap file if you have plenty of disk space; second best is a temporary swap file.

Enhanced mode

Windows can run in either of two modes: standard or, if your hardware supports it, 386 enhanced mode. Enhance mode gives access to virtual memory.

Expansion card

A circuit board that fits into an expansion slot. Typically a sound card or one to drive a scanner, printer or monitor.

Graphics tablet

Used instead of a mouse. A stylus is connected to a port on the computer, in a similar way to the mouse. You draw on the tablet with the stylus; the movements are transmitted to the application you're working on.

Write

This word processor is treated in depth in Chapter 8.

Paintbrush

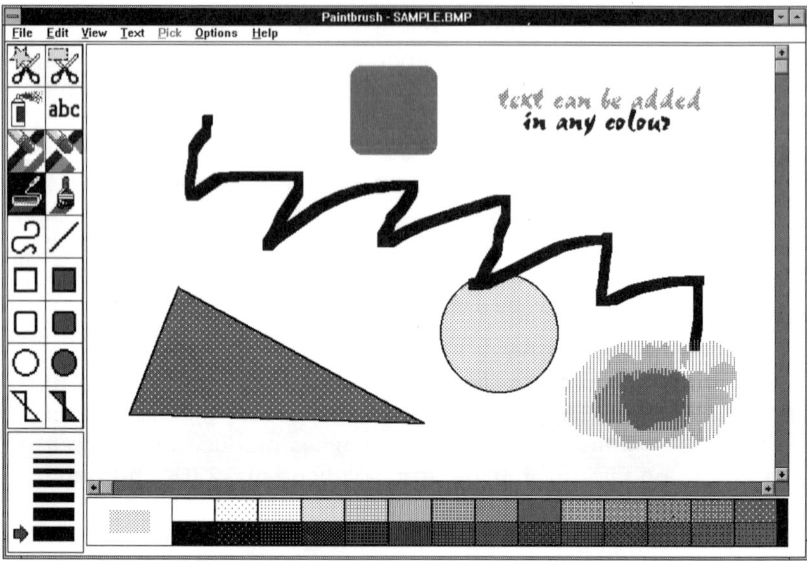

Easy for scribbles like this, but takes some getting used to. For serious work there are specialist painting programs. However, it does come in handy for modifying ***bitmapped*** graphic files; using the 'zoom in' feature you can change individual ***pixels***.

Character map

The character map is discussed in detail on page 121.

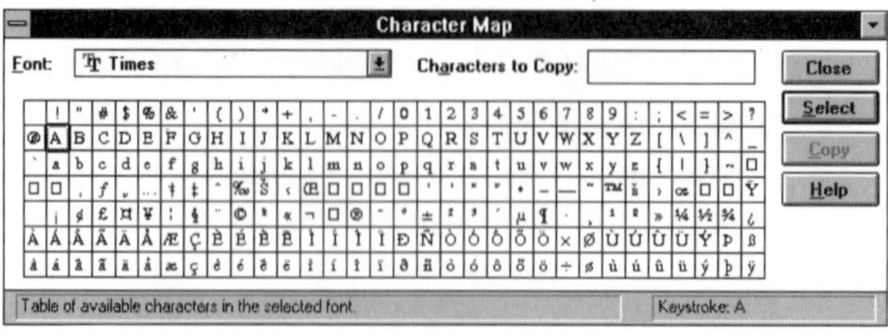

Terminal

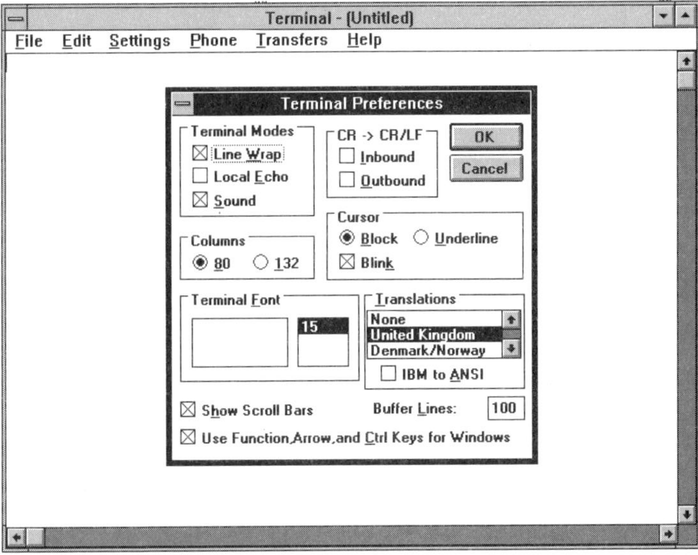

This is all you need for simple operations with a ***modem***: sending (***downloading***) and receiving (***uploading***) files from ***bulletin boards***.

Modem

MODulator/DEModulator, a hardware device that connects to the PC and allows it to communicate worldwide with other computers via the telephone system.

The Terminal Preferences window is one of several to be set up under the Settings menu. Once you have set up the parameters for a particular bulletin board, or fellow computerist, you can save all the details including the telephone number and just call them up from the File menu. Terminal has auto-dialling and will keep trying to make contact as many times as you want until the number you're calling becomes disengaged. All you need now is a modem and you're nearly ready to go for Internet!

Calculator

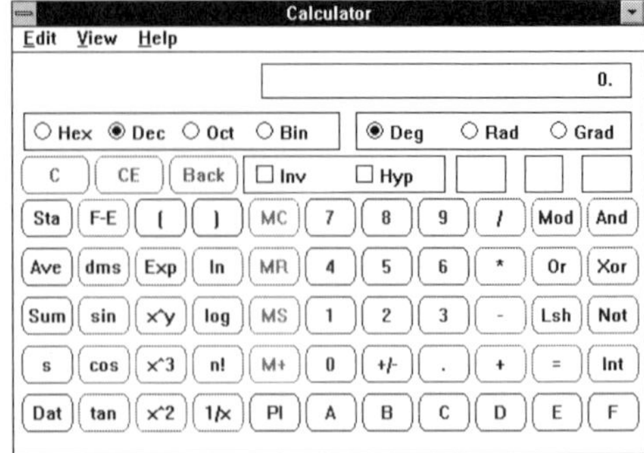

From the calculator's View menu you can choose either the plain or scientific version. Just click on the buttons with the mouse cursor instead of using your fingers.

Calendar

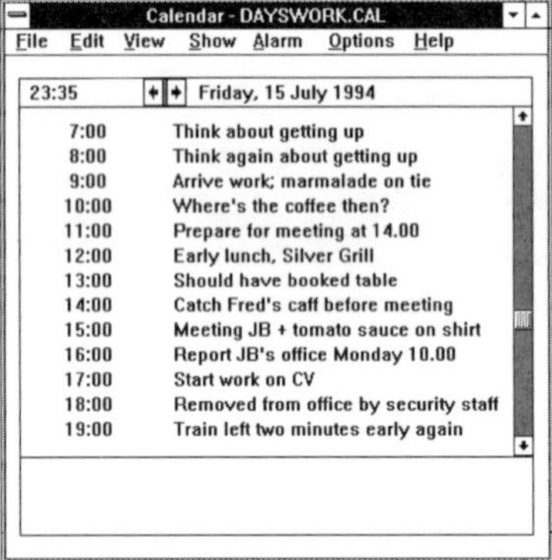

The calendar is multi-faceted; here are two of them. The diary, when used for appointments, can be made to sound an alarm at a predetermined time in advance. You can type up to 80 characters on each line, many more than shown here, and change the time intervals to quarter or half hours.

Cardfile

This 'database' is described in detail in Chapter 9.

Notepad

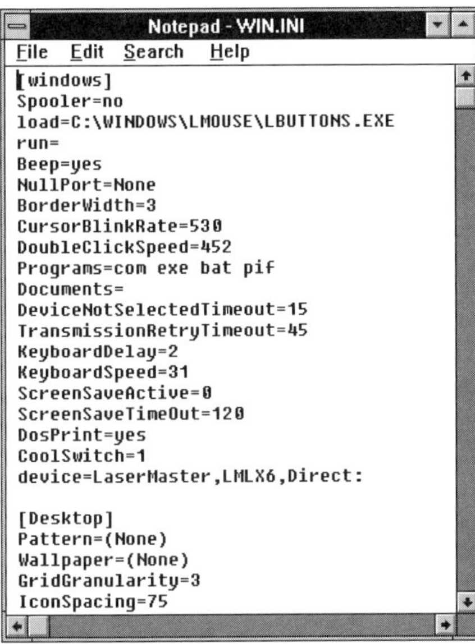
Notepad - WIN.INI
File Edit Search Help
[windows]
Spooler=no
load=C:\WINDOWS\LMOUSE\LBUTTONS.EXE
run=
Beep=yes
NullPort=None
BorderWidth=3
CursorBlinkRate=530
DoubleClickSpeed=452
Programs=com exe bat pif
Documents=
DeviceNotSelectedTimeout=15
TransmissionRetryTimeout=45
KeyboardDelay=2
KeyboardSpeed=31
ScreenSaveActive=0
ScreenSaveTimeOut=120
DosPrint=yes
CoolSwitch=1
device=LaserMaster,LMLX6,Direct:
[Desktop]
Pattern=(None)
Wallpaper=(None)
GridGranularity=3
IconSpacing=75

A handy device for looking at, and editing, text files such as WIN.INI, AUTOEXEC.BAT, CONFIG.SYS.

WIN.INI is described in the glossary; the other two are explained in detail in Chapter 4.

Macro recorder

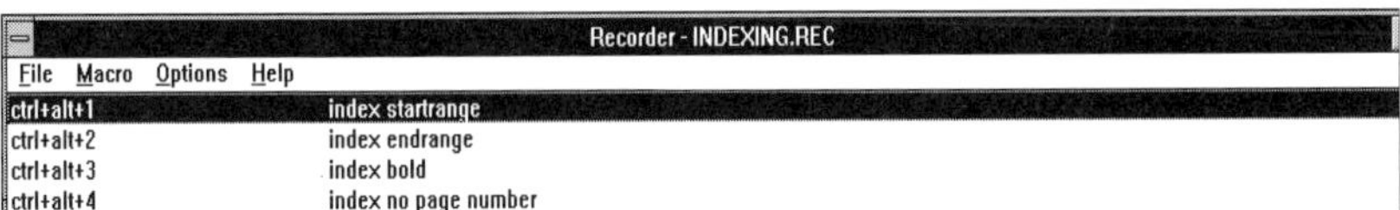
Recorder - INDEXING.REC
File Macro Options Help
ctrl+alt+1 index startrange
ctrl+alt+2 index endrange
ctrl+alt+3 index bold
ctrl+alt+4 index no page number

This lets you store words, phrases and expressions that you need to re-use many times. The four 'macros' shown here were used in producing the index for this book.

WHAT DOES IT MEAN

Macro

A stored sequence of keystrokes that can be replayed by pressing just one or two keys or by entering a short command. It's a short-cut to save typing.

CHAPTER

4

DOS: the operating system

Even if you think you don't use DOS, it is there working for you all the time, from the moment you switch on the computer in the morning until you put it to bed at night.

This chapter contains details of some of the most frequently used commands with examples.

There are descriptions of the 'start-up files': CONFIG.SYS and AUTOEXEC.BAT with an example of each, and valuable information on creating and using batch files.

DOS: the operating system

All main services for the computer

Introduction to the operating system

Even if you spent your entire computing life in *Windows* and its applications, DOS would still be there in the background, beavering away on your behalf.

Engineers and full-time programmers need to know DOS inside out. The rest of us can think of the operating system as a collection of programs we may never see. They provide the essential services in the same way that water, gas and electricity are laid on; we turn a tap and water comes out; we flick a switch and a light comes on.

As well as getting the computer started, or booted up, in the morning and managing its memory throughout the day, the system looks after all the hard disk and floppy disk operations, hence 'Disk Operating System' or 'DOS'.

As techniques improve and more services are offered, so the operating system is upgraded. We have had numerous versions of DOS; at the time of writing we are up to MS-DOS (Microsoft DOS) version 6.

DOS comes on floppy disk and is usually loaded onto the hard disk by the hardware supplier before the computer is delivered. Your first contact with DOS might be when you make a copy of a program, such as a word processor, from the distribution disks onto a reserve set. Even then you could choose to do it from within *Windows*.

Most software houses now use an INSTALL or SETUP program which tells you to insert their disks into the floppy drive in sequence. Although you will not see it happening, these installation programs will be using DOS disk copying facilities to transfer all the appropriate files to directories on your hard disk.

A selection of DOS commands

On the following pages is a selection of some of the most often used DOS commands, to give you a flavour. A full DOS manual will show all of them, together with the 'switches' that let them be used to their fullest extent.

Some DOS commands are internal, or *resident*, which means that you can use them wherever you are in the system without having to return to the DOS directory (C:\DOS). Others, such as FORMAT and CHKDSK are external, but provided you have the DOS directory in your PATH statement (page 61) there is no difference in the way they are used. The only observable difference is that the external commands are shown in the DOS directory listing while the internal ones are loaded into memory and are not shown as individual files.

Help is always at hand

DOS syntax

Don't worry if you've mislaid your DOS manual and can't remember the syntax for a particular command. Just enter **HELP** followed by the command's name:

```
HELP DIR
```

and you get full instructions on how to use it:

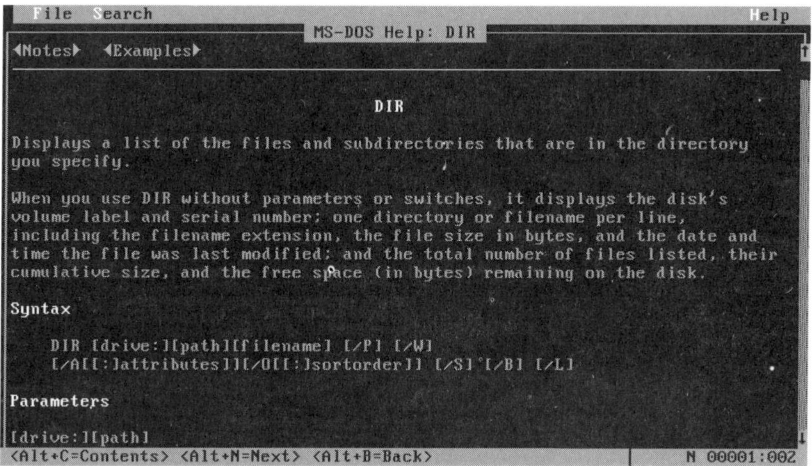

File Search Help
MS-DOS Help: DIR
◄Notes► ◄Examples►
DIR
Displays a list of the files and subdirectories that are in the directory
you specify.
When you use DIR without parameters or switches, it displays the disk's
volume label and serial number; one directory or filename per line,
including the filename extension, the file size in bytes, and the date and
time the file was last modified; and the total number of files listed, their
cumulative size, and the free space (in bytes) remaining on the disk.
Syntax
DIR [drive:][path][filename] [/P] [/W]
[/A[[:]attributes]][/O[[:]sortorder]] [/S] [/B] [/L]
Parameters
[drive:][path]
<Alt+C=Contents> <Alt+N=Next> <Alt+B=Back>
N 00001:002

What the commands do

The 'syntax' of all commands, how to use them correctly, is explained in the DOS manual. This selection shows some of the more popular ones and the occasions on which you might need them.

Although the commands are shown in capitals, with their switches in lower case, DOS is not case-sensitive (except when you want it to search for particular text) so you can use lower case, even mixed case commands.

BACKUP

Here is a true story.

An experienced computerist was in the final stages of writing a suite of database programs. This one was to be used for taking orders over the telephone. The product range was to be displayed on the screen and the operator would key in the items and quantities while the customer dictated them. As each new product and quantity was entered, the program would check to see if the next discount level had been reached, calculating and presenting running totals instantly.

Just one thing troubled the programmer: for reasons of space the discount bands were labelled "1-5", "6-15" etc. How much neater it would be, he thought, if these bands could be made to look more like "1 to 5" and "6 to 15" than "1 minus 5" and "6 minus 15". Then inspiration struck. There is a little right arrow character (ASCII 26) which would take exactly the same space as the hyphen. He would use that to give "1→5" and "6→15".

Unfortunately that character was also used by DOS as an end-of-file marker. For some unaccountable reason these end-of-file markers multiplied like rabbits and wrote themselves into every file and directory on the hard disk. Even the file and directory names were affected; everything had been converted to instant garbage.

There was no recovery system that could rescue the hard disk. It had to be reformatted; all the software had to be re-installed and three weeks programming work had gone up the spout.

If this experienced computerist had backed up the hard disk daily, instead of once a month, then only a few hours' work would have been lost. The following day he bought a tape streamer.

BACKUP

It really is important to back up your work.
That particular set of events will never happen to you because you are now aware of it, but who knows what other disaster might be impending?

The **BACKUP** command is for use on floppy disks, while tape streamers have different backing up software. If you can afford a tape streamer then that is the way to go: you start it running and leave it until it has finished. Disks, on the other hand, have to be inserted and removed from the drive every minute or so until the job is done.

There are several proprietary backup programs in addition to the one that DOS provides. Using one of these will be essential if you plan to use a tape streamer; DOS backup only works on floppy disks.

There is no need to back up the *entire* hard disk daily, only files that have changed since the previous backup. A sensible routine is to do a partial backup of these changed files every day before shutting down and a full backup before close of play on Friday (or whichever day your week finishes).

As well as copying files, **BACKUP** also *compresses* the information. In order to put things back onto the hard disk you have to use the **RESTORE** command (page 63) which *decompresses* them; you can't do it with **COPY**.

Here is a typical command line for a full backup of all files on all directories and subdirectories on drive C: to floppies swapped in and out of drive A:

```
BACKUP C:\*.* /s A:
```

Shown below is the same thing with '∧' added to show where the spaces should be. Anything not so marked is just air between adjacent characters:

```
BACKUP∧ C:\*.*∧/s∧A:
```

This is the command for a partial, or daily, backup of all files on all directories and subdirectories on drive C: to drive A:

```
BACKUP C:\*.* /s /m A:
```

```
(BACKUP∧C:\*.*∧/s∧/m∧A:)
```

CD (Change directory)

The directory currently selected is called the *default* directory because command such as:

```
DIR
COPY A:*.*
DEL *.DAT
```

will apply to that directory by default, thereby saving you the trouble of typing the full path each time:

```
DIR C:\DIRNAME
COPY A:*.* C:\DIRNAME
DEL C:\DIRNAME\*.DAT
```

To change to a different directory use **CD**:

```
CD\NEWDIR
```

To change to the root directory just enter

```
CD\
```

See also:
MD (Make directory) on page 60 and
RD (Remove directory) on page 63.

CLS (Clear screen)

Clears the screen. The DOS prompt (usually **C:\>**, but see **PROMPT** on page 62) moves to the top of the screen.

COPY

There are several reasons for copying files:

1. When installing new or updated software.
2. To duplicate new software distribution disks (this is almost always recommended by the software house).
3. When transferring information from one machine to another.
4. When about to carry out some process whose outcome is uncertain and could result in your losing valuable data.

You can copy from one floppy to another, from hard disk to floppy, from floppy to hard, and from one directory to another on the same hard or floppy disk.

You can also copy a file and give it a different name in the process.

DOS is very accommodating in that it allows you to copy directly from one floppy to another even if you have only one floppy disk drive:

Copying files

1. Put the source disk, containing the file you want to copy, into drive A:
2. Type **COPY A:FILENAME.EXT B:** (substituting the name and extension of your file for **FILENAME.EXT**) and press Return.
3. DOS then reads the source disk and tells you when to insert the target disk into drive B:
4. Remove the source disk from drive A: and replace it with the target disk.
5. If it is a very large file, or there are several files on the source disk, you will be asked to put the source disk back in so that DOS can read the rest of the files from it.

If you need to copy a complete disk, including sub-directories, then use DISKCOPY below.

If you are copying a number of files from one disk to another and have only one floppy drive, it can be quicker to make a temporary directory on the hard disk: type **MD C:\TEMPDIR** at the DOS prompt, press Return. Copy the files from the source disk to **\TEMPDIR**, then copy them from **\TEMPDIR** onto the target disk.

To copy to or from the hard disk you must specify the directory that the files are going to or coming from:

COPY A: FILENAME.EXT C:\DIRNAME

or

COPY C:\DIRNAME\FILENAME.EXT A:

or change to the directory that the file is coming from:

```
CD DIRNAME
```

so that the DOS prompt changes to:

```
C:\DIRNAME>
```

then type:

```
COPY FILENAME.EXT A:
```

The essential thing to remember is the sequence: you are always copying *from* the source *to* the target. DOS doesn't use the words *from* and *to* in the COPY command; you just have to imagine them.

In this next example we shall also change the destination file name:

```
COPY C:\THISFILE.EXT A:\THATFILE.EXT
```

If you have several files to copy you can use the ***wild cards***, * and ?. For example:

```
COPY C:\WINDOWS\*.CDR A:
```

would copy all the files in the *Windows* directory with the extension .CDR to the floppy disk in drive A:.

Windows, by the way, has the command MOVE. This doesn't create a duplicate in another place, as the DOS COPY command does; it removes the file from its present location and places it in another.

DATE

Shows the system date, which is the date based on the date last given to DOS. Gives you the opportunity of changing the system date.

It is good practice to have the date and time set correctly. All files and directories are 'time and date stamped' when they are created, and you sometimes need to know when this was. It only takes a minute to key in the current date and time.

DEL

For one reason or another, unwanted files tend to accumulate on the hard disk. For example, most programs give you the option of generating back-up copies of files you are working on. While it is a good idea to go for this option, when the time comes that you have finished the job there will be a duplicate file, probably with the extension **.BAK**. You can now safely delete it using the **DEL** command.

DIR

This is used mainly for showing a list of files with their size in bytes, and the date and time of their creation. This is useful when you can't remember where you put a particular file or what exactly you called it.

There are file finding utilities, such as QFIND, which locate files for you (they aren't part of DOS and have to be bought separately). If you were in the habit of putting your word processor document files in different directories, and couldn't remember where a particular one was, you would just enter the command:

```
QFIND *.DOC
```

and all the files with the extension .DOC would be listed together with the name of their directory.

However, DOS has its own search facility (see **DIR /s** below) which does the same thing, though less quickly.

The DIR command has a number of 'switches' which give you various different displays. In these examples the listing would be from the default directory. If you wanted to look at a different directory you would have to name it, say: **DIR C:\COREL40\SYMBOLS /p**

`DIR /p`	Pauses when the screen is full. Useful for looking at long lists of files.
`DIR /w`	Gives a wide listing. This shows just the file names in five columns across the screen instead of the usual single column.
`DIR /o:n`	Gives a listing sorted alphabetically by name.
`DIR /o:e`	Gives a listing sorted alphabetically by extension.
`DIR /s`	Searches for files in the named directory and all its subdirectories. If you name the root directory then a search will be made of the entire hard disk: `DIR C:\*.WFN /s`

DISKCOPY

This copies all the directories and files from one disk to another *of the same size and capacity*. It will also delete any files already existing on the target disk.

You can copy straight onto a brand new unformatted disk with this command (and only with this one) because it will format as it copies if necessary.

The command is:

```
DISKCOPY A: B:
```

which, surprisingly, works even if you only have one floppy drive. There can be quite a lot of 'disk-swapping' between source and target disk. Although DOS tells you which one to insert, it pays not to become distracted during the process in case you get out of step.

DOSKEY

In its simplest form DOSKEY keeps a record of your activities on the DOS command line, and pops them up one after another as you press the 'Cursor up' key. When a command that you want to repeat appears, just press Return.

In contrast to the usual command line, where the text is erased as you go back over it to make amendments, a DOSKEY line stays put and allows you either to overwrite or insert characters. It is well worth including DOSKEY in your AUTOEXEC.BAT file so that it is loaded automatically whenever the machine is booted up.

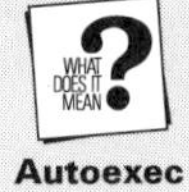

Autoexec

The two special files, AUTOEXEC.BAT and CONFIG.SYS, are consulted by the computer for instructions on the way you want everything set up. This happens automatically when you switch the machine on. There's more on page 66ff.

EDIT

This brings up the MS-DOS Editor, which is an invaluable piece of kit. It is a text editor, as distinct from a word processor, which means that it has no frills: no italics, no bold, no choice of fonts but it is simple and fast and can be used for editing and creating similarly pure files. Furthermore it comes as part of DOS and therefore doesn't cost you anything extra.

Maybe that's something of a eulogy for a built-in text editor, but anyone who has wrestled with its predecessor, EDLIN, will have experienced the same sense of relief when EDIT appeared with DOS 5.

Any time you need to make changes to your CONFIG.SYS (page 66) or AUTOEXEC.BAT (page 66), or you want to create or edit a batch file (page 67), just enter:

```
EDIT CONFIG.SYS
```

(or whatever the file name happens to be) and you're up and running.

FIND

Here's a really helpful command. One scenario for its use could be that you have used a particular word in several documents but you can't be sure which files they're in. Combine **DIR** with **FIND**:

```
DIR C:\ /s /b ¦ FIND /n /i "Wombles"
```

This will find every occurrence of the word "Wombles" in the files on drive C:. The switches work like this:

DIR switches:
/s Lists every occurrence of a file with the word in it
/b Gives the directory and file name
FIND switches:
/n Gives the line number on which the word appears
/i Gives case insensitivity, so it won't matter whether you ask it to search for "WOMBLES", "wombles" or even "WoMbLeS", the word will still be found. Should you wish to find "Wombles" but not "WOMBLES" then omit the **/i** and specify the text string as "Wombles".

That rather complex command was necessary because **FIND** doesn't support ***wild cards***. If you know which file the word (or "text string") is in, use:

```
FIND /n /i "Wombles" WIMBLEDN.TXT
```

which will show line numbers and be case insensitive.

FORMAT

Before using a floppy disk straight from the box, it must be formatted.

In its unformatted state a disk is just an annular (washer-shaped) piece of thin plastic, coated with magnetic oxide and contained in a square plastic (3½") or cardboard (5¼") envelope.

To make it usable the oxide layer must be marked out magnetically into tracks and sectors so that all the information you are about to put on it can be 'written' to the right place on the disk, and later be 'read' from it. This marking out is called *formatting*.

If you format a disk that already has information on it, all that information is deleted. You are given advance warning that this will happen.

In the bad old days before the IBM PC, every computer manufacturer thought he had found the best way of formatting disks for his machine for optimum reading and writing speed. In consequence there are about 1500 different formats. This is one reason why disks from one of those machines can not be read on another.

However, in the world of PCs and their compatibles there are only five formats:

3½" 720 Kilobyte (720K)
3½" 1.44 Megabyte (1.44Mbyte)
3½" 2.88Mbyte
5¼" 380K
5¼" 1.2Mbyte

The higher capacity disk drives will read from, and write to, lower capacity disks of the same physical size, so a 1.44Mbyte 3½" drive will read and write 720K 3½" floppies, but a 720K drive can neither read from nor write to a 1.44Mbyte disk.

Backward compatibility

Incidentally, the concept of an improvement such as the higher capacity disk drive which does not put all earlier versions on the scrap heap, is known as *backward compatibility*. This term is applied to software as well as hardware.

To format a disk for use in your own machine with one drive, just put the disk in the drive slot, close the lever and at the C:\ prompt enter:

```
FORMAT A:
```

Drive letters (A:, B:, C: etc) are always followed by a colon. This differentiates them from file names (you could have a file called just "A").

MD (Make directory)

Before files can be put into a directory, that directory must exist. For example, simply type:

MD MSLANEUS

and you have made a directory ready to accept whatever files you choose to keep in it. If that seems an odd way of spelling 'miscellaneous' it is because directory names have to obey the same laws as file names (shown below). It is interesting to think up names that will describe the contents of a file or directory in eight letters and still be memorable two months later.

File names

File and directory names can be made up from any eight of the alphanumeric characters (A to Z, 0 to 9) and these 17 additional characters (shown in the sequence they appear on the keyboard, starting at top left):

Grave accent	`	ASCII 096
Exclamation mark	!	ASCII 033
Dollar sign	$	ASCII 036
Percent sign	%	ASCII 037
Caret (circumflex)	^	ASCII 094
Ampersand	&	ASCII 038
Parenthesis left	(	ASCII 040
Parenthesis right	)	ASCII 041
Hyphen	-	ASCII 045
Underline	_	ASCII 095
Brace left	{	ASCII 0123
Brace right	}	ASCII 0125
At	@	ASCII 064
Hash	#	ASCII 035
Tilde	~	ASCII 0126
Backslash	\	ASCII 092
Forward slash	/	ASCII 047

See also:
CD (Change directory) on page 51 and
RD (Remove directory) on page 63.

PATH

The **PATH** statement tells DOS where to look for files. If all files could be kept on the root directory there would be no need for it.

The path to a file is its directory location, for example you might have a DOS program called PLANTING.EXE on the C:\FORESTRY\EVRGREEN sub-directory, so its path would be:

```
C:\FORESTRY\EVRGREEN
```

If **C:\FORESTRY\EVRGREEN** was included in the **PATH** statement then PLANTING.EXE, and any other files in that sub-directory, could be accessed regardless of which directory was the default at the time. If it were not in the **PATH** statement then you would get a '**Bad command or file name**' error message.

The best idea is to include the most commonly used paths in the AUTOEXEC.BAT file, where a typical **PATH** statement might be:

```
PATH C:\;C:\DOS;C:\WINDOWS;C:\PAGEMKR4
```

There is an upper limit of 127 characters for this statement, so if you have lots of long directory names you might have to consider shortening them. The down side is that cryptic directory names are much less easy to identify: C:\PM4 is not so immediately recognisable as C:\PAGEMKR4.

You can enter a new **PATH** statement from the DOS command line, but the old one will take over again when the machine is rebooted. If you need to make a permanent change in AUTOEXEC.BAT, you have either to reboot or enter **AUTOEXEC** on the command line before it will take effect.

Entering the word **PATH** on the command line causes the **PATH** statement to be shown on screen.

PROMPT

The usual form of DOS prompt is

```
C:\>
```

This is shown on the left hand side of the screen and is the starting point for the command line. It is here that you type your command and then press Return so that the command is carried out (or 'executed').

The DOS prompt can take many forms, determined by the Prompt command in the AUTOEXEC.BAT file. The line in AUTOEXEC.BAT that gives the standard form of prompt is:

```
PROMPT $p$g
```

The **$p** parameter makes the prompt show the current drive and path, for example:

```
C:\DOS
```

while the **$g** parameter adds the 'greater than' symbol.

In the first heady excitement of discovering how to use the Prompt command, many people put in their name:

```
PROMPT Sarah $p$g
```

gives:

```
Sarah C:\DOS>
```

which might come in handy if you were expecting an attack of amnesia or an identity crisis.

RD (Remove directory)

If you are removing a piece of software and/or all its data files from the hard disk (or from a floppy), you would also want to remove the directory that contained them. Directories can not be removed until they are empty, and an error message will come up if you try to do so. Just enter:

```
RD DIRNAME
```

replacing `DIRNAME` with the name of the directory you want to remove, and it is cleared from the disk.

See also:
MD (Make directory) on page 60 and
CD (Change directory) on page 51.

RENAME

Changes file name. As there can be only one file with a certain name in a directory, it is useful to be able to rename it so that work you have done on this file is secure. You can then do more work in your application program, using the original name, without risk of spoiling something that was good as far as it went.

RESTORE

Replaces files that were saved using the BACKUP command.

For some reason each successive version of DOS had used slightly different versions of the BACKUP and RESTORE combination, which meant that the current RESTORE would not respond to the BACKUP command of the previous version. It was extremely disappointing to find that valuable information held on a set of disks that you backed up under an earlier version of DOS could not be restored by your current system. However, both MS-DOS 5 and 6 will now restore files backed up by any previous version.

To restore everything from a backup set:

```
RESTORE A: C:\*.* /s
```

which puts everything back into the directories from which they came originally.

To restore a selected file you must name the directory from which it came (called **DIRNAME** in the example below) and the name of the file (which has been called **FILENAME.EXT**):

```
RESTORE A: C:\DIRNAME\FILENAME.EXT
```

To restore all the files from a single directory (again substituting the actual directory name for **DIRNAME**):

```
RESTORE A: C:\DIRNAME\*.*
```

TIME

Shows the system time, which is the time based on the time last given to DOS. Gives you the opportunity of changing the system time.

Both time and date are maintained by an internal battery; this will probably last for about three years.

TYPE

You can examine the contents of text files on the screen, or direct them to the printer, using the **TYPE** command.

```
TYPE THISFILE.TXT
```

reproduces the file on screen. To stop the text scrolling off the top of the screen you can use Ctrl + S (a good test of speed of reaction!) then press any key to see the next screenful. Otherwise modify the command to read:

```
TYPE THISFILE.TXT ¦ MORE
```

which will make it wait for you at the bottom of each page.

Use of the '>' symbol, followed by **PRN**, causes the file to be redirected to the printer:

```
TYPE WORDS.TXT>PRN
```

Starting as you mean to go on

There are countless different ways of setting up a computer, depending on how much memory it has, the type of printer and any other devices attached to it, the number of files that different programs need to have open at the same time and so on.

When you switch on the computer you want it to remember the way it was set up, and to act upon it. You don't want to have to spend an hour each morning setting it up all over again. This is where CONFIG.SYS and AUTOEXEC.BAT come into play. They are read automatically when the computer is booted up, and all the instructions and commands they contain are carried out.

CONFIG.SYS is the first to be read; it can be read *only* on start-up, so for any changes to take effect the computer must be restarted. AUTOEXEC.BAT is read immediately afterwards, and can be run on its own at any time by entering **AUTOEXEC** on the command line.

A little knowledge ...

The MS-DOS manual allocates about 35 pages to these two files, giving detailed explanations of how to use them. That is the ultimate reference; it's all in there, and that is where you should look for your particular set-up.

However, here is a foretaste to give you an overview. The examples given here will certainly be *nearly* suitable for your set-up but, equally certainly, they will need some 'tuning' with the help of the manual to get them absolutely right.

CONFIG.SYS

This file contains instructions for configuring (setting up) the computer:

Memory
Device drivers
Country conventions
Files and Buffers

It does contain other information as well, but this is enough to be going on with. Full details are given in the MS-DOS manual.

Here is a typical CONFIG.SYS file:

```
DEVICE=C:\DOS\EMM386.EXE
DEVICE=C:\DOS\SMARTDRV.SYS
DEVICE=C:\MOUSE\MOUSE.SYS
COUNTRY=044,,C:\DOS\COUNTRY.SYS
FILES=30
BUFFERS=20
```

AUTOEXEC.BAT

The .BAT extension shows that this is a *batch file* (see also page 67). This means that it contains a list of instructions to be carried out in sequence. It will take you into a program and, if required, when that is finished it will start up another one for you.

Just like CONFIG.SYS, this is a text file; you can modify it using the MS-DOS Editor; at the DOS prompt type: **EDIT AUTOEXEC.BAT**

The main ingredients of an AUTOEXEC.BAT file are:

The PATH command
Setting up the keyboard (see page 117)
Defining the prompt (see page 62)
Starting TSR (Terminate & Stay Resident) programs
Starting ordinary programs, such as *Windows*

Here is a typical AUTOEXEC.BAT:

```
PATH C:\;C:\WINDOWS;C:\DOS;C:\WORDPERF
KEYB UK,,C:\DOS\KEYBOARD.SYS
PROMPT $p$g
C:\DOS\DOSKEY
WIN
```

Batch files

These are extremely useful for doing regular jobs. You can read, write and modify batch files using the MS-DOS Editor (or any other text editor).

AUTOEXEC.BAT is read and executed automatically; other batch files are treated in the same way as commands. Suppose you had a batch file for setting up a printer in 132 column mode, called PRINT132.BAT. This would be executed by entering PRINT132 on the command line; it could even be included as a line in the AUTOEXEC.BAT file. When you had finished your 132 column printing you could then run another batch file, say PRINT80.BAT, to reset the printer to its normal 80 column mode.

There are three types of file that can be executed in DOS. They are characterised by their extension: .BAT, .COM, .EXE. In each case you type the file name without the extension, then press Return.

Short of writing and compiling programs to do specific jobs, batch files are an ideal way of carrying out one or more commands.

Here is one that sets up a daily backup to the tape streamer, then resets the archive attribute of all changed files so that the same files won't clog up the tape by being saved every day until a full backup is carried out (see also page 49ff).

File attributes

Files can have any combination of four 'attributes'. These carry useful information which you may never need to know about directly, but which help the system in its day-to-day running.

These attributes are:

- r **Read only**, which means that you can examine the contents of the file but can't change them
- a **Archive**. The file has been changed since it was last saved. When next you save it, the 'a' will disappear.
- s **System**. System files, supplied with DOS, also called 'device drivers', can't be changed.
- h **Hidden**. DOS hides some of its files in the root directory. You can see them, if you're curious, by entering this line at the DOS prompt:
  `DIR C:\/a:h`

ATTRIB

You can also use the **ATTRIB** command to hide files yourself, if you have a particular reason to do so.

You can see the attributes of all files in the current directory when you are in either DOS or *Windows*. In DOS, enter the command **ATTRIB** In Windows, go into the File Manager and from the View menu choose 'All File Details'.

```
cls
@echo off
cd pctools
cpbackup daily
cd\
attrib -a *.*/s
rem attrib used here to reset archive
rem attribute so that changed files
rem are saved only on the day they are
rem changed, not for a whole week.
echo.
echo                    Daily Backup Completed
```

Let's take it apart line by line and see what's going on:

```
cls
```

Clears the screen

```
@echo off
```

If you don't put in an '**echo off**', every line of the batch file will be printed to the screen. That can be messy and confusing. The '@' prevents the 'echo off' command itself being echoed.

```
cd pctools
```

Change from the current directory into the PCTOOLS directory, in which is the next file to be executed: CPBACKUP.EXE.

```
cpbackup daily
```

This is the command with an added parameter. Many programs give you the facility of adding one or more parameters on the command line. They are, however, expecting certain specific information. In this case CPBACKUP.EXE is expecting to be told which setup to use; we have told it to use the one called 'daily'.

```
cd\
```

Change to the root directory, from where the next command can be accessed.

```
attrib -a *.*/s
```

This will set the archive attribute off in every file in every directory on the C:\ drive.

```
rem attrib used here to reset archive
rem attribute so that changed files
rem are saved only on the day they are
rem changed, not for a whole week.
```

These lines serve as a reminder of the purpose of using the ATTRIB command. It's all too easy to forget your reasons for doing something! The **rem** (short for 'remark') at the start of each line prevents it from being thought of as a command.

```
echo.
```

The word '**echo.**' with its following full point means 'print a blank line'. In batch files '**echo**' means 'print to the screen'.

```
echo                    Daily Backup Completed
```

Print 'Daily Backup Completed' in the centre of the screen. The number of spaces in front of the screen message should be the number of columns (80) minus the length of the message (22 characters), divided by two = 29 (they aren't all shown here).

You could put in a couple more 'echos':

```
echo.
echo.
```

to keep the closing message clear of the DOS prompt.

Interrupts

Excuse me a tick, I'm pressing a key

We take it for granted that if we are running, say, a word processing program and want to type in some more text, then we just type away and that's that.

However, the wp program is busy displaying what is already on screen, and possibly counting the seconds before it needs to make an automatic back-up copy. *Windows* may also be working out how long it was since you last touched the keyboard or the mouse, so that it can put the screen-saver into operation.

If no means existed of breaking this concentration, you could type all you liked but nothing would happen. So we have 'interrupts'.

Putting it simply, there are many interrupts, each one allocated for a specific purpose; the keyboard interrupt is one, the parallel port (usually with a printer attached) is another. These interrupts are scanned to see if anything is waiting for attention. The scanning speed depends on the speed of the computer clock. Even on a 'slow' machine there is no appreciable delay between pressing a key and seeing its character appear on the screen.

RTFM (read the friendly manual!)

The aim of this chapter has been to ease your way into understanding what DOS can do for you. It has covered some important points, but overall has barely scratched the surface.

The MS-DOS manual contains tons of useful information and tips; please go on from here and dip into it from time to time. It will improve the quality of your computing life.

CHAPTER 5

Storing the information

All the programs you use, and all the data you produce, are stored in files. The files themselves are kept in directories.

These two words do not have exactly the meaning you might expect.

As everything you do on a computer will call for an understanding of files and directories, this short chapter is devoted to getting you off on the right foot.

Storing the information

Grin and bear it

Jargon is inescapable wherever you go and whatever you're doing. Provided it has a logical basis and its roots can be traced back to normal usage then there should be no problem. Take a deep breath and read on.

Files and directories

Computer *files* are kept in *directories*. It will be easier to grasp the concept if we look at directories first.

The diagram below shows the sort of thing you might see if you looked at *Windows File Manager* (which is covered on page 35ff). It is a good representation of the way the directory system works.

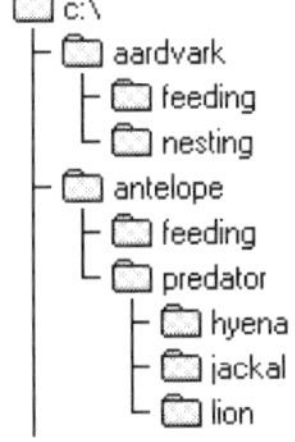

The top part of a typical 'directory tree', showing the main directory, c:\, *with the sub-directory* aardvark *branching off it and the sub-sub-directories* feeding *and* nesting *branching out from* aardvark.

Imagine the main directory, c:\, as the filing department of a large office. Within that office are filing cabinets labelled *aardvark* and *antelope*. These cabinets happen to have two and three drawers each; they could have many more. The drawers of the *aardvark* cabinet are labelled *feeding* and *nesting*; the drawers of the *antelope* cabinet are labelled *feeding* and *predator*. The *predator* drawer is subdivided into three parts, labelled *hyena, jackal* and *lion*.

Computer files aren't like other files

It is at this level that computer terminology and normal filing practice part company. You might have expected those last three subdivisions to be called 'files'. Sorry, they should be but they aren't.

Unfortunately the people who devised many of the terms used in computing do not appear to have had a very strong grip on the English language. As in their choice of the word *file*, they usually came just close enough to be thoroughly confusing. It would have been better to have called it a *'grommet'* or a *'Tibetan Prayer Wheel'* or something else totally unrelated.

A file is a file

The file we are all used to is a container: either a folder made of card, or a box, or else a suspended holder in a filing cabinet drawer. We put things that are related to each other in files to keep them all together; and we can take them out and put them back again very easily.

A computer *file* isn't a file at all

In computing terms, however, a *file* is the thing that is put into the folder, not the folder itself.

A computer *directory* is a container for computer *files*

The container that *files* are put into is called a *directory* (which in the real world is, of course, a book containing names, addresses and telephone numbers).

OK you guys, as of today everyone's a Vice President!

America is a world leader when it comes to promotions, and not just in the field of marketing. They tend to promote the janitor to 'Vice President in charge of Janitorial Operations', they promoted the thousand million to a billion, and in the field of computing they have promoted the letter to being a *file* and the file to a *directory*. So, independent free-spirited breed that we are, what did we do? We copied them.

How *Windows* represents files and directories

Windows File Manager does its best to make sense of *files* and *directories*. It shows document *files* as pieces of paper (african.wri, cubs.wri etc) and the *directories* as folders. This does represent pictorially how computer *files* and *directories* work. You just have to dissociate the accepted meaning of the words from their use in computing.

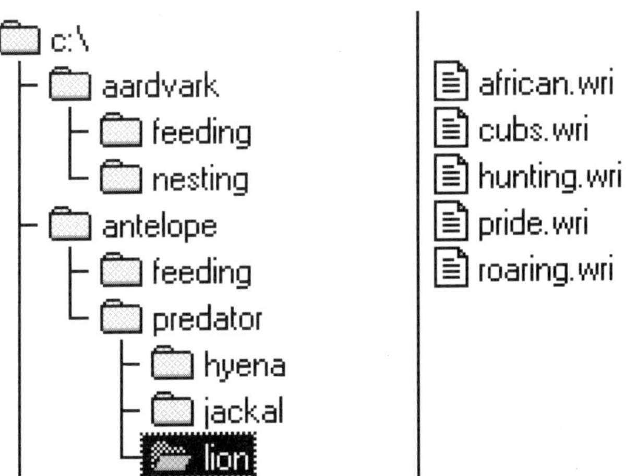

The lion directory, shown highlighted in black, contains all the files with the '.wri' suffix shown on the right. A click on any of the other directories would put up a list of the files those directories contained.

Putting files into directories

All the files on the subject of lions should be kept in the *lion* sub-sub-sub-directory (mercifully you don't have to keep track of all those subs; this one would just be called the *lion directory*). There is nothing to prevent you from putting, say, *roaring.wri* in the *aardvark directory*, but it is more sensible to keep everything on the same subject in the same directory.

Saving files

So put reason to one side, and when you have typed that article for the National Geographical Magazine into your word processor and are about to save it for the first time; don't be surprised when you are asked for a **File Name**. They do mean the name of the document.

You will also be shown a list of **Directories** and asked to select the one in which you are going to keep your file.

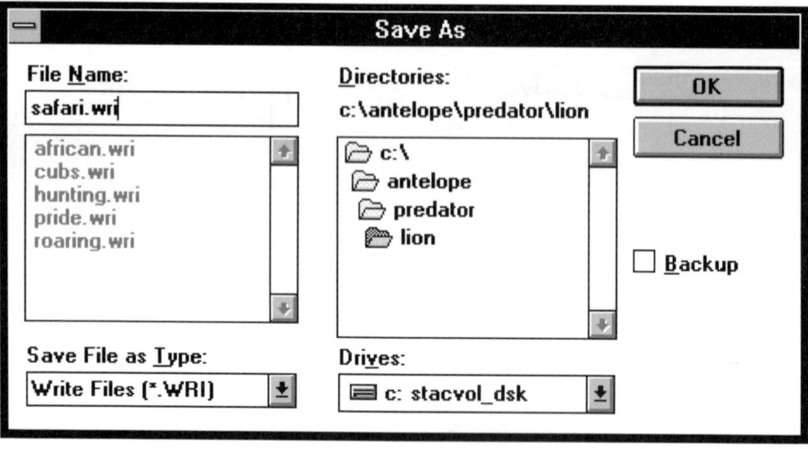

Creating and storing a file is as simple as that: write something and save it. Chapter 4 goes into more details about files, how to copy them from a floppy disk, how to delete them from your hard disk and so on. You will also find more there about creating directories to save your files in, moving files to other directories, and general file handling techniques.

The root directory

Yes, well, the root directory is at the top of the tree. Where else would you expect it to be?

It has been referred to in this chapter so far as the *main* directory, primarily because it *is* the main directory from which all others grow, and secondarily to avoid adding to the verbal confusion. However, following the same *'Alice in Wonderland'* reasoning that gave us files which were actually documents and directories which were really folders, the bottom of a directory tree is always represented as the top. Off with their heads!

Essential contents of the root directory

There are certain files that must be in the root directory so that the computer starts up properly. This is known as *booting*, because in effect it lifts itself up by its own boot straps.

In order that the computer *boots up* correctly the root directory must contain the *system* files: IO.SYS, MSDOS.SYS (or equivalent) and COMMAND.COM. It is also a good plan to have CONFIG.SYS, which sets up the drivers, and AUTOEXEC.BAT which sets up various other bits and pieces. More on all this with the operating system in Chapter 4.

CHAPTER 6

Memory

This chapter explains what memory is and how it is used, with analogies to the human brain as well as the bird brain!

The various different types of memory are shown, together with ways of setting them up.

6

Memory

Computer memory vs human memory

Imagine a robot whose brain was modelled on the perfect human being. It would remember every telephone number, address, post code, birthday and anniversary it had ever come across. It could, as some rare humans can, tell you the square root of 619397; it could work out instantly whether 550 grams of your favourite breakfast cereal for £1.80 was a better buy than 20 ounces for £1.85.

Marvellous. Except that when you tried to wake it up in the middle of the night to tell it the house was on fire, it wouldn't have the sense to take evasive action until you re-connected its batteries. And as you were carrying it downstairs, if you happened to ask what two twos were, there would be no reply.

The difference between computer-controlled robots and us is that we are always switched on (well, more or less) and our memory, however vague, is accessible all the time. Computer random access memory is totally blank until (a) it is switched on and (b) it is told *everything* all over again at the start of the day. Only then can it leave us standing.

Thought processes

While some efforts have been made to understand the workings of the human brain, we still don't really know what goes on in there. We tend to think of it as all-purpose grey matter in which we keep our prejudices, remember how to spell 'Mississippi' and know that we should look left and right before crossing the road. When someone asks us a difficult question we compare the present data with our previous experience and can usually come up with some sort of answer.

Waking up the computer

A computer's 'brain' is organised differently. When switched on it picks up some elementary information on how to deal with its disk drives. This is stored in the ROM BIOS (read-only memory basic input/output system).

From there the contents of the CONFIG.SYS and AUTOEXEC.BAT files (page 66) are pumped into it. These feed it information on how to organise its memory, how to receive and output data, which country it's living in, where to go for instructions.

Even at this stage it can't tell you what two twos are.

If the final item in the AUTOEXEC.BAT file was the instruction **WIN CALC**, then it would go into *Windows* and open the Calculator.

Ready for output

Now it can tell you what two twos are, or the square root of 619397, even (using the scientific calculator) the seventeenth root of 17.

But it couldn't tell you in the same breath where Granny lived; you'd have to switch to the database program for that.

Thinking space

If you had the tiny brain of a bird, your thought processes would very soon reach saturation. It is believed that birds can only count up to one before they run out of memory. If two photographers go into a hide, and one leaves shortly afterwards, the bird is convinced that the hide is empty and resumes normal operations. (According to the RSPB the crows are not so easily taken in. Perhaps corvid memory is a few bytes larger than conventional avian memory.)

Similarly a computer can only process as much information as its memory can hold.

Conventional memory

Standard thinking space

It is unusual for any new computer to have less than 640K, the maximum amount of usable conventional memory. However some essential programs, such as DOS itself, take up part of that space. Other devices such as your mouse, memory manager, country and keyboard drivers will also be using parts of conventional memory.

You can create more space in conventional memory by putting these into the high memory area (HMA). This is done in two stages: first by installing the HIMEM.SYS device driver (add **`DEVICE=C:\DOS\HIMEM.SYS`** as the first line in your CONFIG.SYS file), second by using a memory manager, such as QEMM from Quarterdeck or EMM386 which comes with DOS.

Device driver

A piece of software that loads into memory when the PC starts up, and stays there until it is switched off. In this sense it is like a TSR (terminate and stay resident program), but it usually loads earlier in the boot-up process by being named in CONFIG.SYS. A device driver becomes an extension to DOS, and is therefore more tightly integrated with the system than an ordinary TSR. It has the special purpose of enabling other programs (including DOS itself) to make use of devices they wouldn't otherwise know existed or how to control. A mouse driver is a good example. A device driver may alternatively enhance the use of a device the system already knows about. ANSI.SYS is one example, disk space doublers like Stacker are another.

'High memory' is the area between 640K and 1M that is supposed to be used for controlling hardware, but designers of memory managers have contrived to find empty blocks which they fill with expanded memory so that DOS, mice and other devices can go in there.

RAM: Random access memory

Sounds a bit haphazard doesn't it? As though you might ask the computer to type a list of all the files in the *antelope* directory and it would tell you that the time in Caracas was now 3.43 and 17.28 seconds.

Nothing random about it

RAM

RAM is the part of the computer in which the programs are run and where all the information you are working on is held.

As mentioned on page 10, random access memory is volatile: if you switched off, or if there should be a power failure, all the data in memory would be lost.

The information held in RAM, while the computer is switched on, is addressed and used with pinpoint accuracy. It is 'de-randomised' by the memory addressing system which keeps tabs on exactly where everything goes.

RAM chips

These are the physical components that hold the information. They are plugged either into the motherboard or into a memory card that itself is plugged into the motherboard.

XMS and EMS

'Extended' and 'expanded' are so close to each other in meaning as to be almost indistinguishable in this context (or did they really mean *tall* memory and *fat* memory, and if so, why?). Also they both start with the letters 'ex', so some bright spark decides that one should be abbreviated to XMS and the other to EMS. Not the most sensible thing to do unless the aim was to compound the possibility for confusion. Program manuals will tell you which type of memory they can use. You are unlikely, however, to meet many computer users who can tell you instantly which stands for what and how they differ.

XMS is Extended Memory (page 90), ***EMS*** is Expanded Memory (page 91).

Extra thinking space

Random access memory is the additional space above conventional and 'high' memory in which it holds the programs it is running, and their data. Some programs are able to use this area as extended memory, some need it to be converted to expanded memory, and others are unable to use either.

Virtual memory and swap files

When *Windows* is being run in its 386 ***enhanced*** mode (this happens automatically on 386s and above), memory space can be boosted by using ***virtual*** memory, which means writing to disk the parts of programs that aren't being used for the current operation, so making more real memory available.

This technique is also known as *swapping*. It is carried out by using either a temporary or permanent ***swap file*** on the hard disk. A permanent swap file is preferable because information on it is contiguous rather than fragmented.

Contiguous files

As contiguous means touching, a contiguous file has all its data in an unbroken stream, which can be accessed more quickly than fragmented data. (Yes, a computing word is being used exactly as defined in the dictionary!) Fragmentation occurs when small files have been deleted and newer, larger ones fill in gaps they have left.

As permanent swap file data is 'all in one piece' it can be accessed more quickly than data in a temporary swap file which puts as much as it can into the first available space then finds the next free space, and so on.

You can see, and if necessary change, the amount of hard disk space that *Windows* has allocated to your permanent swap file. Go into File Manager, double click on Control Panel in the Main window, then double click on the 386 Enhanced icon. Click the Virtual Memory button to see the current setting. If you have been advised that this is not enough, click on the Change button and set a new, higher figure. *Windows* puts in its own suggested figure, but provided you know you have enough free disk space then you can safely ignore that. You then have to restart *Windows*, but will be given the chance of saving everything you have been working on.

Make sure you have enough RAM

Some of the very large programs that are being produced these days need a lot of RAM to accommodate them, even before they start producing data which fills it up even further. The standard minimum issue of 4Mb of RAM with new machines to run *Windows* really is just that: a minimum.

If you are using memory-hungry programs for DTP (desktop publishing) or CAD (computer-aided design), or if you are scanning large colour photographs, you will need two or four times that amount of memory, possibly even more. It is best to get advice from the software manufacturers on how much memory they consider necessary for running their programs. You will also need a large capacity hard disk to hold the finished files.

Read-only memory

Stored information

While it is possible, and often desirable, to buy additional RAM for your machine, you will never need any more ROM than the manufacturer fitted.

ROM contains permanent information which the computer cannot change. The ROM BIOS is the Basic Input/Output System, written on to a read-only memory chip.

ROM chips are also used for holding permanent information, such as programs, in hand-held computers which have no room for disk drives. Programs can't be supplied on disk for these small machines, so they are put into ROM and supplied either in the form of plug-in chips or slot-in cards.

How memory is organised

Taking the 'random' out of random access memory

Presumably when the phrase 'random access memory' was coined, it was meant to show that any area of memory could be accessed at any time. In other words information could be reached directly rather than by having to start at the beginning and plough through everything until you reached the place you wanted.

A metaphor for this is the comparison between accessing a particular track on a CD or vinyl recording and reaching the same point on a cassette or reel to reel tape. Similarly any data on a hard disk can be accessed in a matter of milliseconds, whereas many full seconds could elapse while a tape was being wound forward or back to an equivalent destination.

Random access files

There are random access and sequential files, which follow the same line of reasoning. Information can be plucked from any record in a random access file, while sequential files have no pointers or other addressing system and so must be read from start to finish.

Sequential files had their origin in the days when the only portable storage medium for PCs was tape. When floppy disks arrived, it became possible to have random access files using a broadly similar principle to that used for random access memory.

Please use the post code

Every byte of random access memory has an address so the programs will know exactly where to look for the next bit of information.

Extended memory (XMS)

Both extended and expanded memory can only be set up if there is RAM for them to go into.

Extended memory simply adds more RAM on top of the basic 640K which is normally supplied with these PCs and accessed by MS-DOS based programs. MS-DOS and most programs run from it cannot normally use extended memory, or at least can only do so in a very limited way. However, *Windows 3* and OS/2 can take full advantage of extended memory, and by extension so can applications specially written for them.

Expanded memory (EMS)

Expanded memory (also known as LIM EMS, Lotus Intel Microsoft Expanded Memory Specification) can be fitted to all PCs. Hardware restrictions dictate that it works differently to normal memory, and programs have to be specially designed to use it. Expanded memory acts like a notebook which applications can employ for additional data storage capacity, flipping back and forth between pages as required. This is useful, but less flexible than the 'continuous stationery' of conventional memory.

Some programs can use expanded memory but not extended. Use QEMM, EMM386 or other expanded memory manager if you need to convert extended to expanded.

CHAPTER

7

The keyboard

The use of all the 'non-typewriter' keys is explained here, together with ways of typing characters not shown on the keyboard.

There is also an explanation of the software aspects of setting up keyboards for English and other languages.

This chapter goes very much further than you might expect in a beginners' book. However, the information presented here does not (as far as we can tell) exist in one easily accessible place anywhere else. It will be extremely useful to you as you get further into computing.

7

The keyboard

The keys

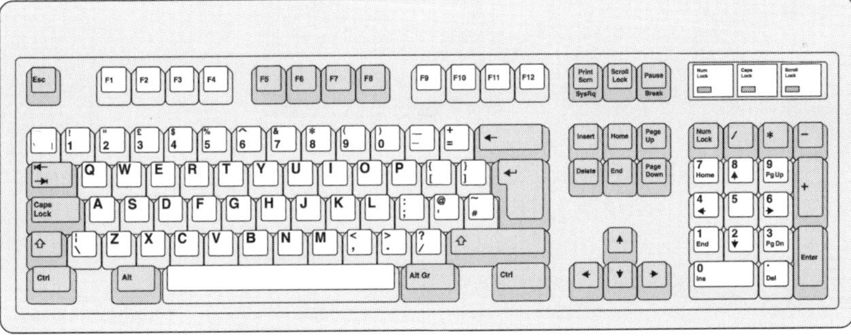

The alphabetic, or 'QWERTY', keys are arranged in exactly the same order as they are on a typewriter. However there are some extra characters within this central area of lighter coloured keys in the main block. Some UK computer keyboards may be slightly different to this one, but only in the positioning of one or two keys. Most of the darker ones are special-purpose keys, and all of these are non-printing keys (they don't produce any marks on screen or paper) except for the slash (/, usually called 'forward slash' to distinguish it from the 'backslash': \), the asterisk and the minus and plus signs around the edge of the numeric key pad.

Programs are written with these special keys in mind. Often they are used to provide ***short-cuts*** to menu items; they are especially useful for accessing items in menus that may be several levels down from the top (see page 136).

The keys are explained in sequence, starting from the top of the keyboard and working from left to right:

Escape key

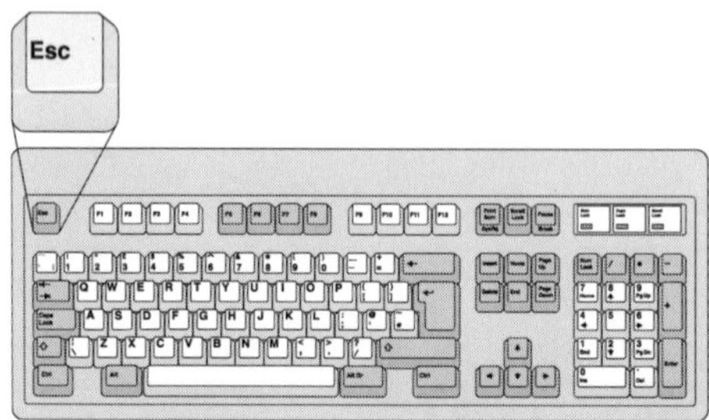

Marked **Esc**; often used literally to escape from what you are doing. If you type something on the DOS command line (see Chapter 4) and want to cancel it, press the Escape key.

Function keys

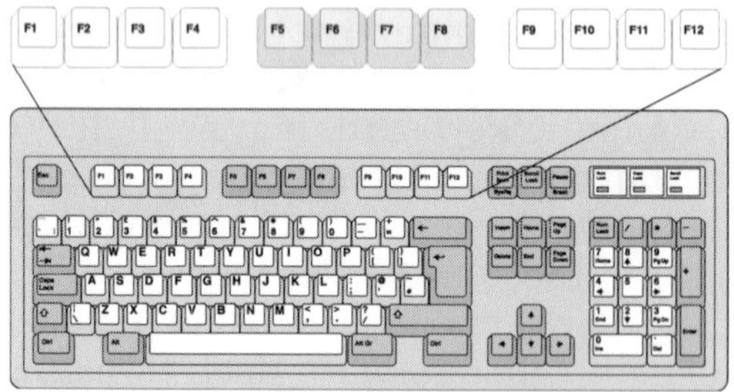

Marked **F1** to **F12** on the drawing. These keys are programmable, which means that they can be preset to do various things, such as acting as ***short-cut*** keys to menu items. They can also be used as ***macro*** keys, pre-loaded with text or instructions which you can access by hitting one key instead of having to type the same thing on many different occasions.

In DOS the **F1** key will retype your last command a letter at a time, while the **F3** key will retype it all from a single key press.

Print Screen key

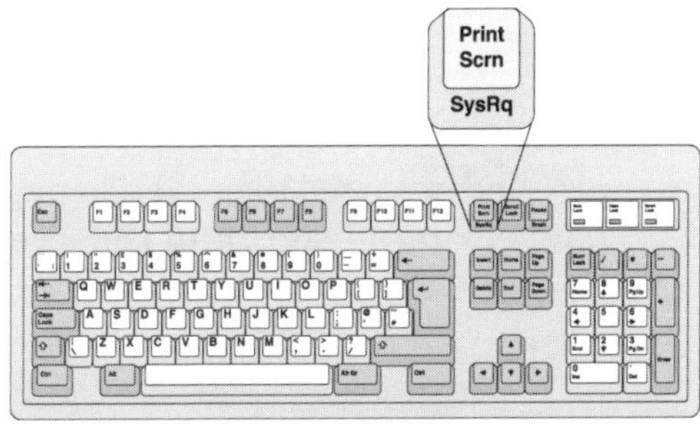

Marked **Print Scrn**. When you are using *Windows*, a press on this key will 'photograph' whatever is on the screen at the time and copy it to the ***Clipboard***. (It is sometimes necessary to hold down the **Shift** key while pressing **Print Scrn**.) The 'photograph' can then be printed directly from the Clipboard or saved as a graphic file for use in a document.

When used from DOS, a press on the **Print Scrn** key will send a copy of whatever is on the screen to your printer. This can be useful if, for example, you need to copy or rename or delete some files: it provides a printed list to work from. Particularly handy if you have used a file finding utility such as *QFIND* which can search an entire hard disk drive and put up a list of files from many different directories.

System Request key

Labelled **Sys Rq** on the front face of the **Print Scrn** key. You probably won't use this key at all. When the keyboard is used with a terminal attached to a mainframe computer, the **Sys Rq** key sends a request for a particular system to the mainframe.

Scroll Lock

A software controlled key used to prevent a page of text or graphics disappearing off the top of the screen.

Pause

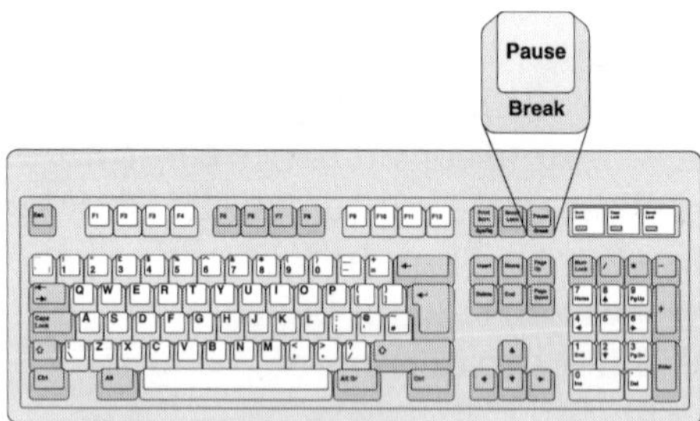

Used in DOS to stay the execution of a command. When using the DIR command to see what files are in a particular directory, **Pause** will freeze the screen. This is useful when the directory contains more than 24 files; the list would otherwise scroll off the top of the screen and you might miss the one you were looking for.

Break

Labelled **Break** on the front face of the **Pause** key. This is used in conjunction with the **Ctrl** key to halt (as opposed to pause) execution of a DOS command. After holding down the **Ctrl** key and pressing **Break** you are returned to the DOS prompt. Holding down **Ctrl** and pressing **C** has the same effect in DOS (but not in *Windows*, where the **Ctrl + C** key combination is often used to copy selected text or graphics to the Clipboard).

Indicator lights

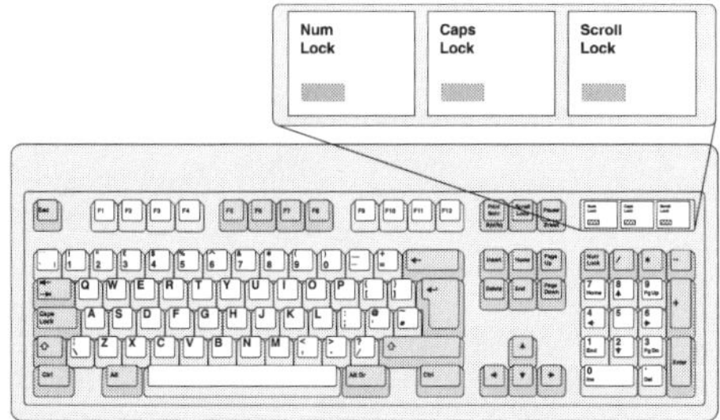

The Num Lock light shows that the key pad is set to respond only with numbers (not cursor movements). But even when it is burning brightly it's still possible to find yourself tapping away half a dozen times on the **Del** key and being surprised to see a row of six decimal points appearing to the left of the text you thought you were deleting!

Logical Not / Grave Accent / Bar

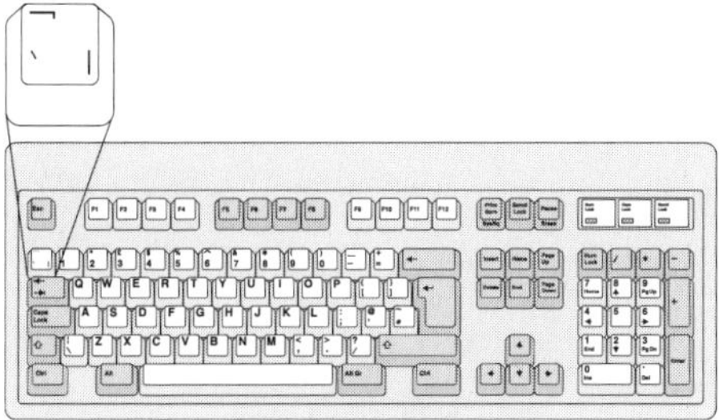

These are hardly everyday characters, which is why you will be one of the very few people in the world to know that in order to type the Bar (which actually comes out as a 'Broken Bar'), you need to hold down the **Alt Gr** or Alternative Graphics key. This is the only function of the **Alt Gr** key on the UK keyboard, apart from being used as a duplicate **Alt** key.

The Logical Not is used in some branches of mathematics; as yet research has revealed no use for the Grave Accent on its own (the normal character set has accented characters, combining the grave with standard characters, such as à, À, è, È).

Circumflex key

Nothing special about this key, but it is worth noting that the circumflex is used sometimes to represent the Ctrl key. Instead of Ctrl + C, you may meet ^C. When you type Ctrl + C at the DOS prompt it shows on screen as ^C.

Asterisk (Star)

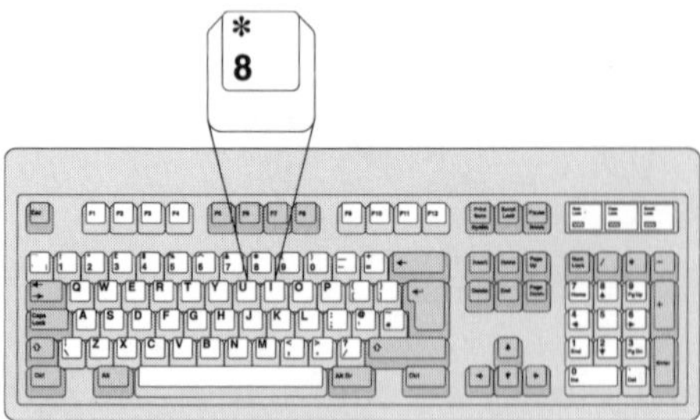

The asterisk is used as a ***wild card*** (page 288) when specifying a number of file names with one or more common characters. If you were referring to *all* the files in a directory or on a floppy disk, you would write C:\DIRNAME*.* or A:*.*. If telling somebody what had been written, the colloquial way of expressing it would be 'C DIRNAME star-dot-star' or 'A star-dot-star' rather than using the uncomfortable 'asterisk-dot-asterisk'.

The other, less powerful, wild card is the question mark. This represents only a single character.

As the asterisk is a shifted character, rather than use both hands it is easier to tap the grey asterisk key on the top line of the number key pad. It will print an asterisk whether the Num Lock is in operation or not.

Underline

The underline character, used in conjunction with the Shift key, is unlike its namesake on the typewriter: it doesn't underline characters. You can have either a character or an underline by using this key, never an underlined character.

If you went back to the beginning of a word in order to underline it, all you would get would be a string of underlines. If you were in Insert mode (see **Insert** key on page 103) they would be added to the left of your word; in Overtype mode (also covered under **Insert** key) they would take the place of the word.

As every word processor and desktop publishing program now has the facility of underlining text (see ***text attributes***, page 285) this key is virtually redundant except for its use as a character in file names and as a separator for variable names in some programming languages.

Aesthetic note: with all the facilities available for altering the appearance of text, it should not be necessary to use any form of underlining. Important words or phrases can be highlighted by being set in italics or bold, or both. Underlining is a hangover from the days of the typewriter when it was the only form of highlighting available, unless you went out and bought a red and black ribbon.

Backspace (Delete right to left) key

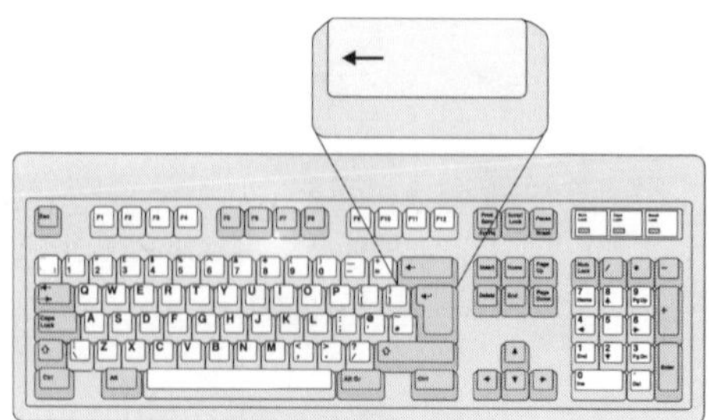

Backspace key

Have a care! This does backspace, but it also deletes as it goes.

To do the customary backspace, use either of the two 'cursor left' keys. The 'backspace' key deletes from right to left; the **Del** key deletes from left to right.

Insert key

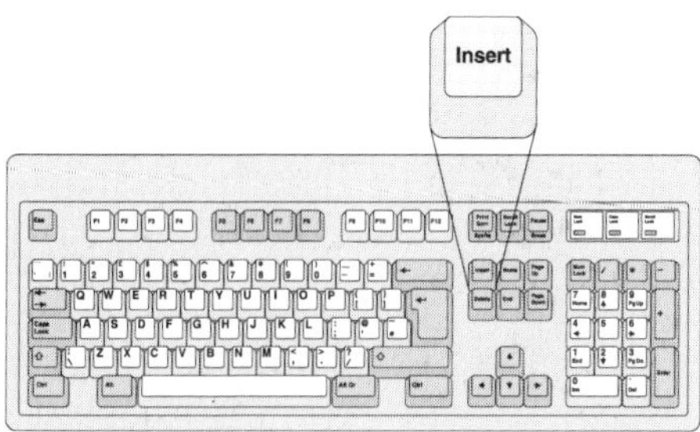

The **Insert** key (like its dissimilar looking but identically acting twin: **Ins** on the number key pad) controls the way that new typing is added into existing material. It acts as a toggle: if you are already in insert mode it switches to overtype mode, and *vice versa*.

It is wise to use insert mode, especially if you are a fast typist. Far easier to delete superfluous text than to recapture that deathless prose you have just charged into accidentally and over-written.

Word processors usually have a status line which, among other things, shows whether you are in overtype or insert mode. DTP programs tend to ignore this switch, keeping you in insert mode all the time.

Home key

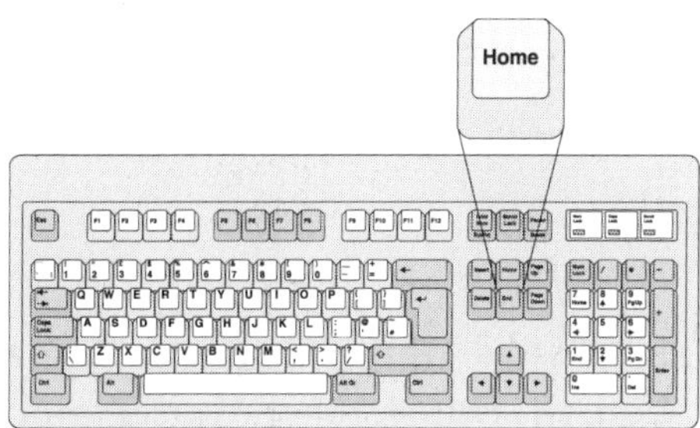

Interpreted differently by different programs. A popular use of the **Home** key is to take the cursor to the start of the current line. Used in conjunction with other keys, such as **Shift**, **Alt** and **Ctrl**, it can take the cursor to the start of the current paragraph, even to the start of the document.

Page Up key

As you won't be too surprised to learn that this key displays the previous page, it can be added that it does have other uses. For example, in *CorelDRAW!* the short-cut key combination (see page 136) Shift + **Page Up** brings the currently selected object (text, line, rectangle etc) to the front of the drawing.

Num Lock key

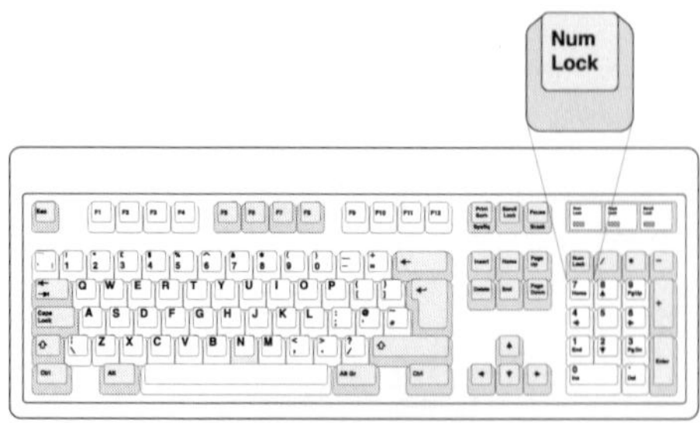

Num Lock toggles the numbers on the key pad on and off. When it is on, the **Num Lock** indicator lamp is lit and the eleven paler keys will make the numbers 0 to 9 and the decimal point available. They will print these numbers to the screen and they will feed them, for example, into maths-based programs such as spreadsheets or the *Windows* Calculator.

Number key pad

If you are keying in a lot of numbers it is much more convenient to have them all directly under your fingers than to have to use the ten numbers across the top of the QWERTY area and then use the full stop for a decimal point. There is even an additional **Enter** key to the right of the pad.

When **Num Lock** is off, the paler keys respond with their lower, non-printing, markings: **Home**, ↑ (cursor up), **Pg Up** and so on.

Next to **Num Lock** is the forward slash (solidus), used for ordinary division. A useful way of avoiding confusion between the / and \ is to refer to them as 'five past seven' and 'five to five' respectively.

The backslash, or 'five to five' slash, is also used to signify ***integer*** division: 10\4 = 2, while the forward slash gives what you would expect: 10/4 = 2½.

To the right of the oblique is the asterisk, used by programs and computer languages as the multiplication sign. On the right hand side are the minus and plus keys, the plus key being larger, in common with standard adding machine practice.

Tab Key

Most word processors and DTP programs will give fine control of tabulation: left tab, right tab, centre tab, decimal tab, all to the nearest tenth of a millimetre. The decimal tab is particularly useful for columns of figures, which will align themselves automatically with the decimal point in the rows above and below.

There is also a wide selection of characters to lead the eye when it could lose its way in the space between the end of one column and the start of another. There are typical examples of the use of leader characters, in this case the full point (full stop), in the Contents and Index pages of this book.

The tab key is often used in programs to move from one input panel or area of the screen to the next.

Return (Enter) key

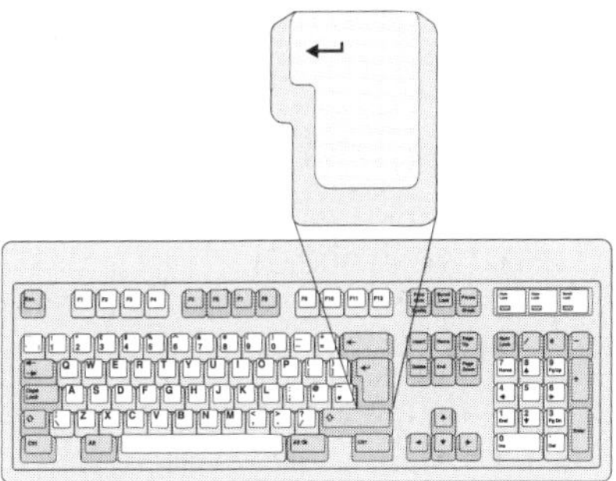

Between the old manual typewriter and the computer came the electric typewriter. It had a large carriage return key which replaced the original mechanical carriage return arm. 'Carriage return' has been abbreviated on the computer keyboard to **Return**; pressing it causes the next character to be placed at the start of the following line. This is the equivalent of bashing the carriage over to the right and simultaneously winding the paper up a notch (see carriage return/line feed, page 108).

However, another name for it is the **Enter** key. This also makes sense in its own way because when you have typed a command in DOS (Chapter 4), you *enter* it into the system by pressing this key. Only after you have entered it will the command take effect (the computer has no other way of knowing when you have finished typing the command).

The bent arrow symbol used for return, or enter, represents the resulting movement of the computer's cursor (rather than the typewriter platen): it goes down a line and shoots across to the left of the screen.

No returns, hard returns and soft returns

Word processors, text editors and DTP programs will automatically 'wrap text around' at the end of a line. You just type away and the text formats itself to the required width between the set margins. There is no need to press **Return** at the end of each line. Pressing **Return** on its own gives what is known as a 'hard return' which starts a new paragraph.

Sometimes you may want to start a new line without going the whole hog and starting a new paragraph; this is where the 'soft return' comes in.

The two most common ways of 'softening' a return are by holding down the **Shift** key while pressing **Return** (Shift + Return) or by holding down the **Ctrl** key and pressing **Return** (Ctrl + Return). The instruction manual will tell you which one to apply, though you won't do any harm by trying to see which one works for the program you're using.

Carriage return / line feed

The code

When you examine text files more closely, using a hex display utility, such as Norton, you'll see hard returns as 0D 0A [ASCII 13 + ASCII 10], representing a carriage return + line feed. Soft returns are shown as 0A [ASCII 10], line feed only.

Delete key

Deletes and closes up a character at a time to the right of the text cursor. Also used as part of the three key combination, **Ctrl + Alt + Delete** which will restart the computer when it fails to respond to anything else.

End key

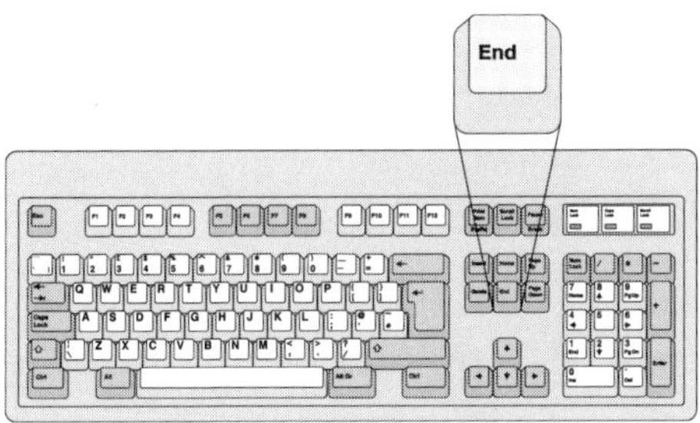

Interpreted differently by different programs. A popular use of the **End** key is to take the cursor to the end of the current line. Used in conjunction with other non-printing keys, such as **Shift**, **Alt** and **Ctrl**, it can take the cursor to the end of the current paragraph, even to the end of the document.

Page down key

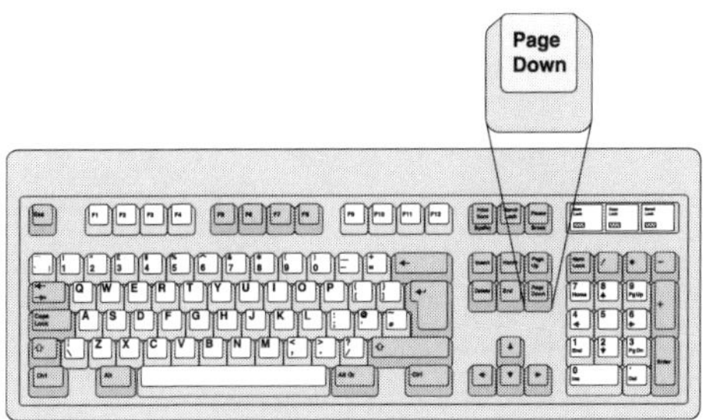

Unsurprisingly, this key displays the next page. Like many other darker, non-printing keys it does have other uses. For example, in *CorelDRAW!* the short-cut key combination (see page 136) **Shift + Page Down** sends the currently selected object (text, line, rectangle and so on) to the back of the drawing.

Caps lock key

This is well named **Caps Lock**, as distinct from Shift Lock, because it locks *only* the alphabetical character keys into being printed as capitals. The top row of number keys print as numbers even when **Caps Lock** is on (indicator light shows).

This is very handy, for example with post codes, where you can type all the letters and numbers without having to shift up and down four times. See also Shift Keys.

Shift keys

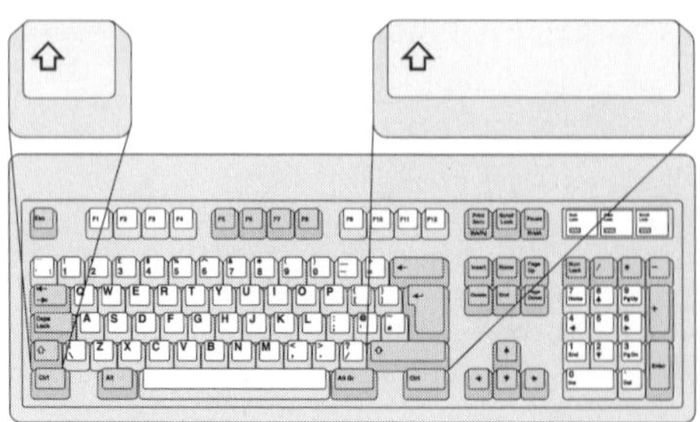

The **Shift** keys give access to the upper (shifted) characters on those keys that have them, except for the keys on the number pad whose 'shifted' numbers become available when **Num Lock** is applied. See also **Caps Lock** above.

Pipe (broken bar) & Backslash key

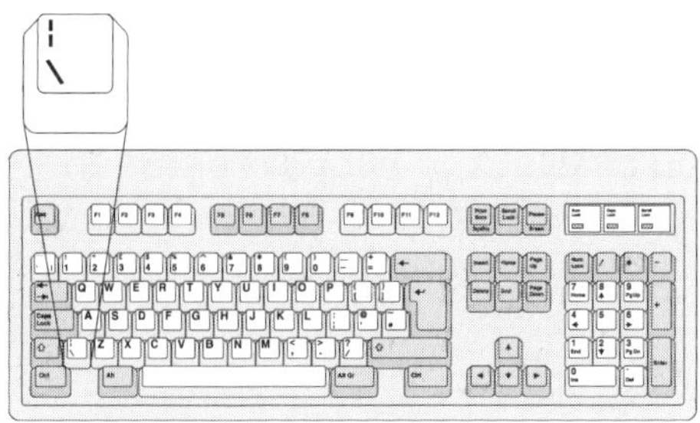

Pipe

The pipe character is used for ***redirecting command input and output***. This is an easy enough idea to grasp if you consider that input is usually applied via the keyboard, and output is usually to the screen. Which is another way of saying that you talk to the computer with the keyboard and see what it has to say by looking at the screen.

Redirecting command input and output is covered in greater detail in the Glossary (page 280), but here is a typical example to be going on with:

Suppose you wanted to look at a text file called README.TXT from the DOS prompt, you would key in the following command:

```
TYPE README.TXT
```

If README.TXT was a fairly large document, most of the text would scroll off the top of the screen and you would be left with the last 23 lines. In order to read the whole file a page at a time, you would make the command:

```
TYPE README.TXT ¦ MORE
```

This redirects the output to a program called MORE.COM which intercepts the text and presents it a page at a time.

The amusing thing is that the pipe, or broken bar symbol is drawn on the key cap, but when you hold down **Shift** and press it, you get a solid bar: | . However it does work for the pipe command. In order to get a broken bar in *Windows*, you must hold down **Alt Gr** and press the **Logical Not** key, which produces the ¦ symbol. In DOS, that produces a thick bar which the command line ignores completely.

Backslash key

The backslash key is used a great deal. It divides a 'path' into the separate directories and sub-directories making up the path to a file. For example:

```
COPY C:\ELEPHANT\FOOTPRNT.TXT A:\
```

would tell the computer that the file FOOTPRNT.TXT on the ELEPHANT directory should be copied to the root directory of the floppy disk in drive A:

Less Than key

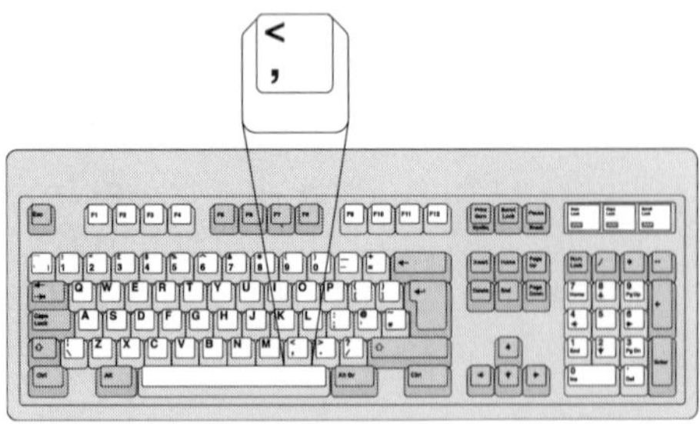

Used in programming to signify 'less than'. Also used in conjunction with the 'greater than' symbol: <> to mean 'not equal to'.

Greater Than key

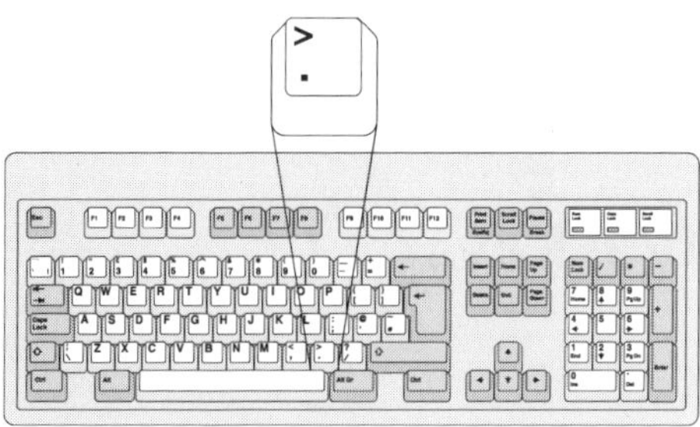

Used in programming as the 'greater than' symbol. Also used for ***redirecting command input and output***, for example:

```
TYPE README.TXT > PRN
```

causes the file to be sent to the printer, not the screen.

Ctrl (Control) keys

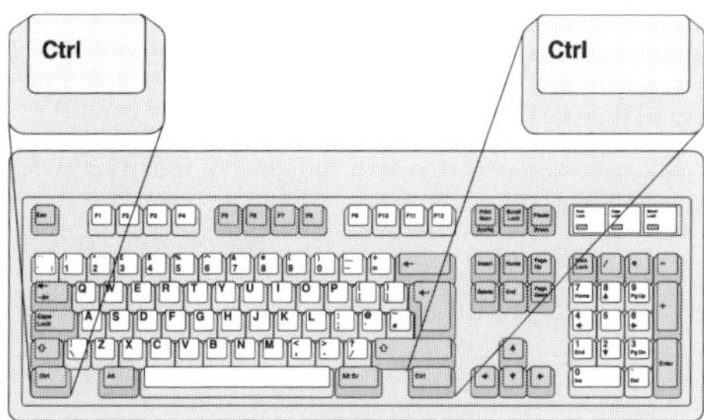

Use of a **Ctrl** key in *Windows* depends on the application that you are running at the time. It is a non-printing key and never does anything on its own, always being used in combination with other keys.

In DOS, **Ctrl + C** is used for cancelling, or escaping from, many operations. It will stop a ***batch file*** in its tracks and ask if you wish to proceed.

Ctrl + **Alt** + **Del** will get you out of situations where, for one reason or another, everything has stopped responding. This key combination restarts the computer, causing loss of anything that has not been saved, so it should only be used when all else fails.

Alt (Alternative) keys

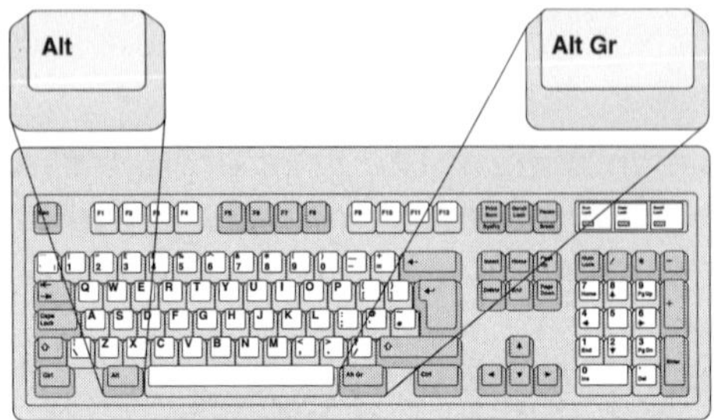

Both **Alt** and **Alt Gr** (alternative graphics) keys may be used in key combinations calling for **Alt**. The **Alt Gr** key accesses the lower right character on keys which have three or more characters on them. The UK keyboard has only one of these (the vertical bar on the **Logical Not** key) but languages with longer alphabets than ours will use them more extensively.

Cursor keys

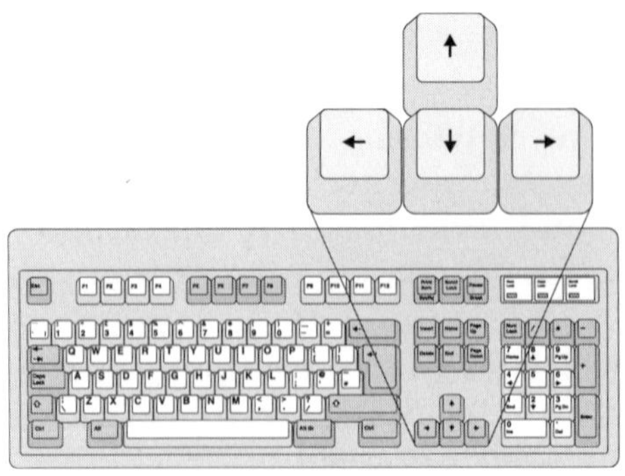

This group of four cursor keys are on the 'extended keyboard', but were not on the original keyboard. Which is why there is another set of cursor keys on the number key pad, available when **Num Lock** is off (indicator light off).

The cursor keys are used, not unreasonably, to move the cursor in the direction in which they point. They are a sensible alternative to the ***mouse*** when it is only required to move the cursor a short distance.

UK, US and other keyboards

The word 'keyboard' has two meanings. The first is applied to the hardware: the *physical* keyboard on the desk in front of you. The second, the *logical* keyboard, refers to the software. It is a shorthand way of describing the instructions given to the computer so that it responds to your key presses in the way you expect. You could, for example, tell the computer that your physical UK keyboard was the keyboard for Switzerland. If you turn to the Appendix in the DOS manual which shows keyboard layouts, you will see illustrations of the different sets of key caps.

Key caps

Some computers allow you to program the keyboard to give different characters to those printed on the keys. You can buy alternative tops (key caps) to replace the standard ones.

If you tapped the corresponding keys on your physical UK keyboard you would have access to the additional Swiss characters. If your work involved translation into several languages it could be worth buying the physical keyboards for those countries and simply swapping them round (not forgetting to switch countries, as explained in the next section).

Getting the right keyboard in *Windows*

Double click on the International icon in *Windows* Control Panel:

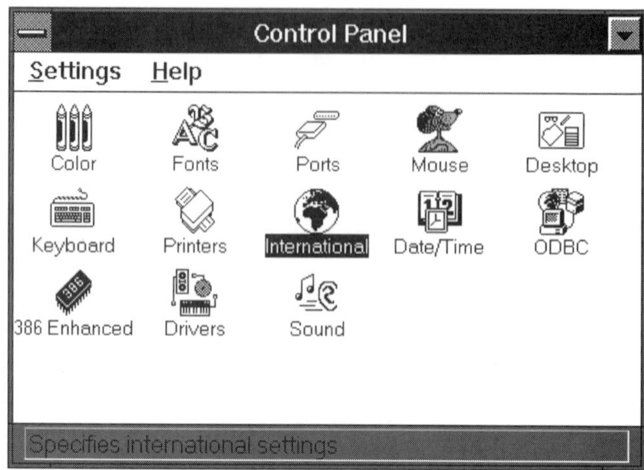

which reveals the International window:

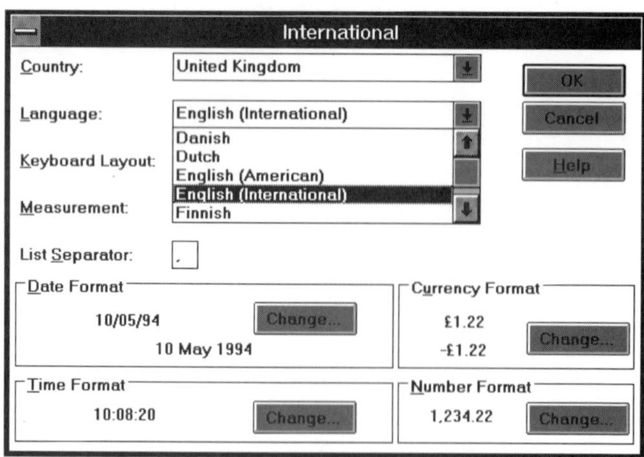

From here you can choose, among other things, how the computer will respond to your key presses.

Getting the right keyboard for DOS

While you can easily override DOS keyboard settings from *Windows*, there is no means of changing your mind within DOS apart from altering AUTOEXEC.BAT and CONFIG.SYS (which load up your choice every time the machine is switched on) or by using the KEYB command at the DOS prompt (which will remain in effect until you switch the machine off).

A standard way of getting your keyboard to respond in English is to write a line each in the AUTOEXEC.BAT and CONFIG.SYS files (see page 66).

Keyboard setting for UK in AUTOEXEC.BAT

```
KEYB UK,,C:\DOS\KEYBOARD.SYS
```

Alternatively you can achieve the same effect by including this line in CONFIG.SYS:

```
INSTALL=C:\DOS\KEYB.COM
UK,,C:\DOS\KEYBOARD.SYS
```

Country setting for UK in CONFIG.SYS

MS-DOS assumes that you are American unless you tell it otherwise. This means that you default to their strange date system: month, day, year (often shown as MM:DD:YY) as opposed to our only slightly less peculiar day, month, year (DD:MM:YY).

The most logical system is used by some UK computerists and by some countries such as Sweden and Poland: year, month, day (YY:MM:DD). This can be followed by the time in hours, minutes and seconds to pinpoint the moment in perfectly descending order.

Problems arise when you don't know which of the two less logical systems has been used. If you are given a file dated 12/12/94 you can be sure that it was created on the 12th December 1994 (or December 12, 1994).

However a date of 04/06/94 could be either 4th June 1994 or April 6, 1994 depending on its country of origin.

94/06/04 is unequivocally 1994, June 4th.

The line that should be in your CONFIG.SYS file to give you the usual UK settings for date, time, currency and decimal point (rather than the European usage of the comma: 22.35 versus 22,35) is:

```
COUNTRY=044,,C:\DOS\COUNTRY.SYS
```

You'll notice a pair of spare commas in that line. This is because the COUNTRY command is in three parts, separated by commas. The commas have to be in there even if there is nothing between them.

Country command part 1

Part 1 is the country code which specifies the country or language:

001 United States
002 Canadian-French
003 Latin America
...
044 UK
045 Denmark
046 Sweden
...
351 Portugal
358 Finland

There is a full list of these in the DOS manual; not all the numbers between 1 and 358 are used.

Country command part 2

This specifies the code page for the country (see Using the keyboard for other languages, page 119 and Character sets, page 125). If you don't enter a code page number between the commas, a Country setting of 044 will default to code page 437 (which is the one you are most likely to want).

Country command part 3

All the country information is contained in a file called COUNTRY.SYS. This normally lives in the DOS directory. You must tell the computer where to find it by specifying:

the drive, in this case **C:**
the path (or route to the directory) in this case **\DOS**
and the file name, **COUNTRY.SYS**

so we end up with:

```
COUNTRY=044,,C:\DOS\COUNTRY.SYS
```

Using the keyboard for other languages

There are three possible ways in which you might want to use foreign language characters:

1 Infrequent use of individual characters, such as é.
2 Occasional need to write in a foreign language
3 The bulk of your work is in a foreign language.

We'll look first at how you would access the hundred or so extra characters that are available but don't show on the keyboard. They're called *extended characters* (which doesn't mean that they are extended, or wider in the typographical sense, only that they are part of the character set in a range beyond those visible on the key caps).

Using characters not on the keyboard

You may need to type foreign characters from time to time, perhaps to write 'café' in preference to 'cafe', or 'Röntgen' rather than 'Roentgen' or 'Rontgen'.

Using accented characters in *Windows*

The following table shows some of the extended characters with their corresponding ANSI (American National Standards Institute) code number.

Some foreign characters and their ANSI code numbers

Character	ANSI code	Character	ANSI code	Character	ANSI code
À	0192	è	0232	Ö	0214
Á	0193	é	0233	Ø	0216
Â	0194	ê	0234	ò	0242
Ã	0195	ë	0235	ó	0243
Ä	0196	Ì	0204	ô	0244
Å	0197	Í	0205	õ	0245
à	0224	Î	0206	ö	0246
á	0225	Ï	0207	ø	0248
â	0226	ì	0236	Ù	0217
ã	0227	í	0237	Ú	0218
ä	0228	î	0238	Û	0219
å	0229	ï	0239	Ü	0220
Ç	0199	Ñ	0209	ù	0249
ç	0231	ñ	0241	ú	0250
È	0200	Ò	0210	û	0251
É	0201	Ó	0211	ü	0252
Ê	0202	Ô	0212	Ÿ	0159
Ë	0203	Õ	0213	ÿ	0255

Find the character you want, press the Num Lock key so that the indicator lamp is lit, put the text cursor where you want the character to appear, hold down the Alt key and keep it held down while you type the code number on the number key pad. Release the Alt key; the character appears in your text.

These tables have been drawn up for *your* convenience; the standard versions are arranged for the benefit of the code! The full set is shown in Appendix A.

It used to be completely straightforward when there was only one extended character set for the UK. Now we have the high (above 127) ASCII (American Standard Code for Information Interchange) set for use in DOS and the high ANSI set for use in *Windows* applications. The lower numbers, which include all the letters of the alphabet, numbers and punctuation marks, are the same for both sets.

The Character Map

In the accessories panel of *Windows* Program Manager is the Character Map icon. When you double click on it you are shown all 224 printing characters. The first of these is ANSI (and ASCII) number 32, the space.

Characters 0 to 31 are non-printing characters, which may seem a bit pointless at first glance. However they all have a use, such as number 7 which sounds the warning 'beep'.

The character map is useful in four ways:

1. It shows all the available characters
2. It shows what they look like in different fonts
3. You can copy and paste from it into your document
4. It tells you the keystrokes for the character you want

It's a long, thin table which suits the screen but will have to be printed in two parts on the next page:

The Character Map

Shown here split into two sections:

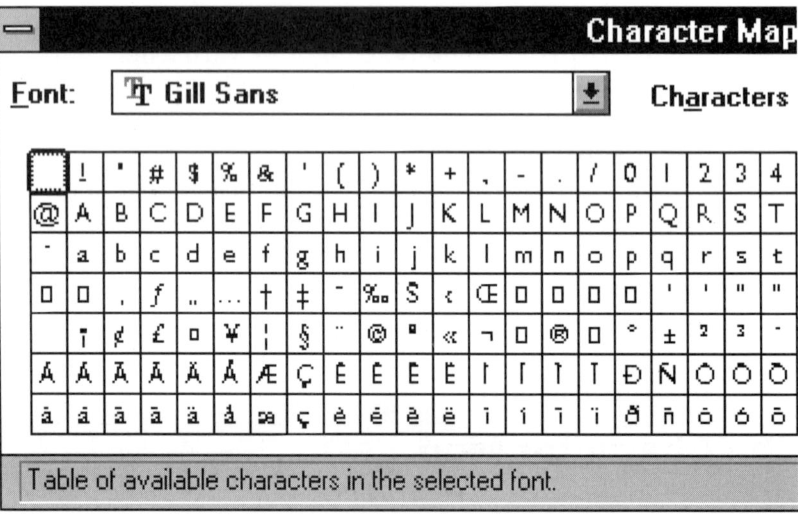

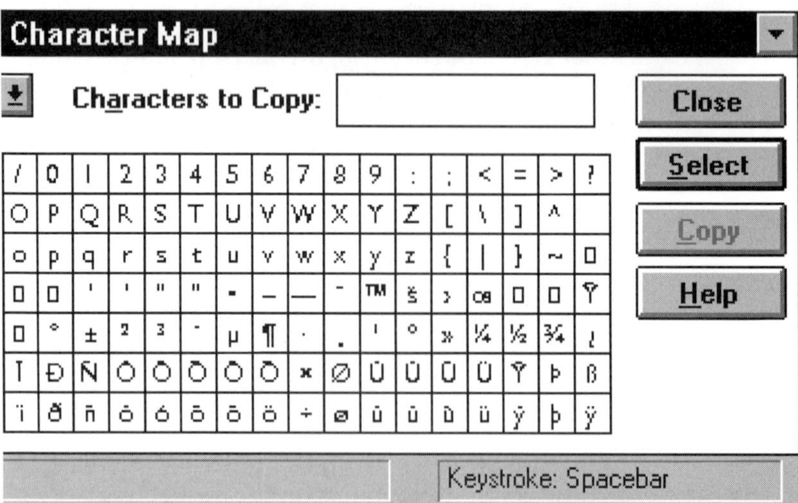

Using accented characters in DOS

Find the character you want, put the text cursor where you want the character to appear, hold down the Alt key and keep it held down while you type the code on the number key pad. Release the Alt key.

The following table shows some of the extended characters with their corresponding ASCII number. The full set is shown in Appendix B.

Some foreign characters and their ASCII code numbers

Character	ASCII code	Character	ASCII code	Character	ASCII code
À	192	è	232	Ö	214
Á	193	é	233	Ø	216
Â	194	ê	234	ò	242
Ã	195	ë	235	ó	243
Ä	196	Ì	204	ô	244
Å	197	Í	205	õ	245
à	224	Î	206	ö	246
á	225	Ï	207	ø	248
â	226	ì	236	Ù	217
ã	227	í	237	Ú	218
ä	228	î	238	Û	219
å	229	ï	239	Ü	220
Ç	199	Ñ	209	ù	249
ç	231	ñ	241	ú	250
È	200	Ò	210	û	251
É	201	Ó	211	ü	252
Ê	202	Ô	212	Ÿ	159
Ë	203	Õ	213	ÿ	255

Writing occasional documents in foreign languages

If you need occasionally to type letters or reports in a foreign language, you can tell the computer that your UK keyboard is, for example, French:

Setting up the French keyboard in DOS

Change **KEYB UK** to **KEYB FR** (see page 117) and change the country from 044 (UK) to 033 (France), see page 118.

Setting up the French keyboard in *Windows*

Go into the International window as described on page 116 and make your selections.

Using the French keyboard

With the DOS manual open at the keyboard for France in the Appendix, you can now use the corresponding keys on the UK keyboard. Notice, by the way, that as well as having accented characters, the French keyboard changes QWERTY to AZERTY.

Other foreign languages

Every country has its code, listed with the Country command in the DOS manual, such as: Germany 049, Spain 034, Italy 039, Denmark 045, Sweden 046, Norway 047.

Working mostly in foreign languages

If most of your work is in one or more foreign languages it will make life easier if you have one or more physical keyboards with the foreign language characters on the key caps. This will remove the need to check with the DOS manual that you are using the correct keys.

Setting up the keyboard(s) is exactly the same as for occasional use, described above.

Character sets (code pages)

Alternative characters from the standard keyboard

This section is here to explain what code pages are. About 99% of UK users can safely ignore it; if you need foreign language characters, go for one of the methods described on page 119ff. That will achieve your object; there is no need to know about code pages in the normal course of events.

The choice of code pages enables you to type some characters (in non-*Windows* applications) that are not available from the standard set-up. In the case of the UK country setting, code page 437 is the default; 850 is the (only) alternative.

This is a swings and roundabouts job: the different characters to which you would have access will take the place of the ones they have displaced on the standard code page. This is because there is a maximum possible number of 256 characters in any set.

Remember that this applies only to DOS and non-Windows applications using the ASCII code. There is only one Character Map for ANSI regardless of whether you have the English language, Swedish, Icelandic, Swiss/French, or choose Brazil as the country with Modern Spanish as the language, using the Latin-American keyboard.

In other words whatever your keyboard setting, the technique of getting characters that are not shown on the key caps is the same; the ANSI character numbers are constant regardless of the code page selected.

What you gain and what you lose

To save you the chore of comparing the two code pages available from a country setting of 044 (UK) here's what you would gain by choosing the alternative page, 850:

Characters in alternative page (850) not in standard code page (437)

Character	ASCII code	Character	ASCII code	Character	ASCII code
ø	155	ı	213	Ù	235
Ø	157	Í	214	ý	236
×	158	Î	215	Ý	237
®	169	Ï	216	¯	238
Á	181	¦	221	´	239
Â	182	Ì	222	-	240
À	183	Ó	224	¾	243
©	184	Ô	226	¶	244
ã	198	Ò	227	§	245
Ã	199	õ	228	¸	247
¤	207	Õ	229	¨	249
Đ	209	Þ	231	·	250
Ê	210	þ	232	¹	251
Ë	211	Ú	233	³	252
È	212	Û	234		

And this is what you lose:

Characters lost from code page 437 to make 850

Character	ASCII code	Character	ASCII code	Character	ASCII code
₧	158	╘	212	Ω	234
⌐	169	╒	213	∞	236
╡	181	╓	214	φ	237
╢	182	╫	215	∈	238
╖	183	╪	216	∩	239
╕	184	▌	221	≡	240
╜	189	▐	222	≤	243
╛	190	α	224	⌠	244
╞	198	Γ	226	⌡	245
╟	199	Π	227	≈	247
╧	207	Σ	228	-	249
╨	208	σ	229	·	250
╤	209	γ	231	√	251
╥	210	Φ	232	η	252
╙	211	Θ	233		

All in all it would be far simpler to change to the country whose accents you needed. European countries other than the UK will default to code page 850 anyway.

CHAPTER

8

Word processing

This chapter starts straight away with 'hands on' experience, which is the only way to find out how to do something and remember it afterwards. Microsoft Windows, *which must be installed on your machine, has an accessory called* 'Write'. *This is your springboard into word processing.*

Word processing

Jumping into *Windows Write*

Following the theme from the introduction that it doesn't *have* to be difficult, here is one way to start writing a letter (or a memo, or a report, or a play, or anything).

1. ***Double click*** the ***mouse*** on the *Windows Write* ***icon***:

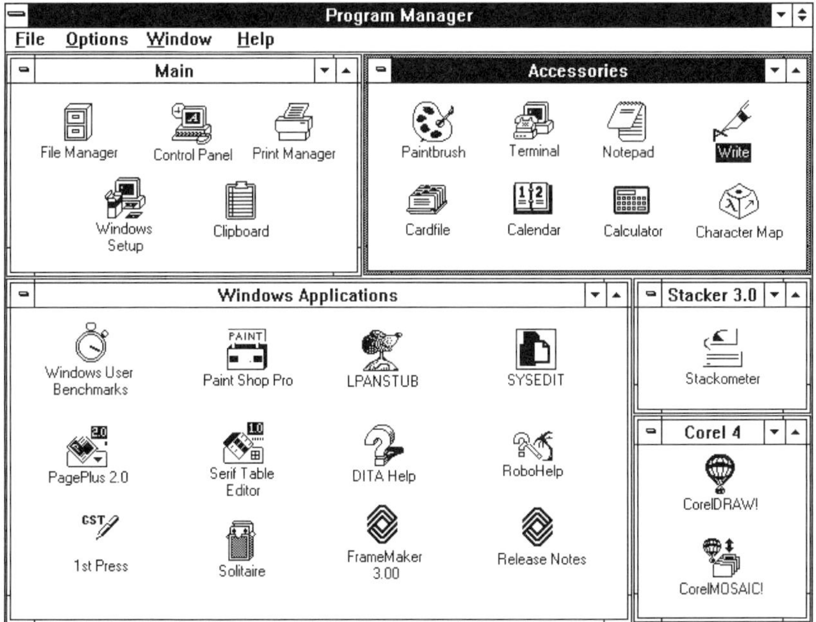

2. Start typing.

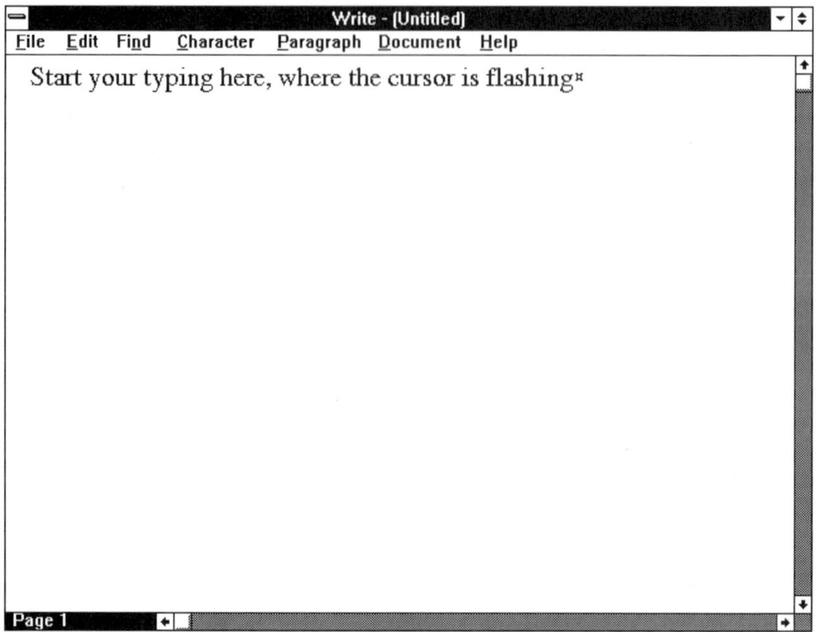

Which wasn't too stressful, was it?

This is typical of computing, or anything else for that matter: when you take the steady approach and do *exactly* what the instructions say, things tend to work.

You'll have noticed lots of italics in the first step. The ***mouse*** and its ***double click*** are explained fully in the Glossary; all it means is to press down the left mouse button twice in quick succession. ***Icon*** (in this case the picture of a fountain pen nib) is also described there.

Beyond the typewriter

Word processors come with varying degrees of sophistication, but even the simplest of them has much more to offer than the humble typewriter.

Selecting text to change

There are various reasons for wanting to select text:

To alter a letter, a word or several words
To change the typeface or type size
To move text from one place to another
To copy text from one document to another
To change a word to *italic* or **bold**, or ***both***.

Text is selected by dragging the ***cursor*** across the words. Move the mouse so that the cursor is at the left hand side of the first word, hold down the left mouse button, drag the mouse to the right until it is at the end of the last word, release the mouse button.

Text can be selected in either direction: from right to left as well as from left to right. You can select a whole word by double-clicking on it. If you are selecting a complete paragraph, say to move it to a more appropriate position, you can select it from the bottom up or the top down.

As the cursor moves across the text each letter is highlighted. Highlighting is also known as reverse video. If you are working with black text on a white background then the text turns white and its immediate background turns black. If you are working with coloured text then the text appears in its complementary colour (for example red text turns green) and its immediate background turns black.

Changing the typeface

The example was set in Times New Roman; you might prefer **the typewriter look (Courier)**, or one of the most elegant typefaces around: Optima. At the same time you could change the type size.

Some of the fonts called up in this chapter may not be on your system. If not, choose the nearest.

Select the text you want to change (the whole document doesn't have to be in the same face or the same size).

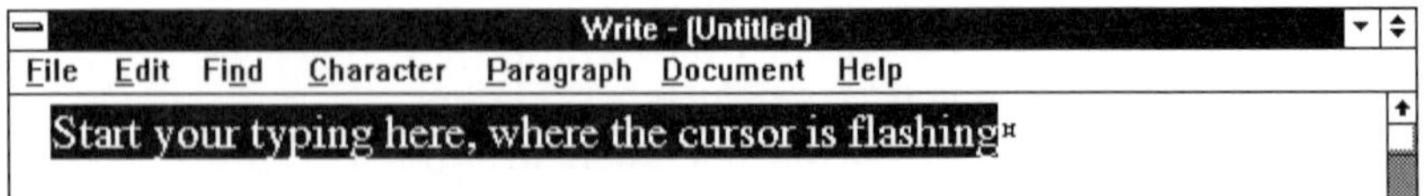

(The bottom of this illustration has been cut off as it doesn't contain any useful information at the moment.)

Click on the **Character** menu. You'll see the word '**Character**' in the menu bar; when you click on it the menu drops down (by the way, the word 'menu' can be used both for the menu title and the items it contains):

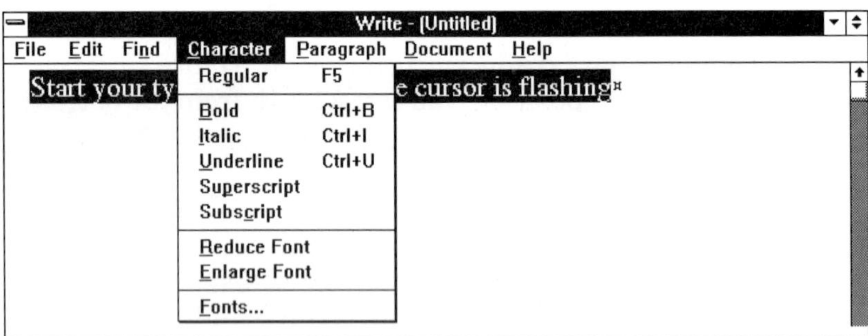

You'll notice that the B of **Bold** is underlined, and that *every* menu item has one of its characters underlined. This is so that you can take a short-cut to getting at the menu, as well as the menu item, without having to use the mouse (see next section, **Short cut keys**, on page 136).

Now click on '**Fonts...**' and a further menu appears (the dots after a menu item always signify that there's more to follow. Had you clicked on, say, **Bold**, then your text would have been converted from the normal weight of Times to **Times Bold**, and the menu would have rolled back out of sight).

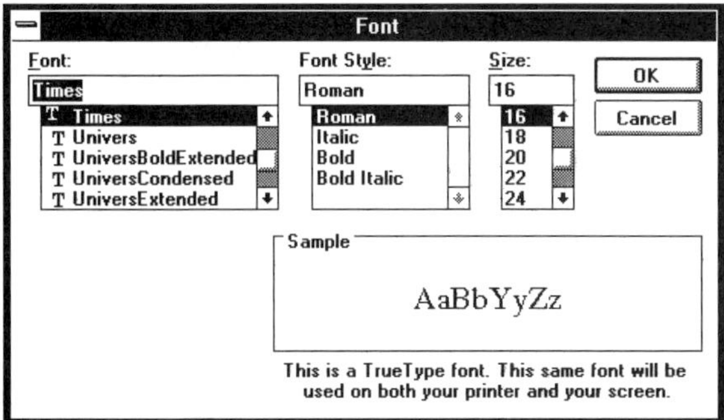

We'll choose Univers Black and reduce the type size from 16pt (16 point) to 10pt. Then click on the OK button.

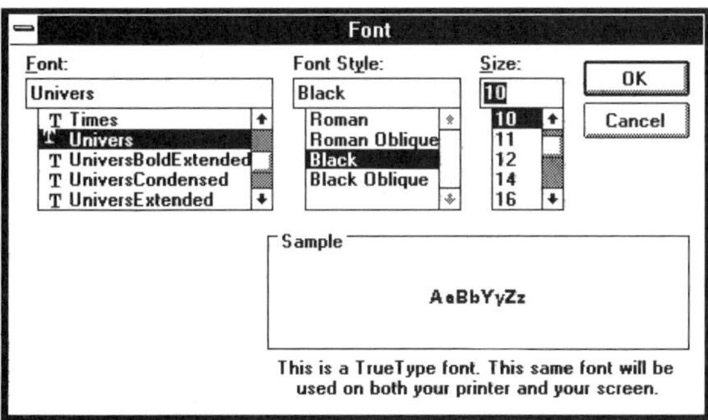

The **Font** window is helpful in that it shows the current setting. This can be useful if you can't remember what you have used: just select a piece of the text, click on the **Character** menu then on **Fonts...**, and up pops the window with all the information you need.

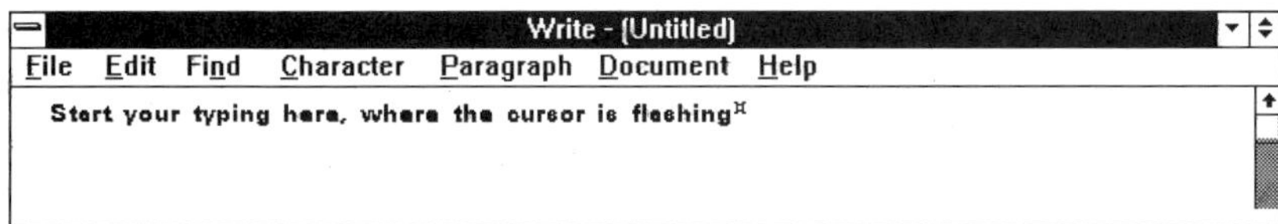

The **Font** window has disappeared whence it came and the text has been changed to Univers Black 10pt.

Short-cut keys

Short-cuts are sometimes useful, sometimes a longer way round if it means letting go of the mouse to use your hand on the keyboard.

Short-cut keys

The short-cut to any Windows menu item is to hold down the Alt Key (or Alt Gr if there's one on your keyboard) and type the underlined character of the menu name, then type the underlined character of the menu item you require.

In the case of popping up the **Font** window you would hold down the Alt key, type the letter C for **Character**, then type F for **Fonts....**

There is one important reservation about the use of short-cut keys: different software houses often use different key combinations. Sometimes the same software house will use different short-cuts in different programs it supplies.

Windows Write uses Alt + T (or Ctrl + X) to cut text, Alt + C (or Ctrl + C) to copy, and Alt + P (or Ctrl + V) to paste. *Microsoft Edit* and *Quick Basic* both use Shift + Del to cut text, Ctrl + Ins to copy, Shift + Ins to paste. *Microsoft Word for Windows* uses Ctrl + X, Ctrl + C and Ctrl + V.

RoboHelp (a programmers' tool for writing help screens, produced by a different software house) works in conjunction with *Word for Windows* but changes *Word's* short-cuts to Ctrl + X to cut, Ctrl + Ins to copy, Shift + Ins to paste! It uses Ctrl + C and Ctrl + V for entirely different purposes.

If you are using one program all the time it's easy enough. Using several can introduce problems.

Saving your work

Save frequently

The importance of saving your work can not be over-emphasised. Accidents can happen: someone might trip over your power cable and pull it out; there can be a glitch in the mains supply. It is even possible to make a complete hash of what you're doing, in which case it would be much quicker to go back to a previously saved version and start again.

The short-cut to saving, or copying your work onto the hard disk, in *Windows Write* is to hold down the Alt key and type F then S. Otherwise you could select the **File** menu with the mouse and then click on **Save**. If you are working quickly then saving every five minutes is a good idea. Without further ado we'll save what we've done so far.

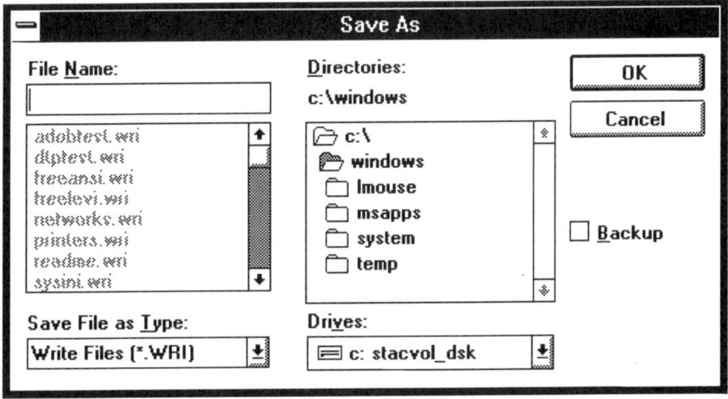

Because this document hasn't been saved before, it has no name, hence **Write - [Untitled]** at the top of the *Write* window.

Files, file names and directories are all explained in Chapters 4 & 5. If you've already been there you'll know that a file name can have a maximum of eight characters plus a three-character suffix (also called 'extension'). The suffix has already been decided for us: as it is a *Write* file this will be '.WRI' (you can see lots of them listed under the **File Name** input panel in the **Save As** window).

Naming files

As this is the first document we have produced, we'll call it FIRSTDOC.WRI; seems reasonable? Do give files sensible names. People are often tempted to call them FRED or RUBBISH or TEABREAK or something else which seems terribly clever and amusing at the time. However, come the dawn three weeks hence, it isn't quite so funny when they can't find the file they're looking for. A certain tester of programs used a scatological four-letter word as the name of a copy of a computer game. This copy was accidentally put onto the CD master, which was run off in its tens of thousands and then distributed as a magazine cover disk. Red faces all round.

Rather than complicating matters at this stage by going into the **Directories** panel (Chapter 5 describes directories), we'll type the directory and file name straight into the **File Name** input panel. There's a directory on the hard disk called ODDSENDS so we'll put it in there.

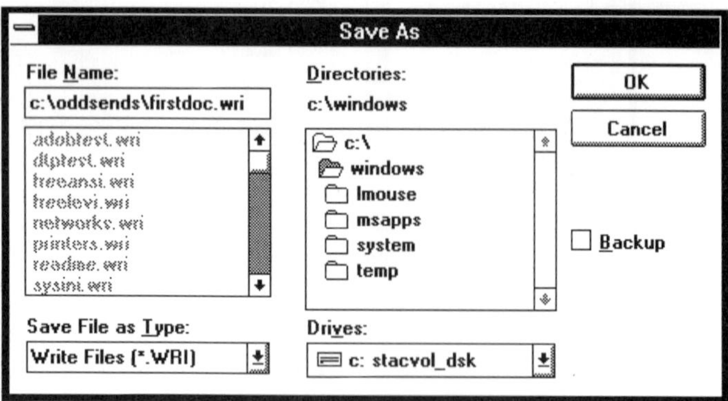

A click on the OK button confirms that the file should be saved, and now its name appears in the title bar:

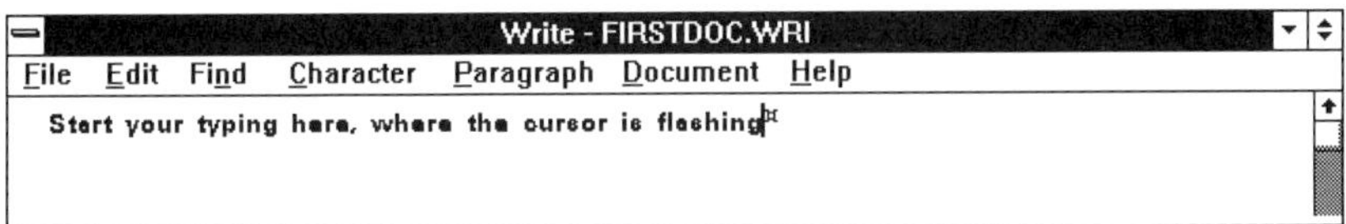
Write - FIRSTDOC.WRI
File Edit Find Character Paragraph Document Help
Start your typing here, where the cursor is flashing

Editing text

If you are making major changes, such as moving a whole paragraph or deleting one, then you will be able to select it as discussed on page 133. We'll take it up from there and go a stage further.

Wipe and type

This is useful when you need to change a whole word or several words. First select the text by dragging the cursor across it (a wiping action):

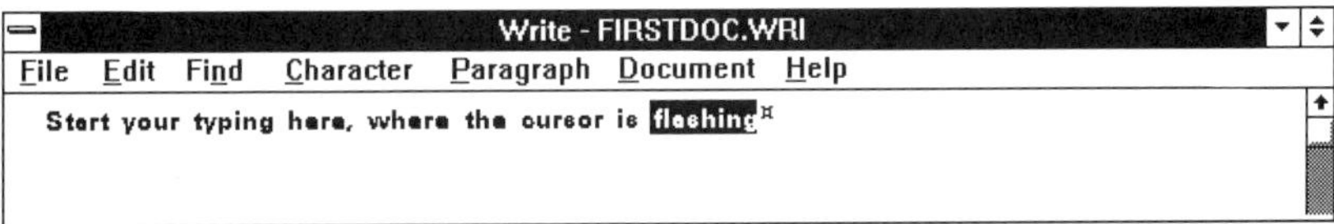
Write - FIRSTDOC.WRI
File Edit Find Character Paragraph Document Help
Start your typing here, where the cursor is flashing

then type the new text. As soon as you start to type, the highlighted characters disappear and the new ones take their place:

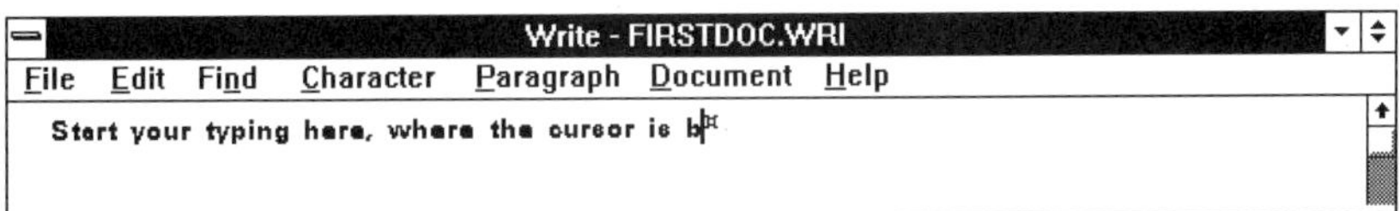
Write - FIRSTDOC.WRI
File Edit Find Character Paragraph Document Help
Start your typing here, where the cursor is b

After you've done this a few times you won't be stopping to watch it happen, you'll just wipe and then type away:

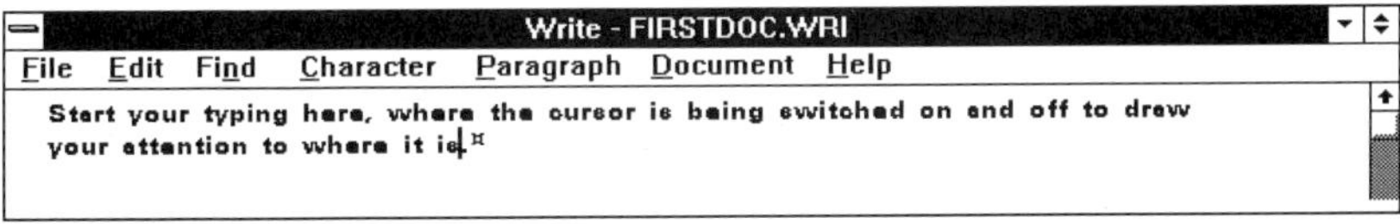
Write - FIRSTDOC.WRI
File Edit Find Character Paragraph Document Help
Start your typing here, where the cursor is being switched on and off to draw
your attention to where it is

Making smaller changes

Making small changes as you go is an instinctive process if you have ever used a typewriter: just backspace over the mistake and type the revised version. The difference here is that there's no need for Tipp-Ex because the characters are cleared as you backspace over them.

'Backspace' is the long grey key with a left-pointing arrow, immediately above the Return key.

The Delete key (there is another one on the number pad of the keyboard, marked 'Del') clears characters in the other direction: from right to left.

If you don't spot the mistake until later, put the cursor to the right of the character(s) and backspace over them, or put the cursor to the left and use the Delete key (or, if Num Lock is off, you can use the Del key).

A complete word can be selected by double-clicking on it. The word then appears in reverse video. You can delete it with the Delete key or type in a new word, as described in Wipe and Type on page 139.

Using italics and bold type

You can alter the appearance of one or more characters by changing the ***text attributes***.

In *Write* these can be Normal (also called Regular), *Italic*, **Bold**, **Underlined**, Superscript or Subscript, and the possible combinations of these six.

To set the attributes, highlight the word(s) with the cursor, click on the **Character** menu then on the attribute you want. The word '**Character**' here goes a stage further by being in a different typeface to the rest of the paragraph. With it still highlighted, go to the bottom of the menu and select **Fonts**.... Pick any one you like; it could even be a different size.

Scroll bars

A little revision: we'll change the typeface for FIRSTDOC.WRI from Univers to Bookman. Select all the text, use Alt + C to get to the **Character** menu, type F for **Fonts...**, then click on Bookman.

Did you manage to get to Bookman? Or did it look as though the only fonts available were four different sorts of Univers and one of University Roman?

To the right of the font list is a scroll bar. In fact there'll be a scroll bar with any long ***pick list***.

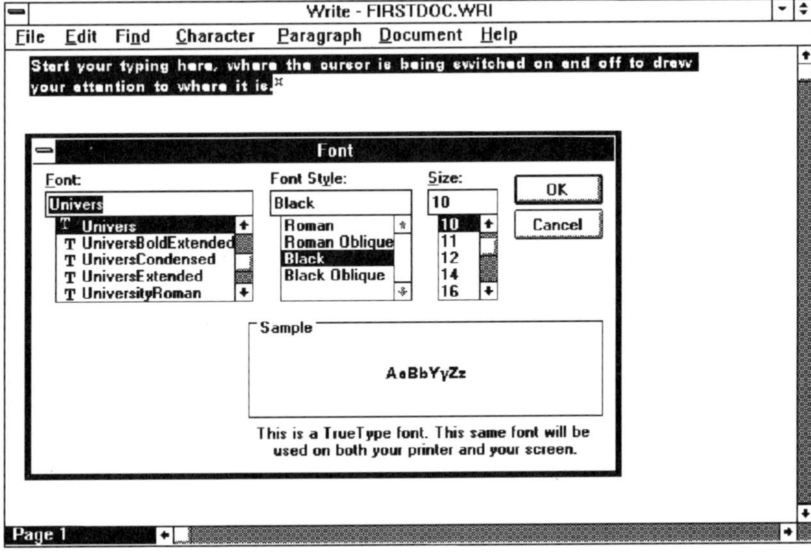

Scroll bars are used for moving to areas which are at present out of sight. They can move lists up and down, they can also move the text in word processor windows up and down. *Write*, in common with other *Windows* applications, also has a scroll bar on the bottom of the window for moving text to the left or right. The next screen shot shows how to use the scroll bars.

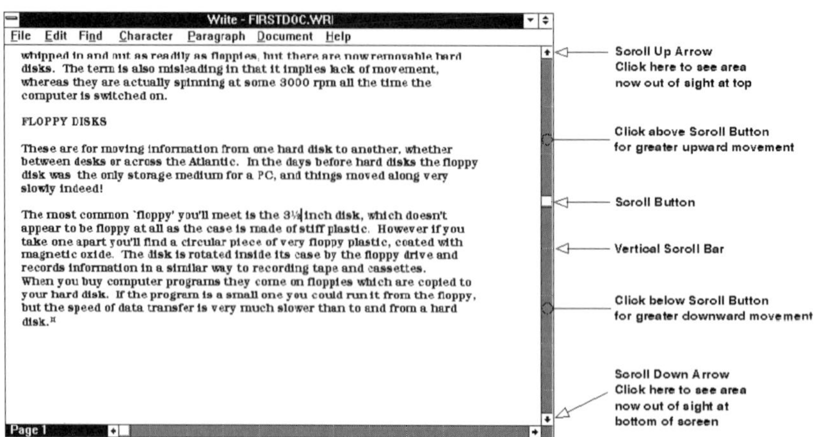

Scroll bars

You'll be using scroll bars a great deal in your computing career. It would be a worth-while idea to practise their use now.

In order to produce the 'How to use scroll bars' picture it was necessary to introduce a whole lot more text so that the scroll button could be brought further down the bar.

This would have involved a considerable amount of typing had it not been for our next trick, which is known as 'cut & paste'.

Cut and Paste

Windows allows you not only to cut or copy something out of a document and paste it somewhere else in the same piece, but also to cut or copy from one ***application*** and paste into another. So you may recognise the text that has been pasted into FIRSTDOC.WRI; it came from Chapter 1 of this book, which was prepared in another *Windows* application: a desktop publishing program called *FrameMaker*.

Imagine trying to do *that* before the age of the personal computer!

This is one of the reasons that computers need a lot of memory. When anything is 'cut' from its current position it is immediately 'pasted' onto the *Windows* ***Clipboard*** for safe keeping:

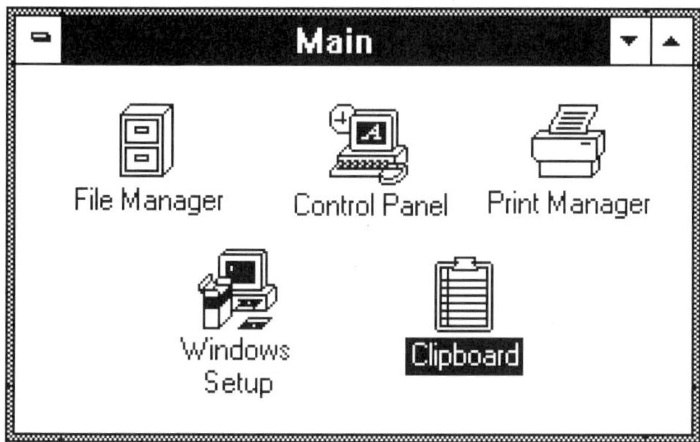

The 'pasted' text or graphics are actually stored in memory, and you can get them out at any time. A double click on the Clipboard icon will show you if there's anything in there:

The process is fully automatic, simply use either of *Write*'s short-cut copy commands (Ctrl + C or Alt + E then C) or click on the **Edit** menu, drag the cursor onto **Copy** and let go the mouse button. You don't have to do anything else: *Windows* takes care of accessing the Clipboard to put things in and take them out.

The single limitation of the Clipboard (prior to *Windows* v3.11) is that there can only be one thing in there at a time. In other words, as soon as you do another 'cut' or 'copy' you will lose (or *overwrite*, as it's known) anything already in there. *Windows for WorkGroups* has a ClipBook; you can now paste things into it from the clipboard, and back out again.

A useful feature is that you can 'paste' from the Clipboard as often as you like and the original will still be there. This is of more use in graphics applications than for text. You could, for example, draw a small grey box, copy it then paste its clones into your illustration as many times as you wanted. Although the term 'paste' is used, they are not glued to the spot but can be moved to different positions in the drawing.

PASTE

Undo

In the **Edit** menu of most *Windows* applications is the magic word **Undo**. This is more immediately forgiving than the process of reverting to a previously saved version of your work.

When you make a mistake, especially in graphics programs where it is possible to move something accidentally, you simply click on **Undo** and are taken back to the moment before you made that false move.

However, the undo facility only applies to your most recent change, whether by mouse movement or keystroke.

Adding pictures to *Windows Write*

Three ways to import graphics

You can add pictures from *Windows Paintbrush* to your document in three ways. The first, Copy and Paste lacks the subtleties of the other two. (*Paintbrush* is described in more detail in Chapter 3.)

In each case use the Scissors tool for making a rectangular outline round the drawing, or part of a drawing, that you want to be incorporated into your document.

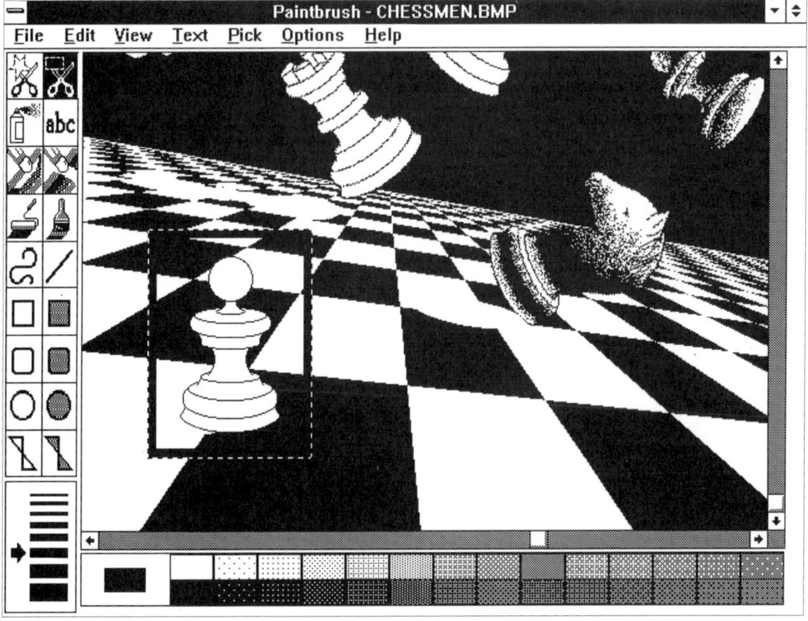

This is a view of part of one of *Windows*' own graphics, called CHESS.BMP and copied as CHESSMEN.BMP so the copy could be modified without affecting the original. The pawn and an added black rectangle have been selected for copying as shown by the dashed box around them. This box was drawn following a click on the

Scissors Tool, shown highlighted at the top right of the toolbox.

To copy this part of the drawing, click on the **Edit** menu and then on **Copy**. This is now ready on the Clipboard for the first of the three different pasting methods:

Copied and pasted graphics

Oddly enough the longest route is used for achieving plain ordinary pasting. With your picture copied from *Paintbrush*, switch to *Write*, click on the **Edit** menu and select **Paste Special**.... Under **Data Type** select **Picture** (as opposed to **Paintbrush Picture Object**) then click on the **Paste** button (not **Paste Link**).

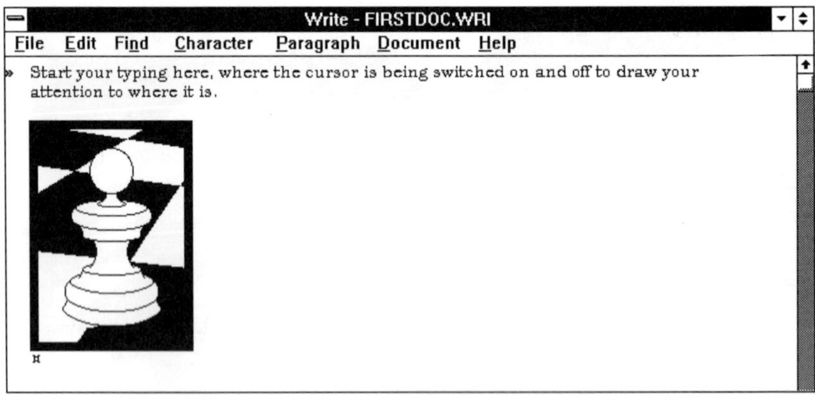
Write - FIRSTDOC.WRI
File Edit Find Character Paragraph Document Help
Start your typing here, where the cursor is being switched on and off to draw your attention to where it is.

This pawn is now independent of any changes made to the original drawing.

Embedded graphics

For this example we'll pick up a rook (Persian: rukh = tower with battlements) from a different part of the CHESSMEN.BMP drawing. Use exactly the same capturing and copying technique as before. To paste, click on *Write*'s **Edit** menu and choose **Paste**.

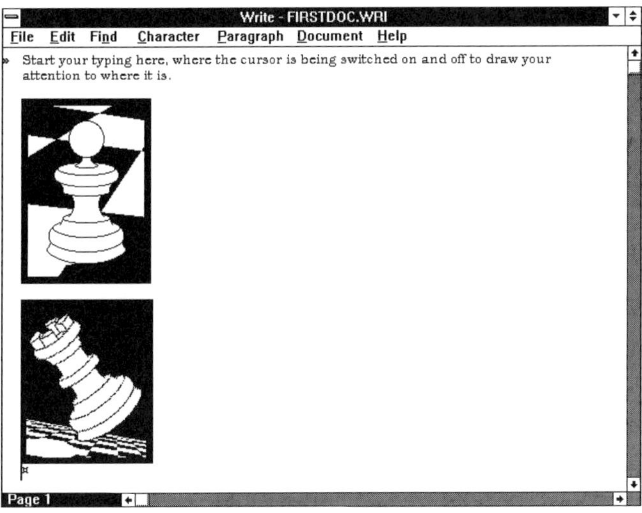

If you double-click on an embedded graphic it will respond by putting you straight into the program that originated it, in this case *Paintbrush*.

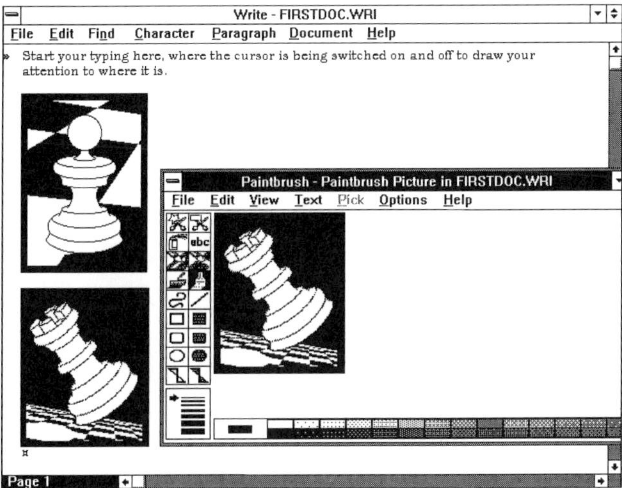

It saves the time spent switching from one program to another and ensures that all embedded versions of the drawing stay the same.

The drawback is that it could be embarrassing if it changed an earlier version that you particularly wanted kept in its unmodified state.

Linked graphics

This is the most powerful method, so we'll use the queen. Copy the drawing from *Paintbrush* as before, switch to *Write* and from the **Edit** menu use **Paste Link**. This establishes a 'dynamic link' between the original drawing in *Paintbrush* and its copy in *Write*. Any changes made to the original are immediately reflected in the copy, so it is always up to date.

This is the 'linking' part of the expression 'Object linking and embedding' (OLE) which you may hear being bandied about. OLE is only available to programs specially written to support the facility.

A double click on the queen in *Write* brings up the original drawing in *Paintbrush*, ready to be changed.

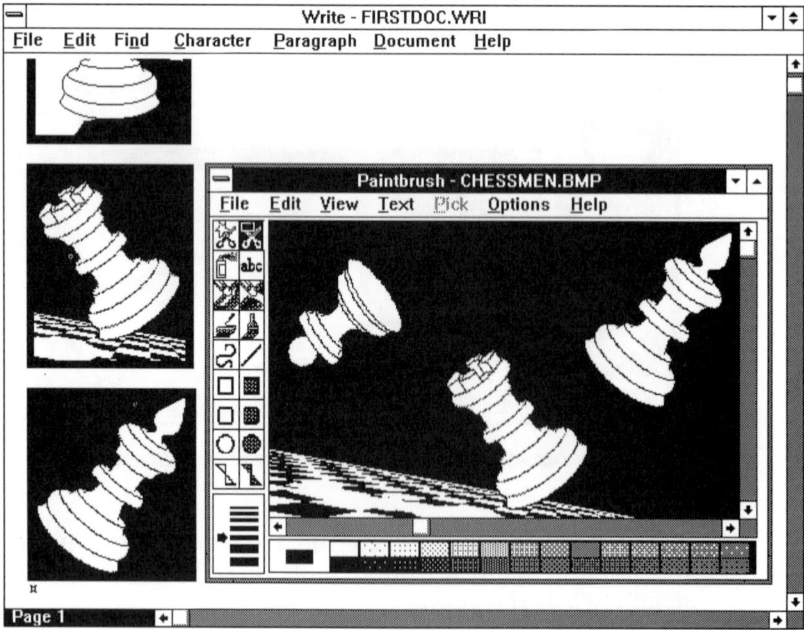

If it were possible to modify the drawing within *Write*, then any changes made there would be reflected back into *Paintbrush*, or whichever other OLE-supported drawing program you had used for the original. It is this reflection in the original that is the difference between linking and embedding.

Moving a picture in *Windows Write*

Although *Write* cannot change the content of drawings it can change their horizontal position on the page and their overall shape and size. They can be pushed further down the page by putting carriage returns above them.

To move a picture horizontally in *Windows Write*, click on the **Edit** menu, then on **Move Picture**. What happens next is peculiar to *Write*: instead of dragging the picture with the left mouse button held down, you just move the mouse. A 'square within a square' cursor and a dotted rectangle follow your movement. When the rectangle is where you want the graphic to be, *then* click the left mouse button.

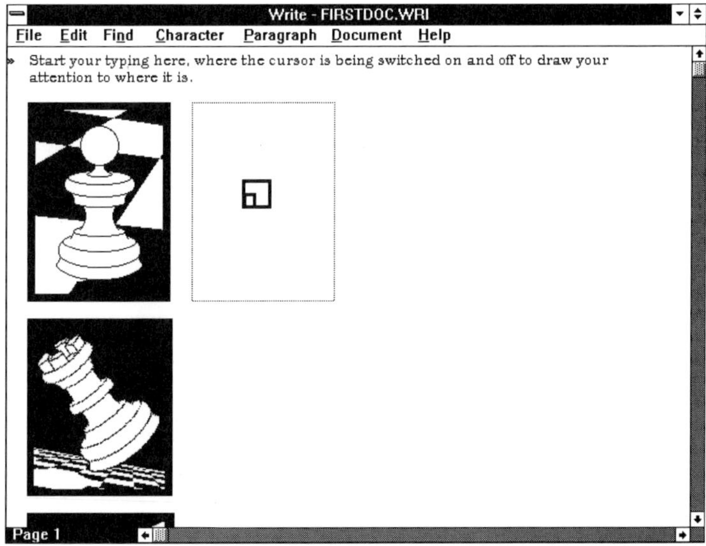
Write - FIRSTDOC.WRI
File Edit Find Character Paragraph Document Help
Start your typing here, where the cursor is being switched on and off to draw your attention to where it is.
Page 1

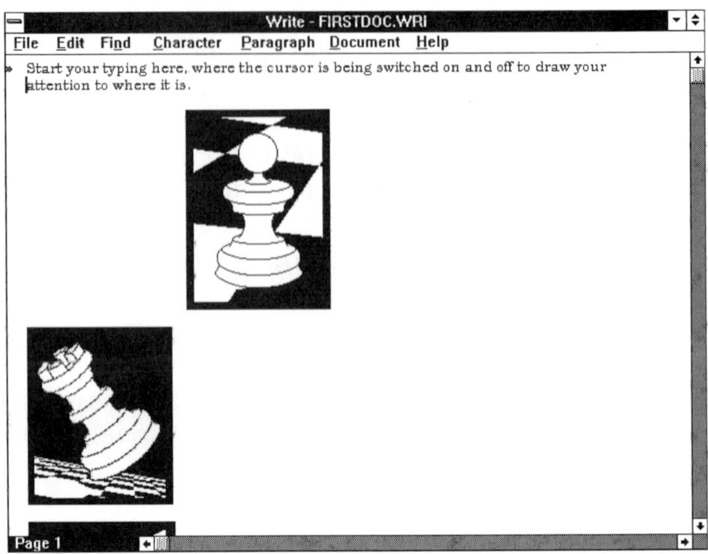
Write - FIRSTDOC.WRI
File Edit Find Character Paragraph Document Help
Start your typing here, where the cursor is being switched on and off to draw your attention to where it is.
Page 1

The graphic is now in its new position.

Changing picture size in *Write*

To change the size, click on the picture and choose **Size Picture** from the **Edit** menu. The 'square within a square' cursor appears, together with a dotted rectangle surrounding the picture. You can increase the size in a downward and rightward direction or just stretch it in one of these directions to change the aspect ratio.

As in the case of moving a graphic in *Write*, the next step is unusual (different to most other word processors, graphics programs and desktop publishing programs): move the mouse with no button pressed.

This time you'll notice a useful indicator at the bottom left of the window, showing how far the picture is being stretched in the horizontal (X) and vertical (Y) directions. **2.0X** indicates double the present width.

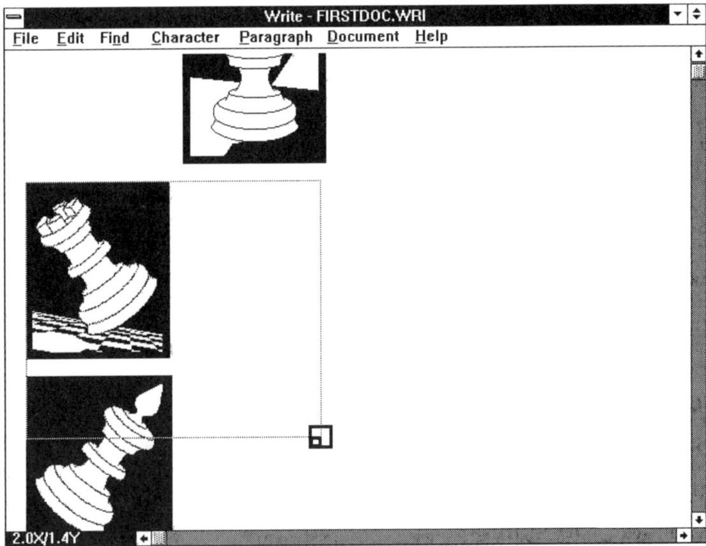

Click on the left mouse button when the size is right.

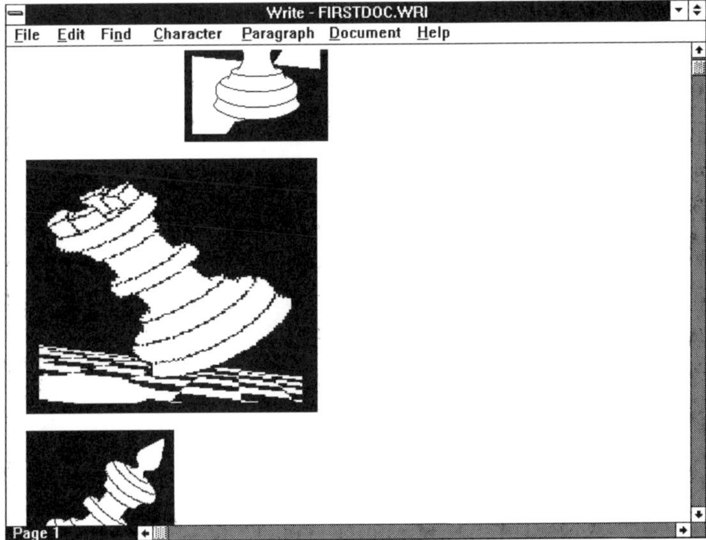

X and Y stretching must be the same to avoid distortion. In this case they were different (2.0 by 1.4).

Moving with the mouse

Do remember that the system Windows Write uses for moving pictures is extremely unusual. Please don't carry it with you to other graphics applications. The normal way is to drag the object while holding down the left mouse button.

After this excursion into graphics we'll have a further look into ways of dealing with text.

Changing the look of a whole paragraph

This is known as paragraph formatting.

A paragraph in word processing and DTP terms is anything separated from the rest of the text by a carriage return, achieved by pressing the Return key. A paragraph can be anything from a single word heading to a whole page of text.

To make a document easier to understand, as well as being easier on the eye, it is customary to use headings, sub-headings, sub-sub-headings and so on. Also lists of items or ideas are better presented by indenting them so their shape is different from the rest of the text.

All of these will use different paragraph formats. Now we shall look at the basic facilities provided by *Windows Write* for paragraph formatting. The word 'basic' there is not meant disparagingly. It is simply that this word processor, thrown in free with *Windows*, could not be expected to have as many features as one costing several times more than *Windows* itself.

The first step in this demonstration will be to start a new document in *Write*, calling it SECONDOC.WRI (maximum eight characters + suffix). Next step will be copying a few paragraphs of text into it.

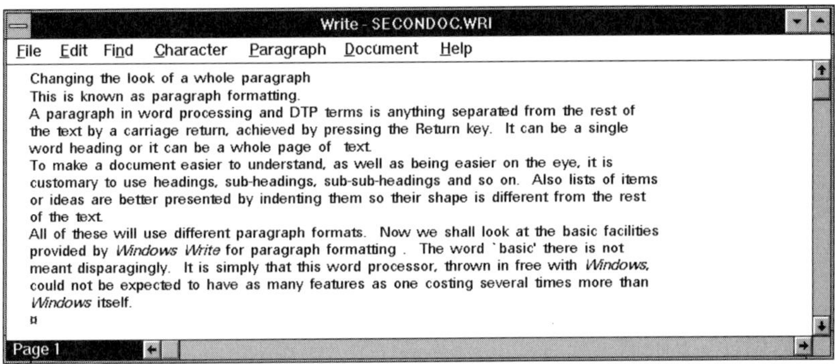
Write - SECONDOC.WRI
File Edit Find Character Paragraph Document Help
Changing the look of a whole paragraph
This is known as paragraph formatting.
A paragraph in word processing and DTP terms is anything separated from the rest of the text by a carriage return, achieved by pressing the Return key. It can be a single word heading or it can be a whole page of text.
To make a document easier to understand, as well as being easier on the eye, it is customary to use headings, sub-headings, sub-sub-headings and so on. Also lists of items or ideas are better presented by indenting them so their shape is different from the rest of the text.
All of these will use different paragraph formats. Now we shall look at the basic facilities provided by Windows Write for paragraph formatting . The word `basic' there is not meant disparagingly. It is simply that this word processor, thrown in free with Windows, could not be expected to have as many features as one costing several times more than Windows itself.
Page 1

You will recognise these paragraphs from the facing page. You'll also notice that they have lost their attributes in the process of being copied, for example the heading 'Changing the look of a whole paragraph' is no longer in a 16pt bold sans serif face, but looks like the rest of the text. Also the body text is not indented from the heading (the computer-speak way of describing the heading in its original form is to say it was 'outdented').

So we'll set about restoring the pasted version in *Write*.

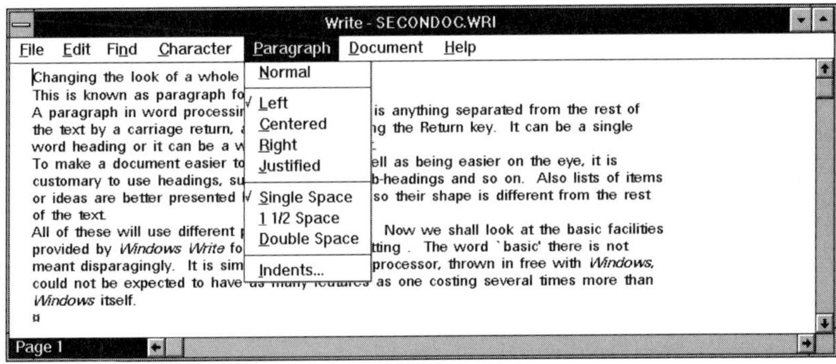
Write - SECONDOC.WRI
File Edit Find Character Paragraph Document Help
Normal
Left
Centered
Right
Justified
Single Space
1 1/2 Space
Double Space
Indents...
Page 1

First thing you notice is that we're not exactly overwhelmed with facilities here (when you look at Chapter 11 on desktop publishing you'll see the sort of things that really sophisticated programs can offer.)

The **Paragraph** menu can give these text attributes:

Text ranged **Left**
like this

Text that is **Centred**

Text that ranges **Right**
like this

And text that is **Justified** so that both left and right sides are straight up and down. To avoid getting funny looks from printers, remember that there is no such animal as 'left justified', or even 'right justified'. The text is either justified or it isn't, in the same way that no-one can be 'slightly pregnant'. Text that is uneven on the right but has a straight left hand edge is 'ranged left' and text that is uneven on the left but with a straight right hand edge is 'ranged right'.

The **Paragraph** menu also offers standard typewriter style line spacing: single line space, line and a half space, double line space and indents.

We'll start by putting back the indents. Select everything except the heading, then pop up the **Indents** window: 1.5 cm left and 3.0 cm right should do it. Click on the OK button.

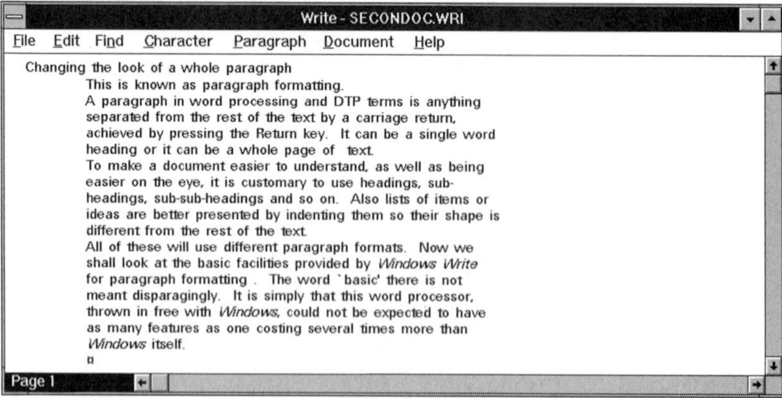

Changing the look of a whole paragraph

This is known as paragraph formatting.

A paragraph in word processing and DTP terms is anything separated from the rest of the text by a carriage return, achieved by pressing the Return key. It can be a single word heading or it can be a whole page of text.

To make a document easier to understand, as well as being easier on the eye, it is customary to use headings, sub-headings, sub-sub-headings and so on. Also lists of items or ideas are better presented by indenting them so their shape is different from the rest of the text.

All of these will use different paragraph formats. Now we shall look at the basic facilities provided by *Windows Write* for paragraph formatting . The word `basic' there is not meant disparagingly. It is simply that this word processor, thrown in free with *Windows*, could not be expected to have as many features as one costing several times more than *Windows* itself.

The remaining restoration work would be a paragraph formatting job if the facilities were here in *Write*, but unfortunately they aren't, so they will have to be done manually.

Put the cursor at the end of each paragraph and press Return. This will add the (approximate) space we had between paragraphs before. Then select all the header text, select **Fonts...** from the **Character** menu and choose Univers Black 16pt. Now select all the body text and change it to New Century Schoolbook 11pt.

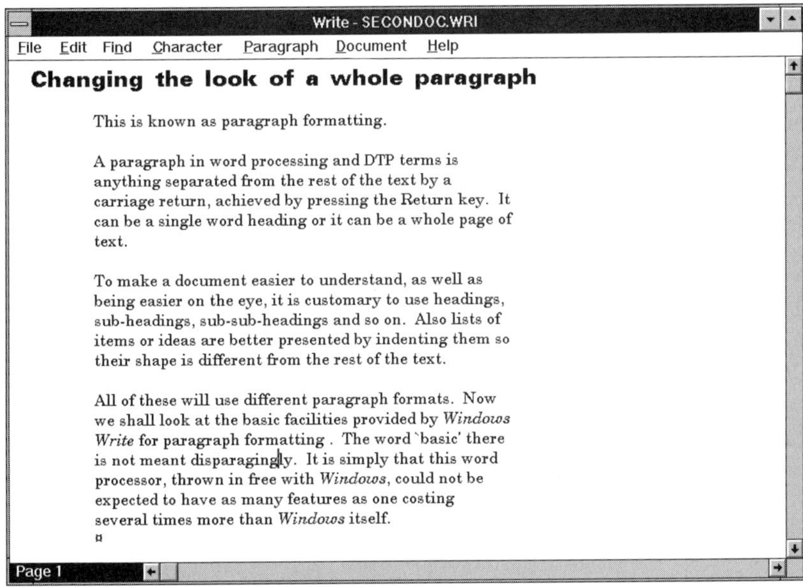

Changing the look of a whole paragraph

This is known as paragraph formatting.

A paragraph in word processing and DTP terms is anything separated from the rest of the text by a carriage return, achieved by pressing the Return key. It can be a single word heading or it can be a whole page of text.

To make a document easier to understand, as well as being easier on the eye, it is customary to use headings, sub-headings, sub-sub-headings and so on. Also lists of items or ideas are better presented by indenting them so their shape is different from the rest of the text.

All of these will use different paragraph formats. Now we shall look at the basic facilities provided by *Windows Write* for paragraph formatting . The word `basic' there is not meant disparagingly. It is simply that this word processor, thrown in free with *Windows*, could not be expected to have as many features as one costing several times more than *Windows* itself.

The instructions in the previous paragraphs were a little more cryptic, weren't they? This is so that you begin to find your own way around the menus. A further test of how you are getting on will be to add the finishing touches: the words '*Windows*' and '*Write*' are in italics; 'DTP' is one point size smaller than the rest of the text. See how you make out.

Printing from *Windows Write*

Setting up the printer

Before any *Windows* application can print anything it has to be told what sort of printer you have and which port it is connected to. If you're lucky this will all have been sorted out by someone else before you need to do any printing. Just in case it hasn't been set up, here's what you do to 'install' a printer.

Telling *Windows* the name of your printer

Go into Program Manager (click on the button top left of the screen), double-click on the Control Panel icon:

then on the Printers icon:

This brings up the **Printers** window:

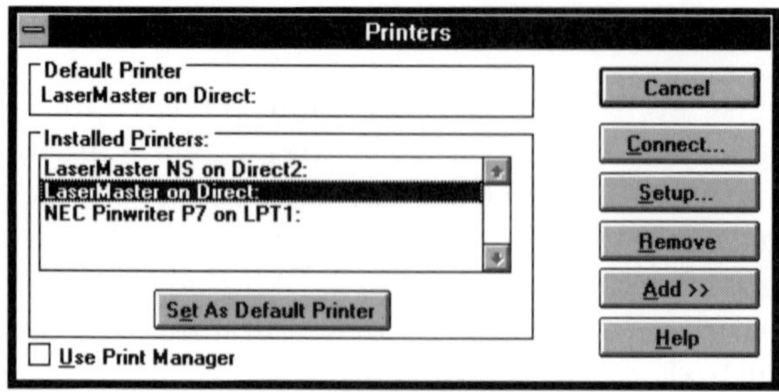

Click on the **Add** button and the **List of Printers** appears:

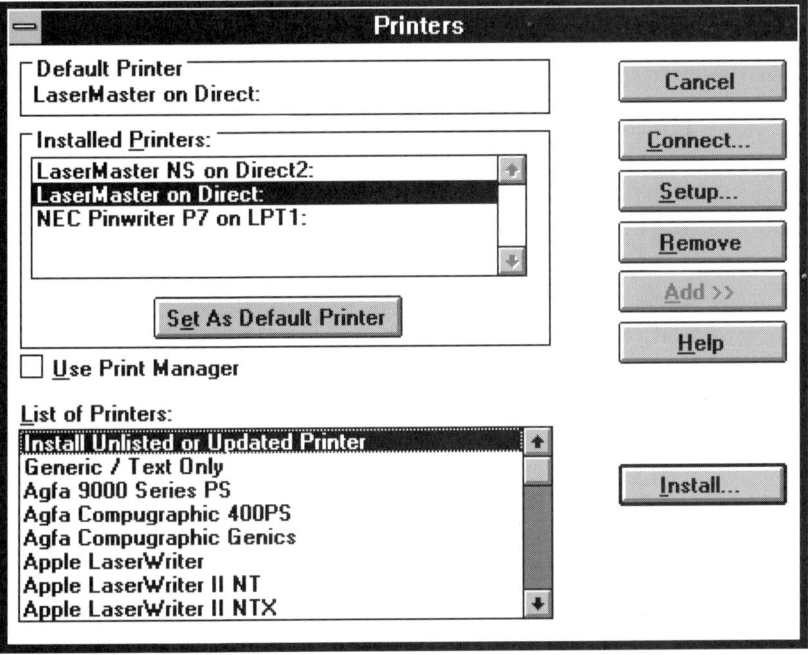

For the next step you will need to have the *Windows* installation disks standing by. The installation procedure calls for information from these disks and will probably be asking you to insert Disk 1; later it may ask for some of the others in the set.

Use the ***scroll bar*** on the right of the list to reach the name and model number of your printer; when you have selected it, click on the **Install** button.

If you have searched through the entire list and not found it, then you will need the printer manufacturer's *Windows* installation disk.

Go to the top of the list and select **Install Unlisted or Updated Printer**. *Windows* tells you what to do next.

Once the printer has been installed its name will appear in the **Installed Printers** list. With the printer name selected, click on the **Set As Default Printer** button.

Connecting the printer

The power cable and the cable between the computer and the printer must be plugged in, but the computer also has to be *told* which port the printer is using. You might expect it to know that, but it doesn't.

Click on the **Connect** button, which brings up the **Connect** window:

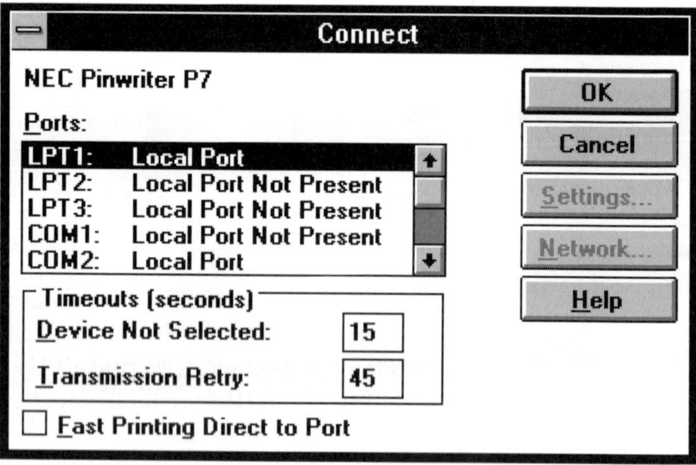

Most printers are connected to a parallel port, such as 'LPT1:' as shown above, but you should check the manufacturer's instructions. Once satisfied that you have made the correct decision, click on the OK button.

Setting up the printer

Click on the **Setup** button which will bring up details of the capabilities of your printer. It may be a dot matrix printer, or a laser, even a colour printer; it may print in all paper sizes up to A3. The details shown will reflect only those features which it can cope with.

The important one to choose is paper size. If your paper is A4 but the printer thinks it's using American Letter (11 x 8½ inches) then your margins and page layout are going to be hopelessly adrift.

Paper size

Choose the paper size you are going to be using. Many a strong man has been reduced to tears because he couldn't get his A4 page layout to come out properly and didn't realise the printer had not been changed from its default American Letter setting!

Two points confuse the issue here: first because it's an American program they just call it 'Letter', second is that the standard way for people in the printing business over here to give sizes is height by width. Our transatlantic friends do it the other way round, hence their 8½ by 11 versus our 11 by 8½ (at least the inches are the same!).

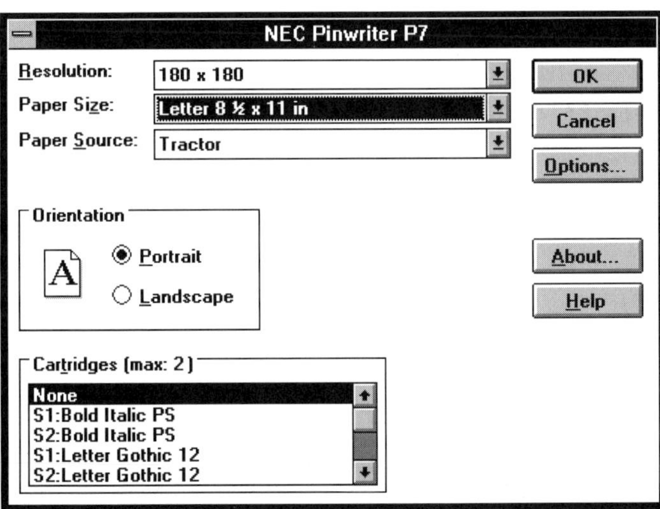

So click on '**Letter 8½ x 11 in**' whereupon a list of other sizes will drop down. Your most likely choice is A4. Click the OK button or press Return. The printer is now installed and ready for use.

What if the printer doesn't print?

The most frequent causes of printer errors are that they haven't been switched on or they have run out of paper. Next most popular is the paper jam, either as a result of using too lightweight a material so that two pieces go through together, or possibly the paper has become dog-eared so it jams between the rollers.

Dot matrix printers will go on printing for ever, even if the ribbon is totally exhausted of ink or has jumped out of its guides. They'll beep if they run out of paper, but tend to plough on whether it's flowing through or not.

Laser printers will stop, usually telling you what's wrong by displaying an illuminated symbol, if they run out of toner or have a paper jam.

Timeout: waiting for something to print

Whatever the problem, the computer will give you more or less time to rectify it depending on the setting of **Timeouts** in the **Connect** window that pops up from within the **Printers** window of the **Control Panel**. Unless there is a special reason, such as several people sharing the same printer and having to wait their turn in the queue, leave these at the ***default***. In this case it will be the 'factory setting': 15 seconds for **Device Not Selected**, 90 seconds for **Transmission Retry** on PostScript printers, 45 seconds for **Transmission Retry** on non PostScript printers.

PostScript

PostScript is a type of computer programming language which is understood by some laser printers. Commands in PostScript do such things as print text, draw lines and fill areas. PostScript printers are often much slower to produce results than those using other languages.

Device Not Selected
This is the length of time that elapses before the computer stops trying to communicate with the printer. It then puts up an error message to let you know that it can't get through.

Transmission Retry
The length of time that the computer will wait for a printer to finish printing a previous job before accepting the next one. There is nothing wrong with the printer, it is just too busy.

Printing the document

The Setup procedure has to be done only once for each printer, assuming that you won't need to change paper sizes between print runs.

Here follows the easiest part of all:

1. Switch on the printer
2. Make sure it has some paper
3. From the **File** menu select **Print**

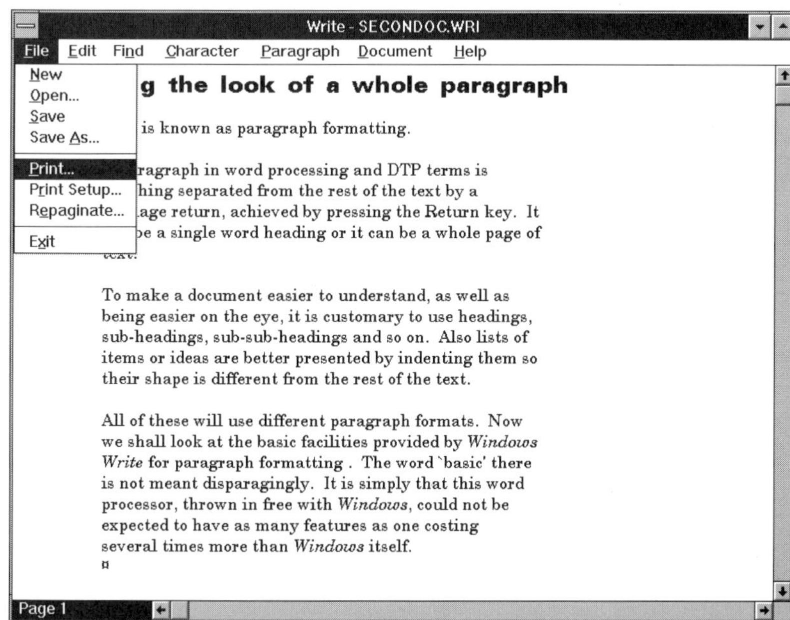
Write - SECONDOC.WRI
File Edit Find Character Paragraph Document Help
New
Open...
Save
Save As...
Print...
Print Setup...
Repaginate...
Exit
g the look of a whole paragraph
is known as paragraph formatting.
ragraph in word processing and DTP terms is
hing separated from the rest of the text by a
age return, achieved by pressing the Return key. It
be a single word heading or it can be a whole page of
To make a document easier to understand, as well as being easier on the eye, it is customary to use headings, sub-headings, sub-sub-headings and so on. Also lists of items or ideas are better presented by indenting them so their shape is different from the rest of the text.
All of these will use different paragraph formats. Now we shall look at the basic facilities provided by Windows Write for paragraph formatting . The word 'basic' there is not meant disparagingly. It is simply that this word processor, thrown in free with Windows, could not be expected to have as many features as one costing several times more than Windows itself.
Page 1

4 The Print dialogue box pops up

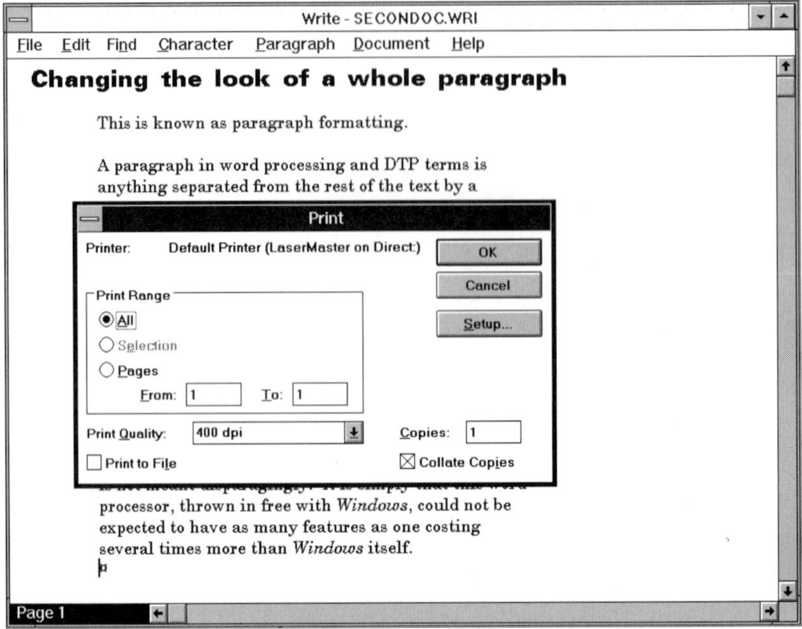
Write - SECONDOC.WRI
File Edit Find Character Paragraph Document Help
Changing the look of a whole paragraph
This is known as paragraph formatting.
A paragraph in word processing and DTP terms is
anything separated from the rest of the text by a
Print
Printer: Default Printer (LaserMaster on Direct:)
OK
Cancel
Setup...
Print Range
All
Selection
Pages
From: 1 To: 1
Print Quality: 400 dpi
Copies: 1
Print to File
Collate Copies
processor, thrown in free with Windows, could not be
expected to have as many features as one costing
several times more than Windows itself.
Page 1

5 If you only want to print part of the document, select the page numbers to be printed

6 Click on the OK button.

Features of other word processors

Apart from a passing mention on page 14 of dedicated word processors (those hardware devices which can process words and nothing else), 'word processor' and 'word processing' in this book will always mean *using a word processing program that runs on a PC*, such as *WordPerfect, Word for Windows, Ami Pro* etc.

Word processing beyond *Write*

Paragraph styles

Do you remember the **Paragraph** menu in *Write* (page 153)? It offered:

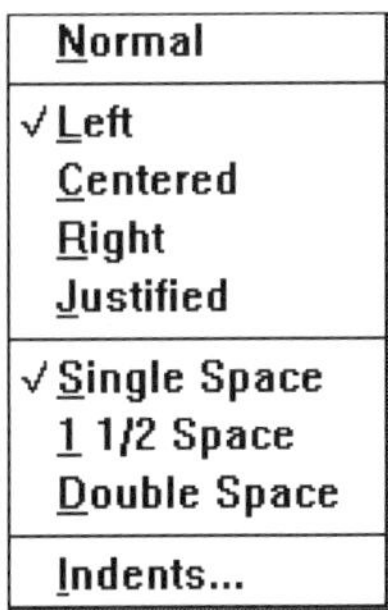

We are now going to experience two quantum leaps: one in the number of options on offer, the other in the application of those options. The first needs no explanation, the second is a simple enough concept.

Wouldn't it be nice if you didn't have to format every single paragraph? Suppose you could store different sets of ***text attributes*** and somehow apply them to different paragraphs? One paragraph could be in *Times New Roman 11pt Medium*, set to the full width, another could be in *Helvetica 10pt Medium*, indented left and right by a couple of centimetres. A third could be a single word heading in *Helvetica Bold 14pt*.

Paragraph

A paragraph is any number of words separated by a carriage return from the word(s) above and below it.

Well, you shall go to the ball! Those three hypothetical sets of attributes can be applied in reality when you use *paragraph styles*, otherwise known as *paragraph tags*. *Write* doesn't have this facility, as we have seen, but most other word processors and desktop publishing programs do.

What happens is that you give each paragraph style a name, such as *Body Text*, *Main Heading*, *Indented List*, and go through the **Format** menu picking out as many attributes as you want for each one. (The menus may have slightly different names in different word processing programs, but they all do the same job.)

These attributes are added to the selected style. If you decide later that you want to change the look of every Main Heading in the document, you have only to change the paragraph style and every one with that tag will be changed instantly. This is how Microsoft *Word for Windows* version 2 tackles it:

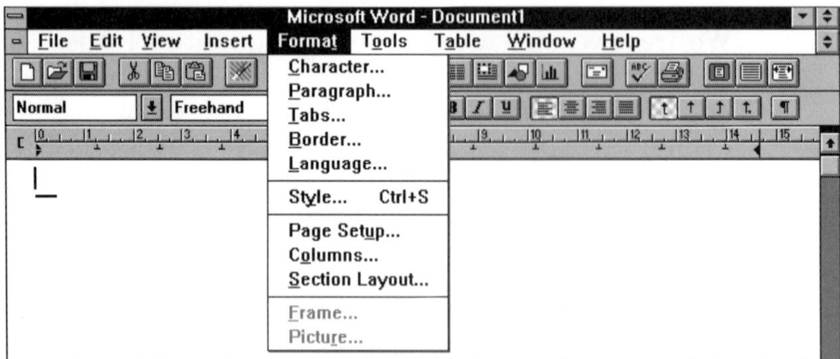

One easy mistake to make, by the way, is to set everything up very carefully under **Paragraph** and then find that what you've done has only changed the selected paragraph. To change a style you must go into the **Style** menu and from there to its multiple windows.

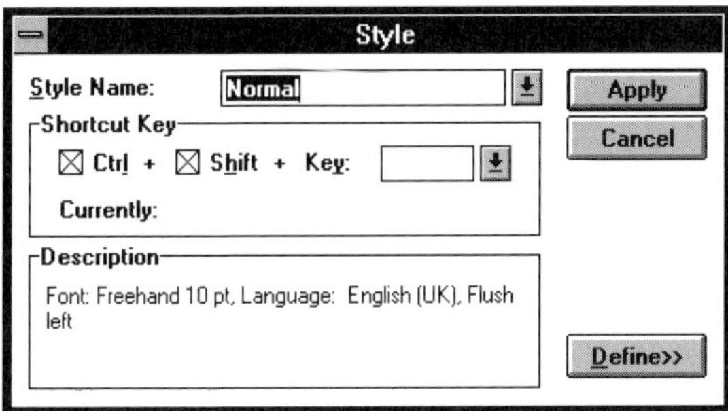

This is the tip of the iceberg; it shows you a summary of the current settings and offers a **Define** button which leads to:

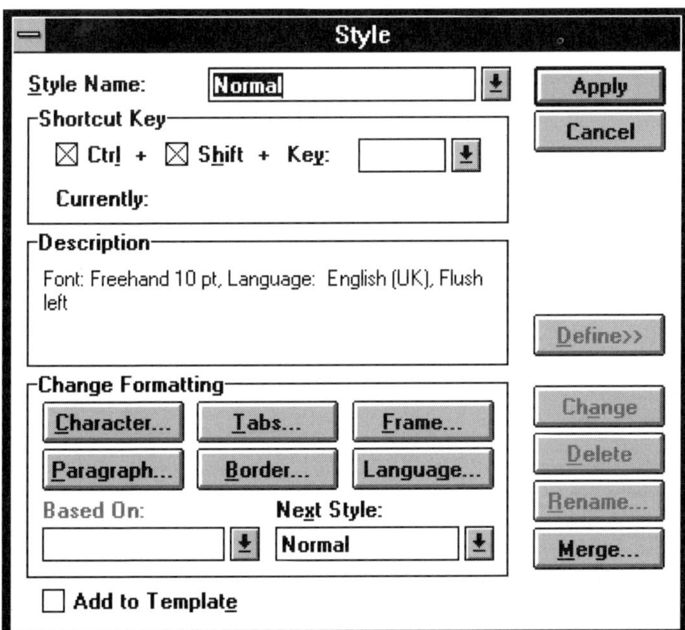

A click on the **Character** button leads to:

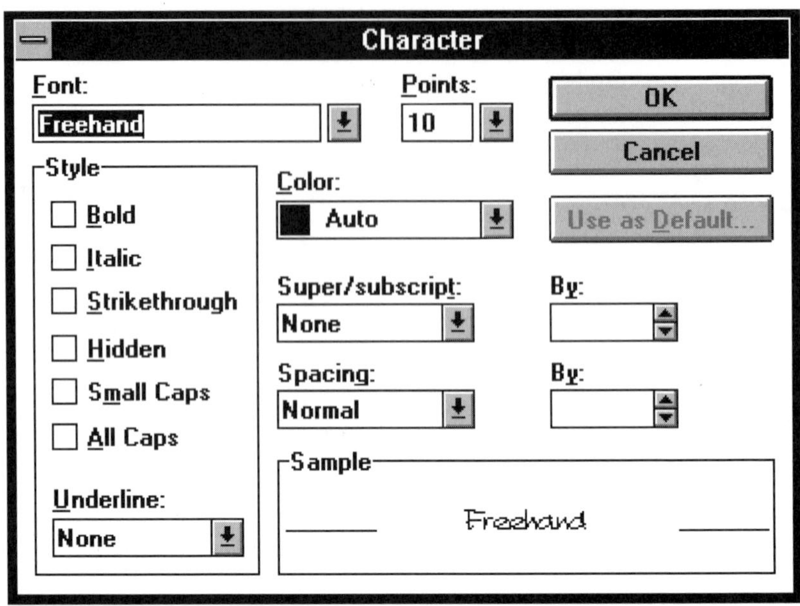
Character
Font:
Freehand
Points:
10
OK
Cancel
Use as Default...
Style
Bold
Italic
Strikethrough
Hidden
Small Caps
All Caps
Underline:
None
Color:
Auto
Super/subscript:
None
By:
Spacing:
Normal
By:
Sample
Freehand

While the **Paragraph** button takes you to:

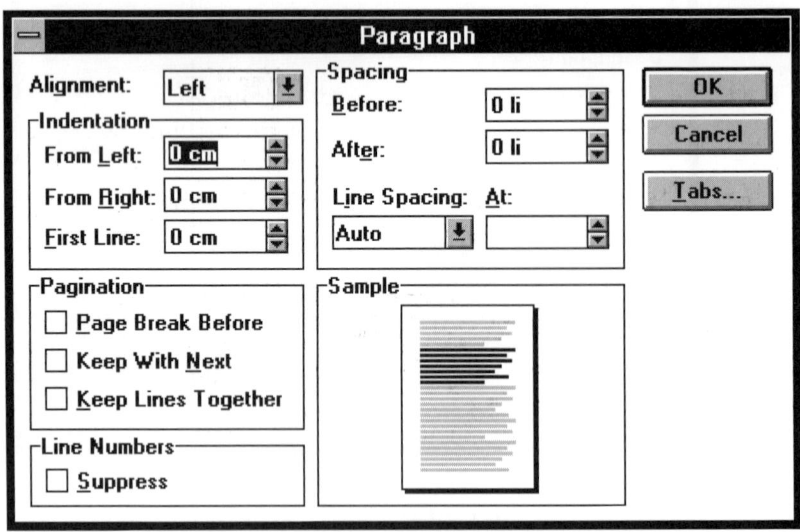
Paragraph
Alignment:
Left
Indentation
From Left:
0 cm
From Right:
0 cm
First Line:
0 cm
Spacing
Before:
0 li
After:
0 li
Line Spacing:
At:
Auto
OK
Cancel
Tabs...
Pagination
Page Break Before
Keep With Next
Keep Lines Together
Line Numbers
Suppress
Sample

From the **Paragraph** menu, a click on **Tabs** reveals:

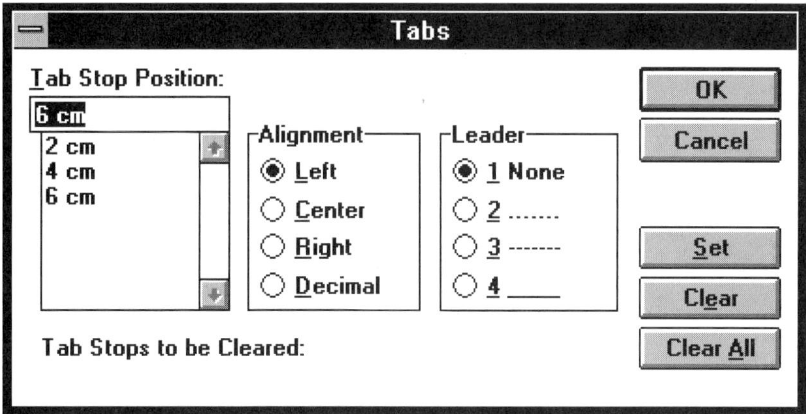

Your next step in word processing

That is just a sample of some of the powerful tools available to you from 'fully-featured' word processors. Books in this *'Need to Know'* series are in hand for *Word for Windows* version 6, *Ami Pro* and *WordPerfect 6 for Windows*.

CHAPTER 9

Databases

This chapter will give you an understanding of why databases are so useful and how they work.

There are examples of the use of *Windows Cardfile*, a computerised card index system, and a demonstration of the use of *FoxPro*, which is an all-out, no-holds-barred database with every imaginable facility.

You may not come out at the end as a fully-qualified database programmer, but you will have done enough of the necessary groundwork to whet your appetite. (And if you read the whole chapter, you'll discover the basics of programming a coffee machine!)

Databases

What is a database?

Records and fields

Database

A database is a program that stores information, for example a list of names and addresses or a book catalogue, in such a way that it can easily be retrieved by using its searching and sorting facilities.

The information is stored in records. A record would contain the same details that you would find on any one card in a conventional card index system.

Within each record are one or more fields. If the database contained a list of names and addresses, for example, the first field would probably contain their surname, the second their first name, the third the first line of their address and so on.

Every single piece of useful information would have its own field.

A database proves its usefulness by the ease and speed with which data can be retrieved from it. Once you have put all the information in, you can ask for it back again in all sorts of different ways.

It is the system of putting individual pieces of information into separate fields that makes this possible.

A 'people' database

Let's suppose you are using a database to keep records of everyone you have ever known; family, friends, business colleagues, customers, suppliers, plumbers, electricians, doctors, veterinary surgeons, whoever you can think of.

It is approaching Christmas and you want to know how many cards to buy. Now, if you had thought of this possibility in advance, you would have had a field called 'Christmas Card List' or something similar. This field would have had one character in it: 'Y' or 'N'.

Without going into the technicalities (which aren't complicated, be assured) you would ask the database to count the number of records whose 'Christmas Card List' field had a 'Y' in it. The answer would come out in a fraction of a second. When you came back with the shopping, you would ask it to print the first name, surname and address lines of everyone with a 'Y' in that field.

If you had fallen out with anyone during the previous year, but still wanted them in the database for other reasons, you might have changed the 'Y' to an 'N' so they wouldn't get one (it would be possible to build in a facility to print out "Oh, come on, it *is* Christmas!" to give you a chance to relent).

A 'things' database

You have this wonderful collection of compact discs. There are so many that they are stacked all over the house in different rooms. Your musical taste ranges from Gregorian chant to the latest subtle variation in Reggae. You've just got to have a database, or you'll lose track of what you've got and may never hear some of it again. (Sorry, vinyl addicts, but putting records in records would have been too confusing. The principle will work for you too though.)

Well, it's not hard to imagine, is it? The fields would include Album Title, Album Number, Where Is It? (cupboard under stairs, box labelled 'D' in attic), Track Title, Composer, Artist, Accompanist / Backing Group / Orchestra, Recording Date, Recording Location, and so on and so on.

When you come home in the evening and need the soothing tones of your favourite singer, your faithful database will tell you exactly where they are.

Storing and retrieving information

We'll look first at *Windows Cardfile*. This is a useful accessory if you need a simple record system, and it's only a couple of mouse clicks away.

Windows Cardfile

Using *Cardfile*

From Program Manager, double click on the Cardfile icon in the Accessories window.

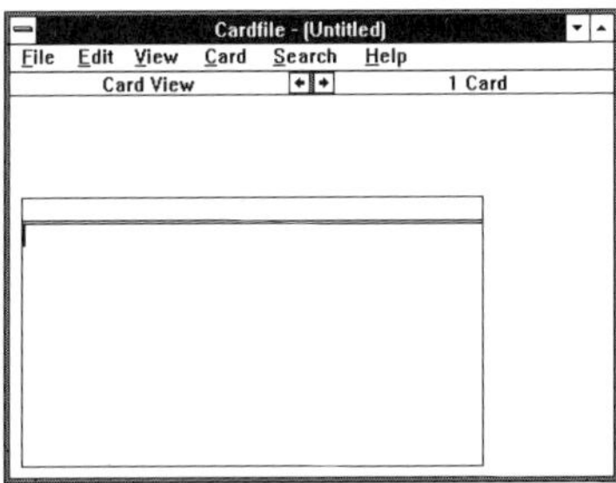

A blank card appears, ready for you to type in a recipe, a football match result, a name and address; anything that you might want to record with similar information so that you could find it again easily.

The header tells you that there is one card in the system. In other words, so far you have one *record*.

Records

This word, *record*, is used in database terminology. Now you know exactly what it means. When you add a second recipe you will have two records.

Big databases, such as the one kept by the Inland Revenue, can have millions of records, holding all our personal details in separate *fields*.

Index field

Cardfile has two fields: the index field and one that we'll call the information field. The way you fill in the index field (using up to 39 characters) is crucial to the operation of the system.

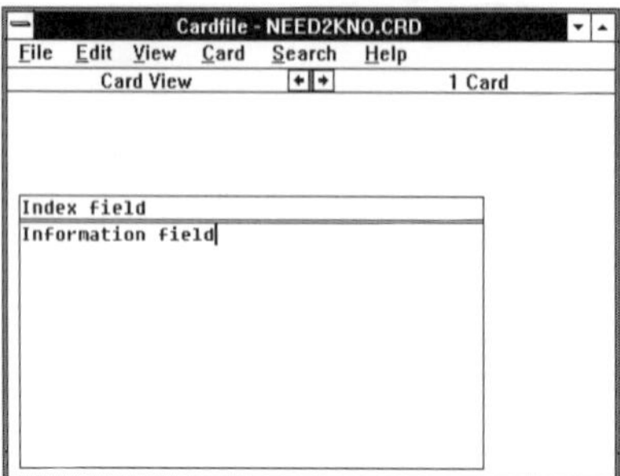

The cards are sorted into alphanumeric (letters and numbers) order based on the text in the index field, so it pays to think about what you are going to call each one. If you were setting up a file of names and addresses you would put the surnames first every time, so that your records appeared in a sensible sequence.

Using *Cardfile*

You can take the 'bottom up' or the 'top down' approach. Although the first of these always seems the easier, it usually goes like this: have a rough idea of what you want; bash in the data straight away; discover some twenty cards later that this wasn't quite the way you wanted it; start again from scratch.

The 'top down' method involves planning:

What are we trying to achieve?
What information are we going to put in?
What are we hoping to get out of it?

The answers to these questions govern the way your database should be laid out.

A real database should have no limitation on the ways in which it will present data culled from its records. *Cardfile*, on the other hand, is only a card index system on a computer.

Cardfile's facilities

Indexing (sorting) records

A new card is sorted into its alphanumeric sequence as soon as the data on its index field has been entered. Don't be misled by an apparent lack of order: when a card is brought to the front by clicking on it, the following cards go back in order. After the last card, the sequence starts again with the first card:

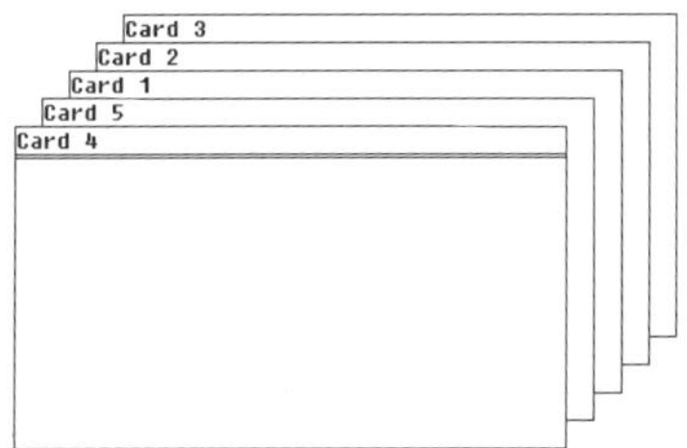

Finding records

Cardfile can search for a word. Suppose, for example, that all the shops are shut; unexpected guests arrive. You rush to the kitchen cupboard, finding a 5Kg bag of lentils and not much else. You open your recipe file and do a search on 'lentil'. Of the three records found containing the word 'lentil', there is one with only two added ingredients: salt and boiling water. *Cardfile* has proved its worth. Lentil soup all round.

Adding pictures

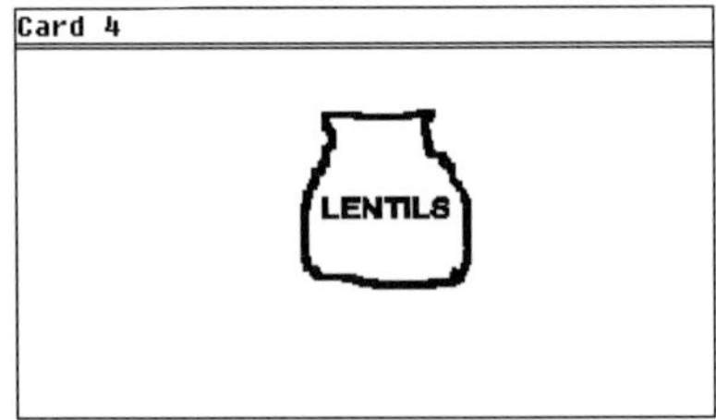

This is not the easiest thing to do because Paintbrush insists that the empty space around the subject is part of the picture. This surrounding space goes with the picture when you put it into *Cardfile*, acting as a sort of force field which obscures the text.

As the text can not be formatted to fit around the picture, the results are dismal. You have either to know in advance the exact proportions and size of the finished drawing or go through the clumsily-contrived procedure of resizing. However, with perseverance it can be done.

The best way is to use a bitmapped file produced in a more sympathetic drawing program, such as *CorelDRAW!*.

Setting up a *Cardfile*

Let's set up some records of cars, using *Cardfile's* limited facilities. We'll have the car name in the index field, with price, horsepower and depreciation in the 'information field'.

This information would be in separate fields in a proper database, but it is at least accessible here if we use the Search command.

Here is the end result:

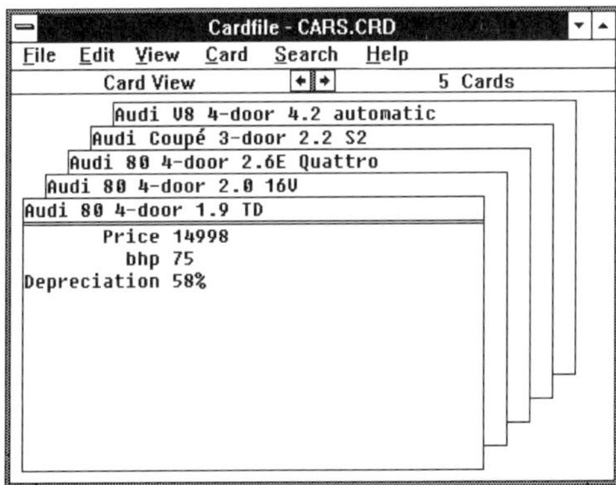

and these are the steps taken to produce it:

1

Type in the headings. We are going to save time by duplicating these cards with the headings on; the details can be put in later.

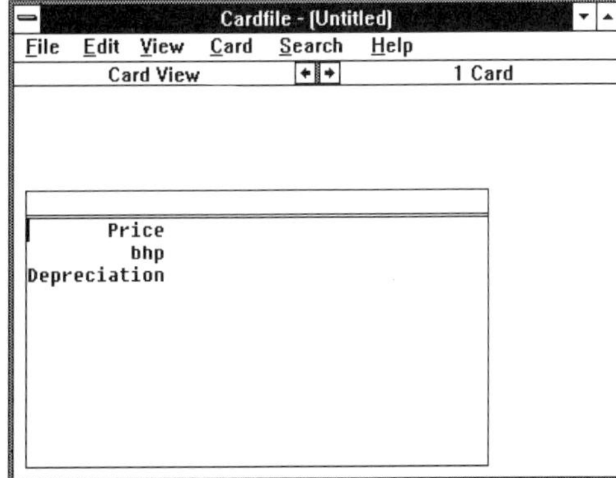

Duplicating cards

We can save a lot of time by preparing a card with the headings and then duplicating it for as many entries as necessary.

2

Click on the Card menu and select Duplicate. Notice that these two words have under-lined characters. Hold down the Alt key and type C then P to make as many duplicates as you will need.

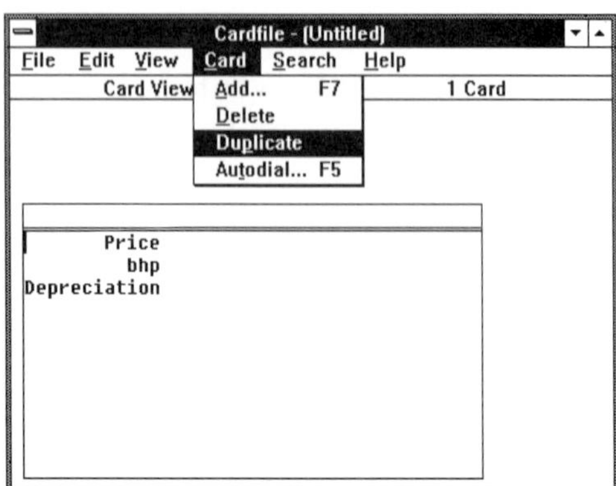

3

The Alt+C, P short-cut key combination has been used to create a further four cards. The header tells us that we now have a total of five cards.

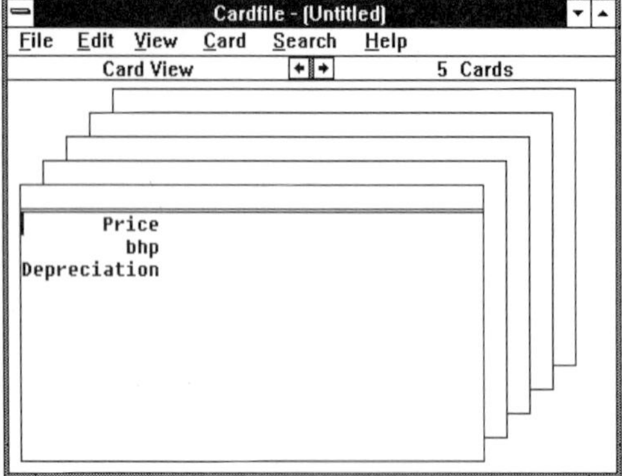

Saving the file

As well as showing us that we now have a total of five cards, the information at the top of the window, in the Title Bar, shows that the *Cardfile* has not been given a name. This also shows that the information typed in so far could be lost if there was a power failure. We should save this at once.

4

Click on the File menu and select Save As...

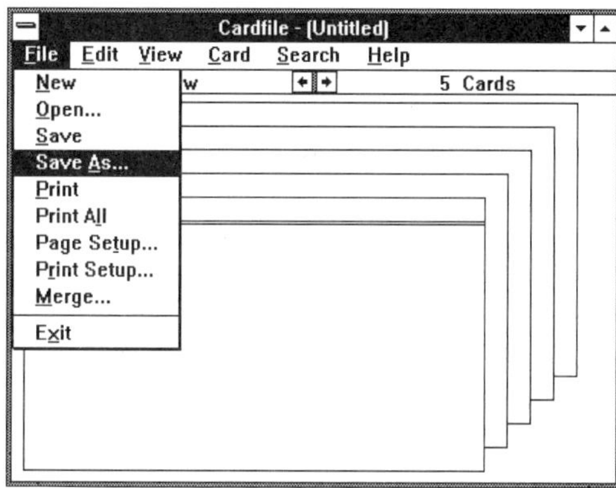

'Save As...' leads to the Save As window. The next time you save (do this every five minutes to be safe), you can just click on 'Save' in the File menu; your work will be saved to the chosen file name.

Short-cut keys

An alternative way of saving in *Cardfile*, and in many other *Windows* accessories and applications, is to use the short-cut key combination Alt + F, S. The F of the File menu name is underlined, as is the S of Save.

This principle of holding down the Alt key and typing an underlined character is used in every menu system everywhere. Sometimes there are alternative short-cuts in addition to this standard method.

5

Click on the File menu and select Save As... Use the maximum of eight characters wisely. In this case we shall only need four: CARS.CRD sums it up nicely. Keep the standard extension, .CRD.

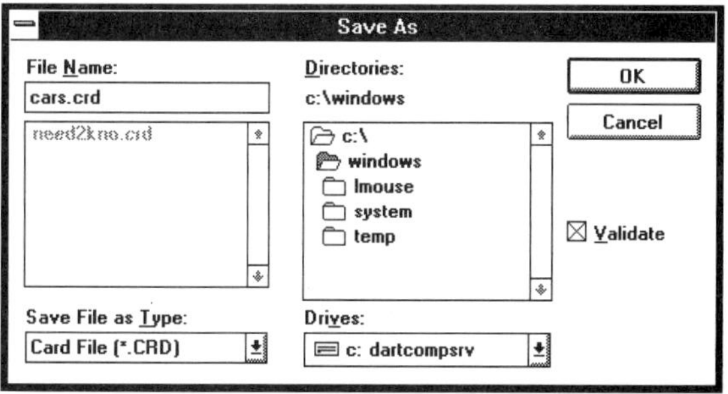

6

The Title Bar now shows the name of the file containing our five record cards. Clicking on 'List' in the View menu changes the window to a list of index details

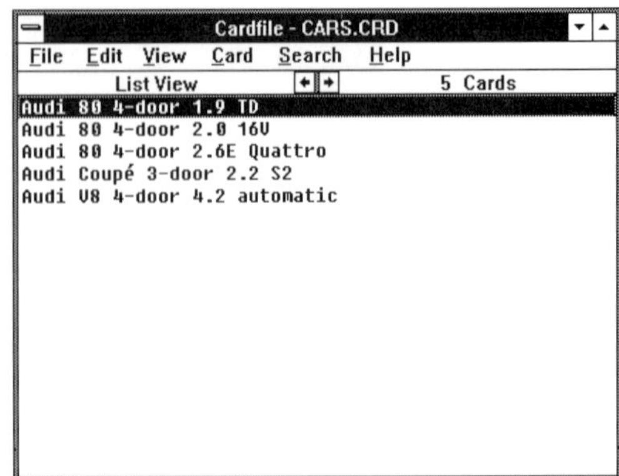

Now is the time to fill in the Index Line of each card with the car name.

7

Getting to the Index Line via the Edit menu. The quicker alternative, as shown in the menu, is to tap function key F6.

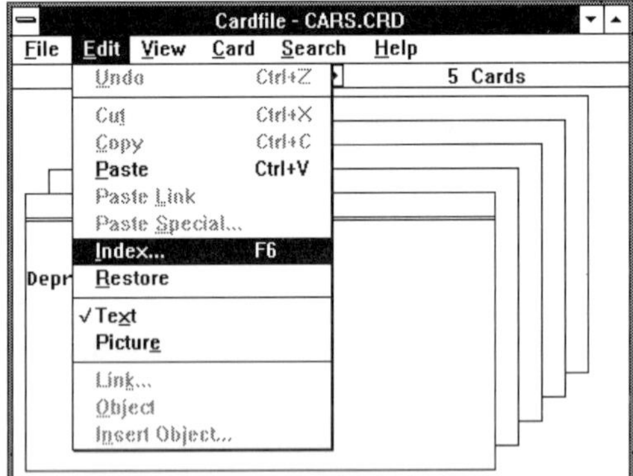

8

The Index window pops up, and we fill in the details. This window was put in its present position by placing the cursor in the Title Bar and dragging with the mouse. All windows can be moved this way.

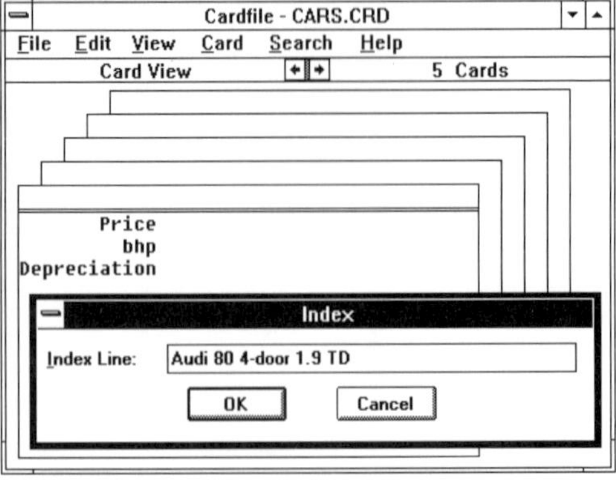

9

When the Index Line has been entered, the cursor moves down to the main body of the card, where can type in the details.

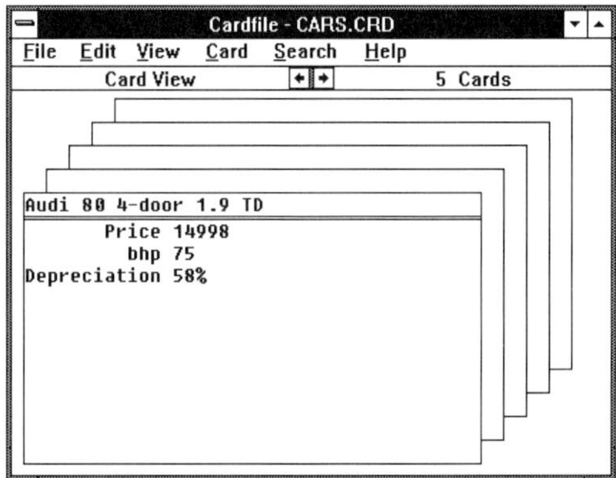

10

To bring another card to the front, just click on it. The first card takes up its correct position. Blank, or 'null', is a lower value than 'A', so the uncompleted cards precede the completed one.

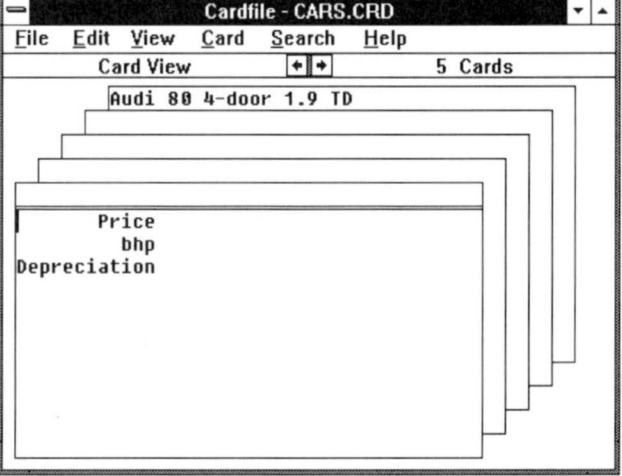

11

All the cards have now been completed and sorted into alphanumeric order by Cardfile. *Note that numbers come before letters, so '80' is earlier in the stack than 'Coupé'.*

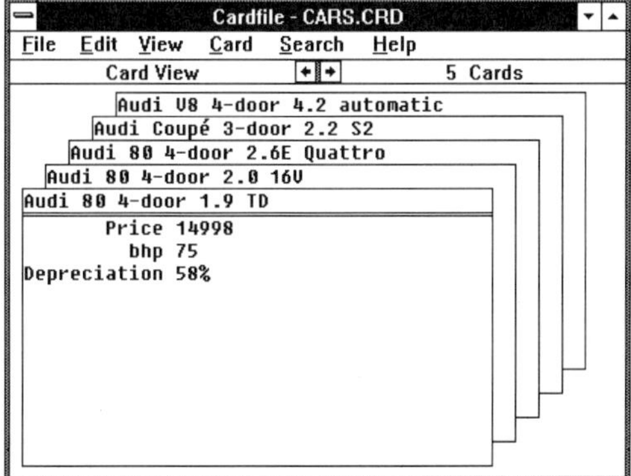

Extracting information from *Cardfile*

Now that we have our stack of record cards, what can we do with them?

Browsing

Browse and Browsing are database terms, meaning the ability to select one record here or there and just look at it to see what it says.

Cardfile allows us to browse by clicking on the Index Line of any card to bring it to the front. As the maximum number of cards visible at any time is five, the only way of browsing on records beyond number five is to go into List mode.

Listing *Cardfile* records

'Listing' is generally used in computing to mean 'printing a list', usually of program lines. The printed result is also called a 'program listing' or just a 'listing'. Here it means 'showing a list on the screen'. However, you can choose **Print All** from the **File** menu and do a listing of this list!

To get into List mode, either click on the **View** menu then on **List** or take the short-cut Alt + V, L. To put up any card, click on its name in the list, then either click on the **View** menu and select **Card**, or use Alt + V, C. The selected card comes to the front.

Searching

Cardfile can only show one found item at a time. It does not search the index field, so you may want to repeat the contents of the index line in the 'information field'.

Go into the **Search** menu and choose **Find** (or use the short-cut Alt + S, F). Enter one or more words or figures. You may have to drag the **Find** window down so that it doesn't obscure what has been found. You can also press cancel after the first find, then use F3.

Using a real database

Fields

All databases have an index field, chosen by the person who is managing the database. Many of them give you the opportunity of choosing other fields to index on, depending on your *query*, in other words what you are looking for at the time. The more powerful databases will have as many records and fields as you need.

The user decides what each field will be called. Typical examples for records in a personnel database might be:

last_name
first_name
department
nat_ins_number
occupation
date_first_employed
hourly_weekly_monthly
married_single
address1
address2
address3
address4
address5
post_code

Queries

The beauty of a good database is that you can ask it all sorts of questions: 'How many left-handed lorry drivers are there living in Letchworth?'; 'What is the average age of the inhabitants of Aviemore?'.

This brings us to a philosophical moment: as with life, you only get back what you have put in. So the first query could only be answered if you had a 'handedness' field as well as an 'occupation' field and a 'town' field. Also, of course, you would have to have carried out a survey of the people who lived in Letchworth and entered the results into the database.

These searches are called *queries*, and are easily set up thanks to SQL (Structured Query Language). A good database program will translate your parameters:

handedness = left
occupation = lorry driver
town = Letchworth

into SQL which will then search through each of the chosen fields in every record in the database and present you with the names of the people who answer to that description.

From the sample opposite (shown in two sections) you could set queries to find out a number of things *without having to scan all the information by eye* (this database could have thousands of entries):

Where does Phil Putnam live?
Who has spent more than $5000 with us this year?
How many customers do we have in Minnesota?
Who is our contact at Yonkers Software Inc?
Who does Nancy Wright work for?
What is Zwladislaw Polski's telephone number?

Working with *FoxPro*

There are many database programs about, and several of the larger software companies have been so impressed by the performance of some of them that they have bought out the originating company, or at least the particular product that interested them.

Foxpro is one of these, bought up by Microsoft. It goes like the wind and has added many extensions to the standard *dBase* language. dBase is a database that has been around for many years, and on whose construction several later databases have been, er – based.

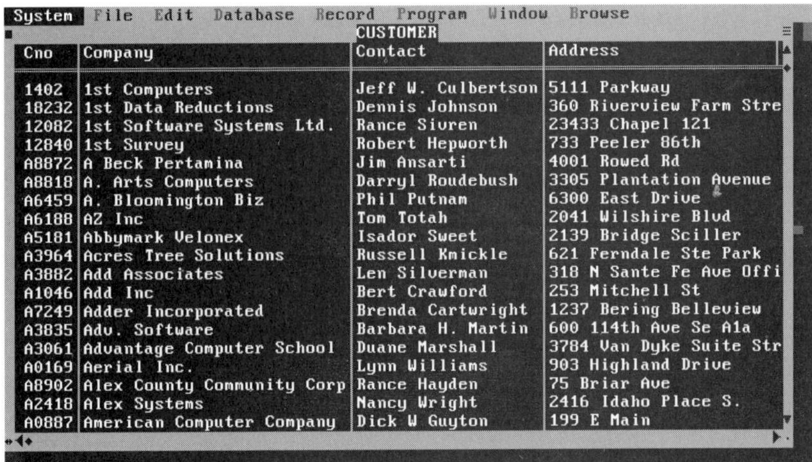

System File Edit Database Record Program Window Browse

CUSTOMER

Cno	Company	Contact	Address
1402	1st Computers	Jeff W. Culbertson	5111 Parkway
18232	1st Data Reductions	Dennis Johnson	360 Riverview Farm Stre
12082	1st Software Systems Ltd.	Rance Sivren	23433 Chapel 121
12840	1st Survey	Robert Hepworth	733 Peeler 86th
A8872	A Beck Pertamina	Jim Ansarti	4001 Rowed Rd
A8818	A. Arts Computers	Darryl Roudebush	3305 Plantation Avenue
A6459	A. Bloomington Biz	Phil Putnam	6300 East Drive
A6188	AZ Inc	Tom Totah	2041 Wilshire Blvd
A5181	Abbymark Velonex	Isador Sweet	2139 Bridge Sciller
A3964	Acres Tree Solutions	Russell Kmickle	621 Ferndale Ste Park
A3882	Add Associates	Len Silverman	318 N Sante Fe Ave Offi
A1046	Add Inc	Bert Crawford	253 Mitchell St
A7249	Adder Incorporated	Brenda Cartwright	1237 Bering Belleview
A3835	Adv. Software	Barbara H. Martin	600 114th Ave Se A1a
A3061	Advantage Computer School	Duane Marshall	3784 Van Dyke Suite Str
A0169	Aerial Inc.	Lynn Williams	903 Highland Drive
A8902	Alex County Community Corp	Rance Hayden	75 Briar Ave
A2418	Alex Systems	Nancy Wright	2416 Idaho Place S.
A0887	American Computer Company	Dick W Guyton	199 E Main

System File Edit Database Record Program Window Browse

CUSTOMER

City	State	Zip	Phone	Ono	Ytdpurch	Lat	Long
Brookline	MA	02146	617/232-5053	1	1509.67	42.3396	71.1149
New Orleans	LA	70113	504/524-3966	4	1608.35	29.9486	90.0773
Houston	TX	77035	713/723-1288	5	2272.06	29.7503	95.3662
Dallas	TX	75234	214/243-7247	5	754.81	32.9246	96.8909
Arlington	MA	02174	617/643-6920	1	3991.66	42.4143	71.1518
Melrose	MA	02176	617/662-0157	1	3922.04	42.4563	71.0647
Tallahassee	FL	32301	904/222-9457	3	684.47	30.4421	84.2850
Taunton	MA	02780	617/823-5180	1	370.73	41.8980	71.1007
Dallas	TX	75201	214/922-4927	5	1390.17	32.7815	96.7947
Sparta	NJ	07871	201/786-0785	2	272.48	40.9882	74.7445
Novato	CA	94947	415/897-2810	6	5487.46	38.1075	122.5647
Boulder	CO	80303	303/499-2086	5	161.70	40.0233	105.2741
Warren	MI	48093	313/573-5873	4	722.25	42.4925	83.0373
Arlington	MA	02174	617/646-7974	1	4820.51	42.4143	71.1518
San Jose	CA	95131	408/946-1317	6	4635.01	37.3317	121.8871
Wayne	NJ	07470	201/696-7378	2	1921.26	40.9166	74.2699
Lanham	MD	20706	301/459-4484	3	1637.64	38.9513	76.9498
Erie	PA	16505	814/838-3116	2	8505.03	42.1214	80.0870
Lubbock	TX	79413	806/799-7706	5	5496.99	33.5821	101.8535

You can browse (and change the data) either in the wide view above, or in the individual entry view shown here. To change any field, just select it with the mouse and type in the new information.

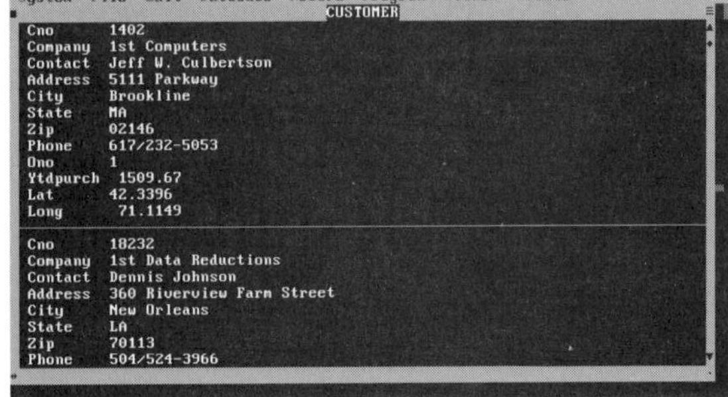

System File Edit Database Record Program Window Browse

CUSTOMER

Cno	1402
Company	1st Computers
Contact	Jeff W. Culbertson
Address	5111 Parkway
City	Brookline
State	MA
Zip	02146
Phone	617/232-5053
Ono	1
Ytdpurch	1509.67
Lat	42.3396
Long	71.1149
Cno	18232
Company	1st Data Reductions
Contact	Dennis Johnson
Address	360 Riverview Farm Street
City	New Orleans
State	LA
Zip	70113
Phone	504/524-3966

The 12 fields of the first record are shown, with a partial view of the second record.

Setting up a query

This will use *FoxPro*'s RQBE (Relational Query By Example) facility; it is far less terrifying than it sounds, the key being in the 'By Example' part. We'll ask the Customer database to give us details of everyone who has spent $5000 or more in the year to date. Some answers could be derived simply by browsing, but this one would take some time and involve handwritten notes, so we'll let *FoxPro* do it all for us. The results can be shown on screen and printed.

Set up query, stage 1

From the File menu select 'New'. A list pops up, showing all the things we could set up from scratch. Choose 'Query':

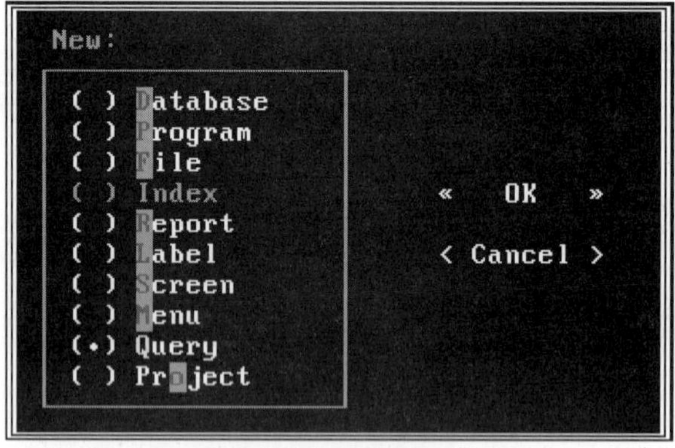

Set up query, stage 2

If a database has already been opened, the next screen will be skipped. We'll assume that *FoxPro* has just been started up and that no databases have been selected.

The Customer database, shown on the previous page, has already been set up for us as an example in the Tutorial directory.

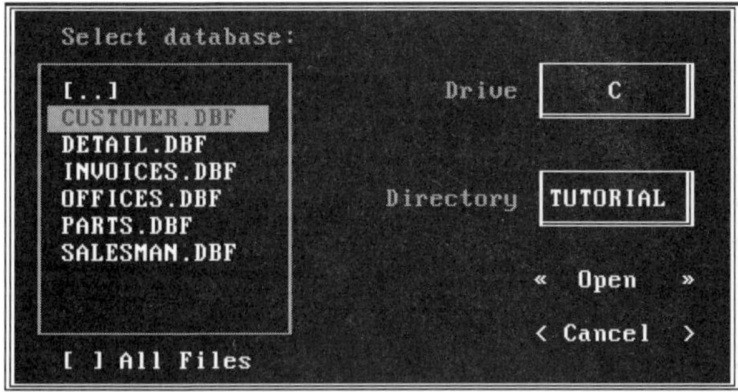

Set up query, stage 3

As soon as a database has been selected, the Relational Query By Example window pops up:

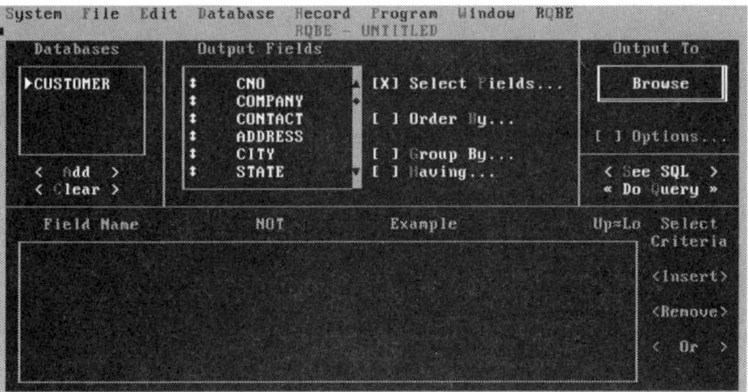

Click on 'Select Fields'. All the fields have been selected by default; click on 'Remove All'.

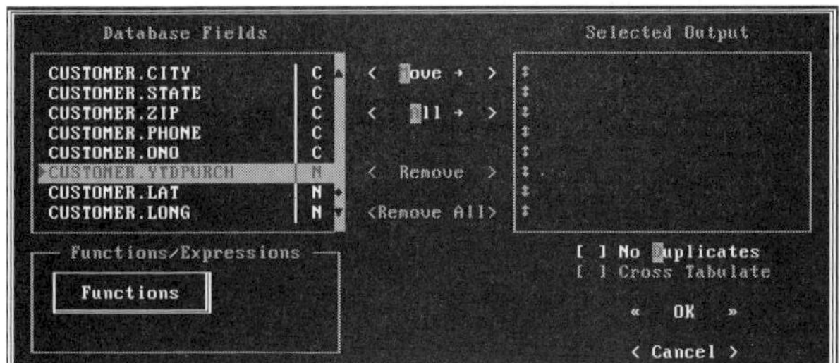

Select CUSTOMER.COMPANY, then click on 'Move' to put it into the 'Selected Output' box. Scroll down and select CUSTOMER.YTDPURCH. Click on 'Move' again.

All the fields could be displayed, but we are interested only in the name of the company and how much it has spent, if $5000 or more.

The screen looks like this after both fields have been moved across to the Selected Output box:

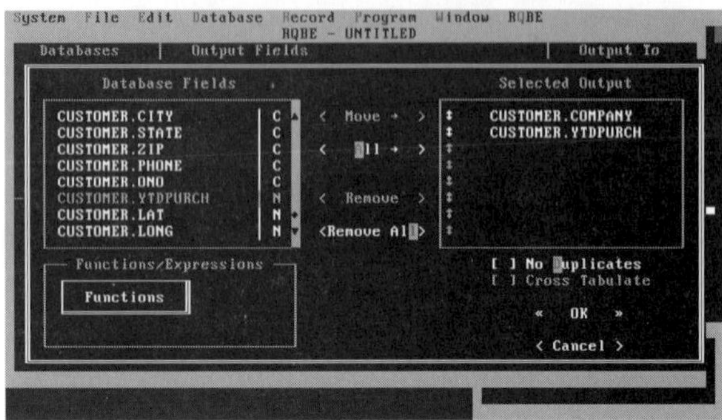

Set up query, stage 4

Click on OK in the previous screen, put the cursor on the horizontal bar in the box below 'Field Name' and keep the left-hand mouse button held down. This brings up the Field Name pop-up.

Select CUSTOMER.YTDPURCH, the field which contains data we are interested in, and for which we are about to set up an example of Boolean Logic (also known as Boolean Algebra).

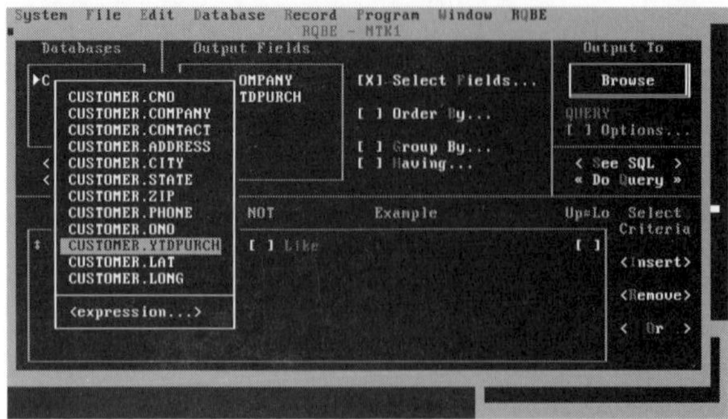

Boolean Logic

Boolean Logic or Boolean Algebra was devised by George Boole: born 1815, died 1864. It forms the logical basis of computer design. At its heart it uses simple English words: AND, OR, NOT.

Let's look at an example in process control using a single AND gate. This one has two inputs; if both are TRUE then the gate opens. The first is fed with the level of the contents of a hopper. If the level is high enough, the first input of the AND gate is set to TRUE.

The second input is given the output of a device measuring the temperature of a heated vessel containing water. When the temperature reaches 100 degrees centigrade, the input becomes TRUE. At that moment the AND gate opens, releasing a quantity of material from the hopper into a receptacle below. At the same time it releases a measured quantity of boiling water into the same receptacle. And there we are: the basic principle of the office coffee machine! Add a third input to the AND gate for coin weight and you're in business.

Set up query, stage 4

Hold the mouse button down while the cursor is on 'Like' and five more operators are revealed. This is what they all do:

Like
If you wanted every Smith, Smythe and Smyth, you would choose 'Like' and under Example you would put Sm?th?. (This particular database file surprisingly does not have a separate field for CUSTOMER.SURNAME, and therefore *wouldn't* find them.)

Exactly Like
Finds precisely what you are looking for. This could be a name or a quantity.

More Than
This is the one we shall be using to find customers who have spent $4999.99 or more with the company. Had we been looking for someone who had spent precisely $5000, we would have used 'Exactly Like'.

Less Than
The reverse of More Than. You could click between the square brackets under 'Not' and put $5000 under

'Example' so that the search was for not less than $5000.

Between

All the variations of Smith could be found between 'Smh' and 'Smz', though other names would appear in the list. Similarly you could search for amounts between $5000 and $10,000.

In

Searches for a nominated word or number in the chosen field. 'CUSTOMER.ADDRESS in 5111' would bring up Jeff Culbertson of 1st Computers, whose address is 5111 Parkway. It would have been easier if the syntax had allowed it to be '5111 in CUSTOMER.ADDRESS ('item in field' rather than 'field in item').

As with 'Like', 'CUSTOMER.CONTACT in Jim', will find all the Jims and Jimmys. It will not, however, find text that does not start with the search example, such as their surnames.

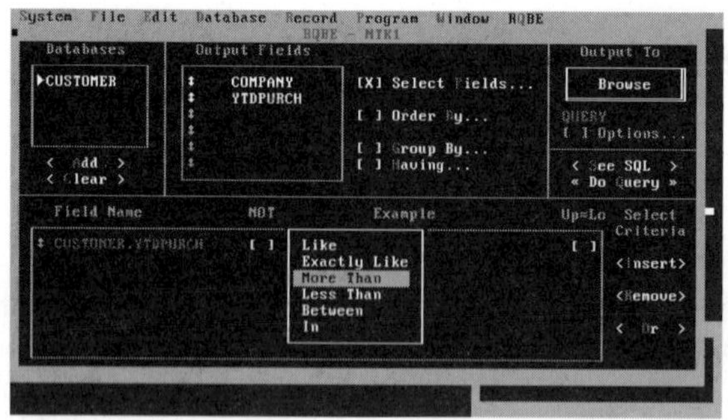

We have chosen 'More Than'...

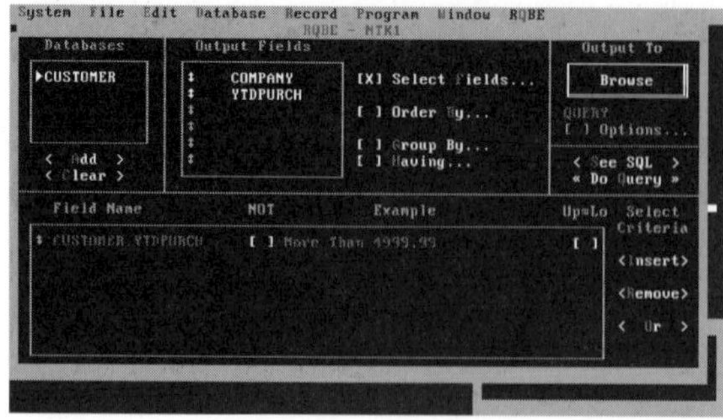

... and put $4999.99 under 'Example'. A click on 'Do Query' brings up the information we wanted.

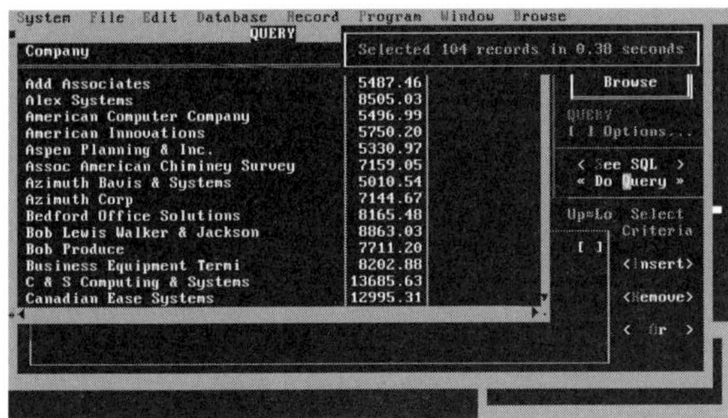

FoxPro prides itself on the speed of its searches. It uses its patented '*Rushmore*' system, and lets you know how little time it took to search every record in the file and come up with an answer.

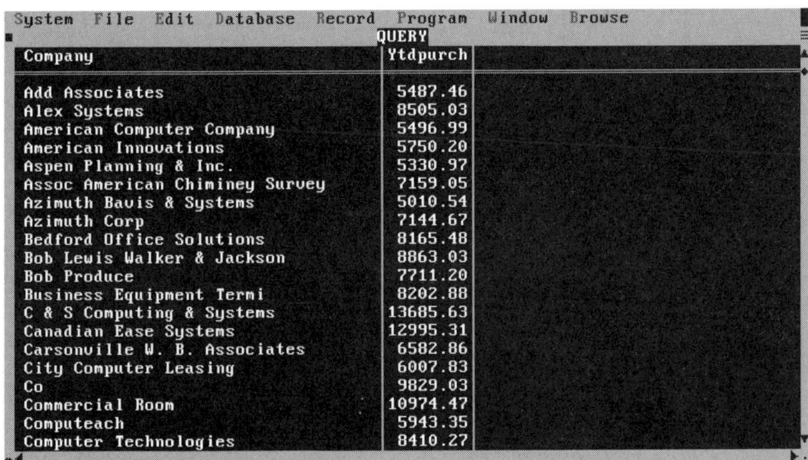

The window can be re-sized by dragging the dot in the bottom right-hand corner of the window.

First step to programming in *FoxPro*

Close the Query window by clicking on the small square at the extreme left, just below the System menu.

Now click on 'See SQL':

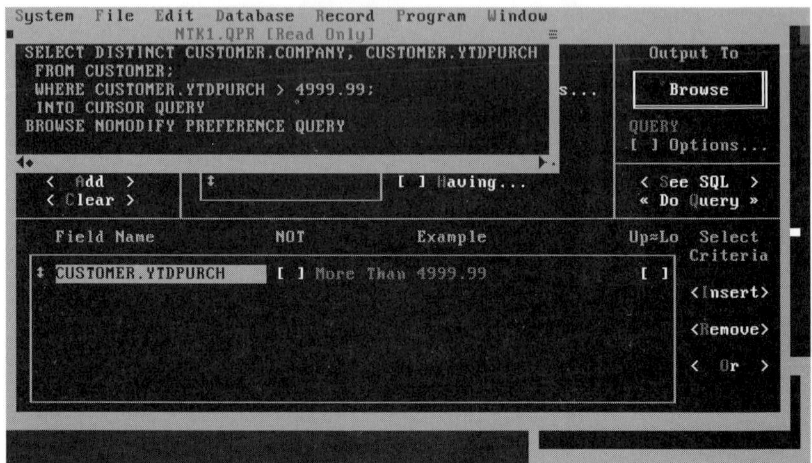

A new window appears over the top of the RQBE window, showing the program code that *FoxPro* has generated from your query.

```
NTK1.QPR [Read Only]
SELECT DISTINCT CUSTOMER.COMPANY, CUSTOMER.YTDPURCH
 FROM CUSTOMER;
 WHERE CUSTOMER.YTDPURCH > 4999.99;
 INTO CURSOR QUERY
BROWSE NOMODIFY PREFERENCE QUERY
```

Remember that *FoxPro* has done all this for you, and will do it again, even under entirely different circumstances. You only have to click on 'See SQL' and all will be revealed. You don't really have to know what it all means, but here it is for your interest:

SELECT
Retrieve data from one or more databases. The second line of code tells us that in this case it will be from **CUSTOMER.DBF.**

DISTINCT
This was derived from choosing 'No Duplicates' in the Select Fields window. It is possible that one or more records in a database could satisfy one or more of the criteria in a query. You need only one copy of the record (or of selected fields from the record) to prove that it meets the case.

CUSTOMER.COMPANY
Show the **COMPANY** field of the **CUSTOMER** database in the query output.

CUSTOMER.YTDPURCH
Show the **YTDPURCH** (purchases in the year to date) field of the **CUSTOMER** database in the query output.

FROM CUSTOMER
Use the **CUSTOMER** database.

WHERE
This has the same meaning as in algebra, for example:
Egg Quantity = Bnum x EPBnum
where Bnum = Number of boxes
and EPBnum = Number of eggs per box.

YTDPURCH > 4999.99
As mentioned on page 189, this is a Boolean expression, which means that the result is True or False. There are no in-betweens with Mr Boole: it either satisfies the case or it doesn't.

You can use other Boolean operators, such as **AND** and **OR** to build up a compound query. We might have included Luton in our search for left-handed lorry drivers. The query then might have said:
WHERE HANDEDNESS = "Left" AND OCCUPATION = "Lorry Driver" AND (TOWN = "Letchworth" OR TOWN = "Luton")

INTO CURSOR QUERY
Show the results on screen. The results could have been sent to an array (see page 242), to a file, to a printer or to another database.

BROWSE NOMODIFY PREFERENCE QUERY
There are more than 30 different **BROWSE** commands. **NOMODIFY**, as you might have guessed, prevents any modifications being made to the database (except for appending or deleting records). **PREFERENCE** lets you save a Browse window's attributes in the form you have chosen, rather than using the standard set-up.

You have done the groundwork

The aim of this chapter has been to show the main principles of databases, to explain some of the jargon and to demonstrate a few of the ways in which they can be useful.

It will have prepared the ground so that you will be on familiar territory when you come to your first database user manual.

CHAPTER

10

Spreadsheets

Lotus 1-2-3 *is used in this chapter to show some of the uses of spreadsheets for calculations. This program includes some of the text handling features of word processors; it also has the ability to manipulate data from some of the leading databases.*

We look at ways of creating a budget worksheet, making calculations from the data, and of enhancing its appearance to highlight key areas.

10

Spreadsheets

What spreadsheets do

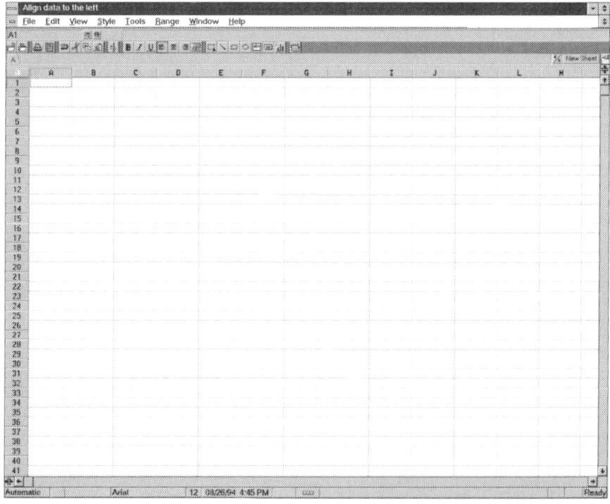

This is an empty worksheet, ready for an entry to be made in cell A1. The entry could be a mathematical or logical formula or it could just be text. Up there in the top row it is more than likely to be the heading for a column or group of columns. But any cell could contain either words or numbers.

formula

The word 'formula' is used quite often in this chapter. As ever, it will be something you knew already, though probably in a different context.

A mathematical formula is exactly what you think it is: a prescribed sequence of adding, subtracting, multiplying or dividing certain numbers, often represented by symbols. However, the 'symbols' here are usually spreadsheet cell references. So if it was required to multiply the contents of cell A1 by the contents of cell B2, the formula would be: A1 x B2, which in the language of Lotus *1-2-3* is **=A1*B2**.

Logical formulae only ever give one of two answers: 1 if the result is true and 0 if it is false. You might want to carry out some further mathematical operation if the value of cell A1 was greater than the value of B2, so your formula would start **A1>B2**.

Spreadsheets process numbers: amounts of money; quantities; measurements; populations; statistics; anything that can be expressed numerically. They can act as simple records or they will process the figures you feed into them, giving you projected results for the following week or far into the future.

Imagine a blank sheet of paper on which you could write a list of items with their individual costs. Instead of having to add them up, the total would just appear. Suppose it came to more than you could afford, so you trimmed the cost of some of the items. Or perhaps you cut some of them out altogether. A new reduced total would be presented to you, instantly.

A spreadsheet processes the information you give it, in any way you want. So it can be as simple or as complicated as you like, and will do virtually anything depending on your ingenuity.

Applications

These are some of the things you can do with a spreadsheet program:

- Budgeting
- Planning
- Projections ('What if' scenarios)
- Performance processing

Lotus *1-2-3* has been used here to demonstrate the power and usefulness of spreadsheets. You can have as many sets of calculations as you want, on the same or different subjects. Each of these is saved with its own title, and is called a 'worksheet'.

Let's explore some of the ways in which these worksheets can be used, without going into great detail, but showing you enough to give you an insight into how you might apply them.

Budgeting

Two columns will be used for each month; the first to contain text, the second to contain amounts of money. At the head of the first pair of columns we'll type in 'January', the second pair 'February' and so on.

Cell A1 will be taken up by 'January', and it would be neater to leave A2 and B2 empty. In A3 we can put in the first regular item of expenditure, say 'Food', and in B3 we'll type in the amount we expect to spend on food during January.

Continue down the 'A' column with Rates, Mortgage Repayments, Motor Expenses, Telephone, Clothing, Entertainment, Holiday Fund. In the 'B' column enter the corresponding amounts, except for Telephone.

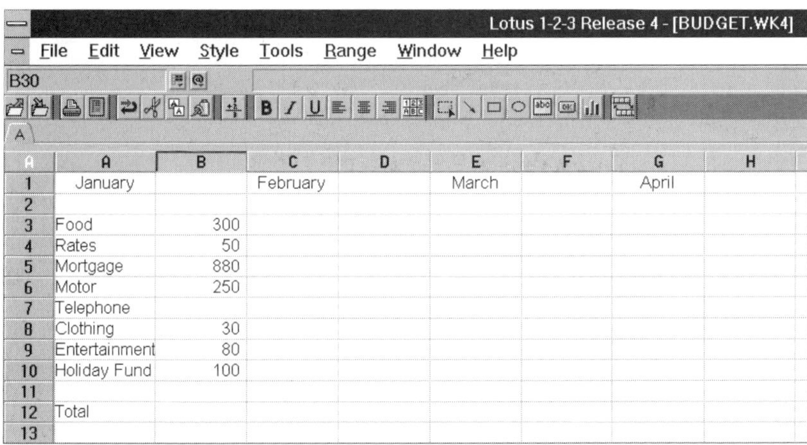

	A	B	C	D	E	F	G	H
1	January		February		March		April	
2								
3	Food	300						
4	Rates	50						
5	Mortgage	880						
6	Motor	250						
7	Telephone							
8	Clothing	30						
9	Entertainment	80						
10	Holiday Fund	100						
11								
12	Total							
13								

Adding cell contents

We shall put a 'formula' in cell B12 which will add the contents of cells B3 to B10 and give us a total for January. Building an formula, using words from the spreadsheet language, is a form of programming.

The easy way

Lotus *1-2-3* gives us a simple way of building expressions. Click on the cell where you want the result of the formula to appear, then go up to the Edit line of the control panel and click on the @ button. This brings up the @Function menu:

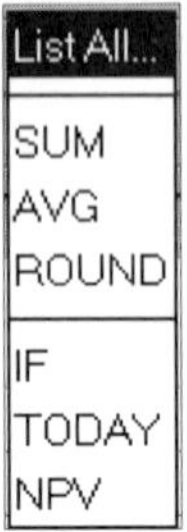

Click on **SUM**, then click on the first cell in the range to be added, B3, and drag the cursor down to the last, B10. Click on the green tick in the Edit line. The total appears immediately in B12.

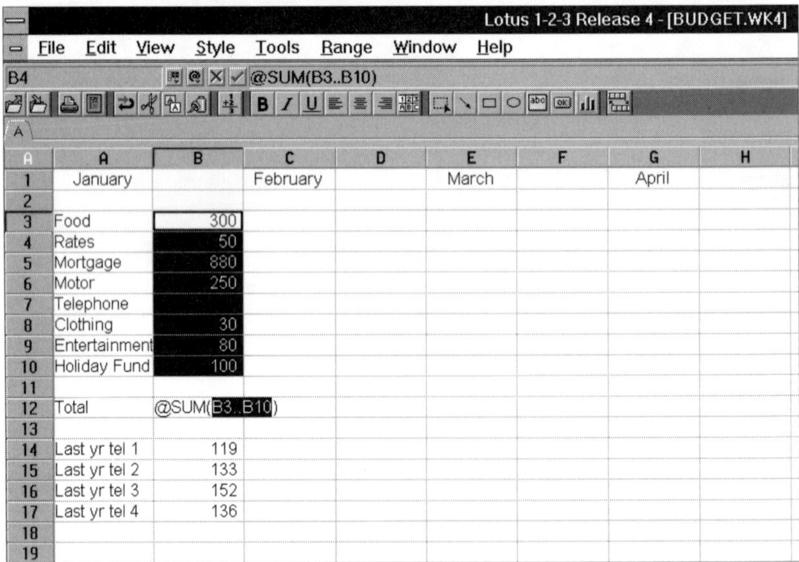

The thinking way

Type **@SUM(B3..B10)** in B12. Press Return. The total appears immediately in B12.

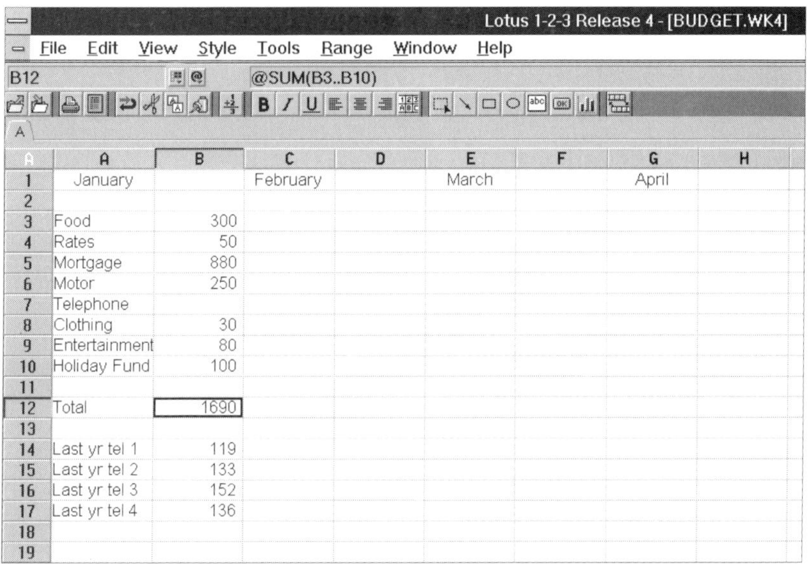

Using data from other cells

Now we can start adding refinements. For example, you probably don't pay your telephone bill monthly. What we can do here is to use four cells to input the amounts of the telephone bills for the last four quarters.

They should be in an area of the worksheet that doesn't show, but for simplicity we'll have it 'on the front page' with everything else.

Hide cells

You can 'hide' cells so they are invisible but will still do their job.

Having input last year's bills, the worksheet can add them together and divide them by 12 to give us a figure for the monthly cost. In cell B7 we put the formula **@SUM(B14..B17)/12**.

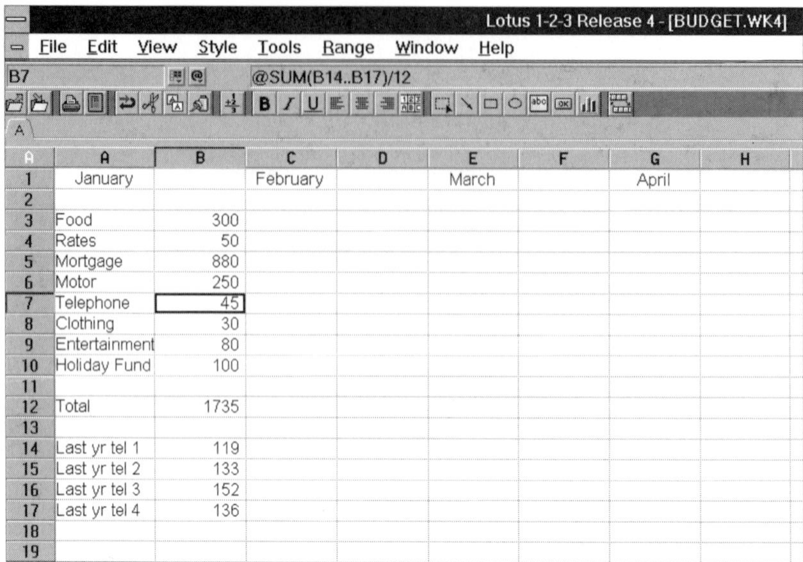

	A	B	C	D	E	F	G	H
1	January		February		March		April	
2								
3	Food	300						
4	Rates	50						
5	Mortgage	880						
6	Motor	250						
7	Telephone	45						
8	Clothing	30						
9	Entertainment	80						
10	Holiday Fund	100						
11								
12	Total	1735						
13								
14	Last yr tel 1	119						
15	Last yr tel 2	133						
16	Last yr tel 3	152						
17	Last yr tel 4	136						
18								
19								

As soon as Return is pressed, or the green tick in the Edit line is clicked on, the answer appears in B7. At the same time the total is updated from £1690 to £1735.

As you see, a cell can contain text, figures or a formula. The formula could even be another cell reference, such as '**`M17`**'. Suppose the total expenditure for the year was in cell Y14, you could put 'Annual Total' in cell A19 and '**`Y14`**' in cell B19 so that the end result would be repeated on the 'front page'.

Viewing other areas of the worksheet

The cells you see may be only the tip of the iceberg. Calculations could be going on in cell ZZ1 or A200 and beyond, depending on the resources of your computer and the spreadsheet program.

Each program will have its own way of getting to areas currently out of sight. *1-2-3* lets you jump to any cell by pressing the F5 function key and typing in the destination:

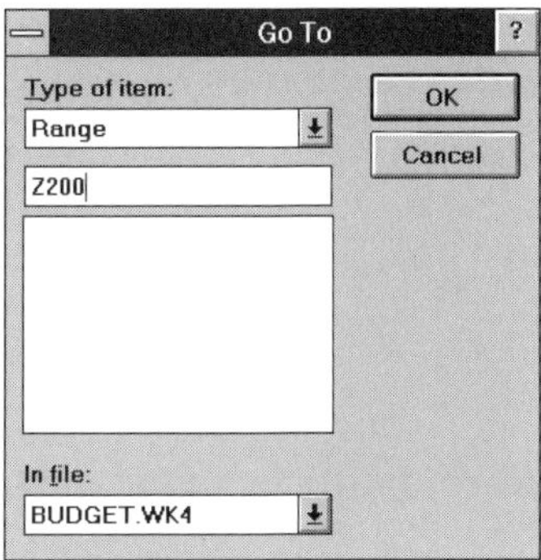

If the cell is in view, just click on it; then you can add the necessary word(s), number or formula.

Changing the look of a worksheet

You can change:

- The format of numbers
- Fonts and text attributes
- Colours and patterns
- Alignment
- Column widths
- Row heights
- Visibility or invisibility of cell contents

You can even add borders, frames and pictures.

Number formats

Click on the **Style** menu and select **Number Format**. This brings up its dialogue box:

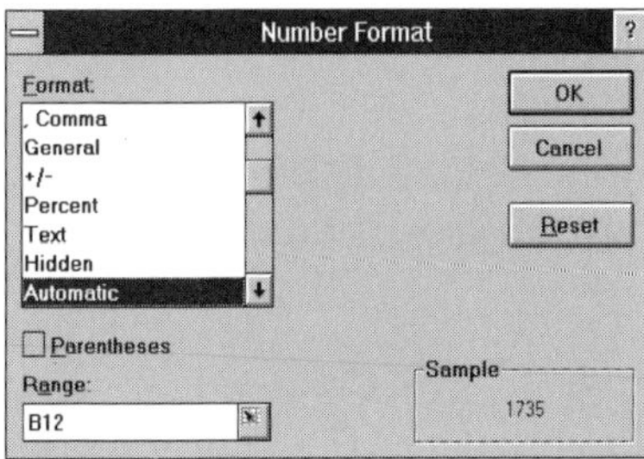

You'll notice that it tells you the present format of the selected cell. You now have a choice of:

- Automatic
- Comma
- Currency
- Percent
- Scientific

There are also five different date formats and four time formats.

The cell range B14 to B17 has been selected for change to Currency using the Number Format dialogue box.

The first cell in any selected range is always outlined; subsequent cells are reversed out into white on black.

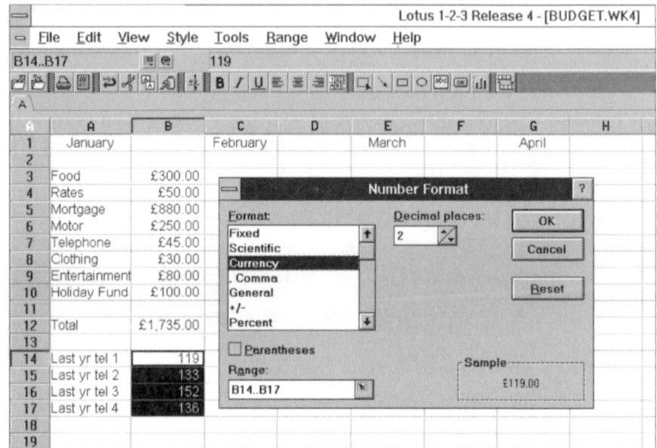

Fonts and text attributes

Click in the **STYLE** menu, select **FONT & ATTRIBUTES** to get a dialogue box similar to those used in word processing and desktop publishing programs. Here you can change the typeface, the size and these attributes: normal, bold, italic, single and double underline.

Colours and patterns

From the **STYLE** menu select **LINES & COLOUR**. Here you can highlight selected cells on the screen.

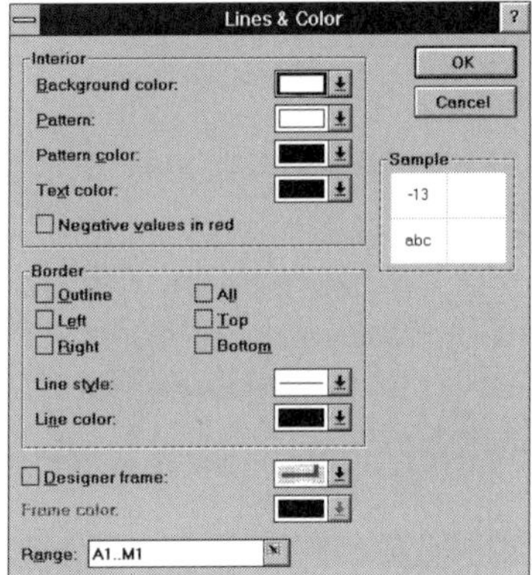

Alignment

Choose **ALIGNMENT** from the **STYLE** menu. Another dialogue box pops up, allowing you to have the cell contents aligned horizontally by the left, centre or right. At the same time they can be aligned vertically with the top, centre or bottom of the cell.

Column width

COLUMN WIDTH is also in the **STYLE** menu, where you can select a numeric value for the width. Alternatively, take the mouse cursor to the left or right-hand edge of the column letter. The cursor changes to a black two-headed horizontal arrow. Drag the column to its new width.

Row height

This is adjusted automatically to accommodate the amount of material in the cell. However, it can also be selected numerically from **ROW HEIGHT** in the **STYLE** menu, or the lower border of the cell can be dragged into a new position.

Hiding data

Distracting information can be hidden, and 'sealed' so it's not deleted accidentally. Choose **NUMBER FORMAT** from the **STYLE** menu.

Adding pictures to worksheets

Graphics are brought into Lotus *1-2-3* via the *Windows Clipboard*, so you have to make sure you have put your picture in there first.

We'll import a piece of clip-art from the *CorelDRAW!* CD-ROM, copy it to the clipboard and import it from there into our worksheet as a *Windows Metafile*.

Black coffee might be appropriate for budgeting.

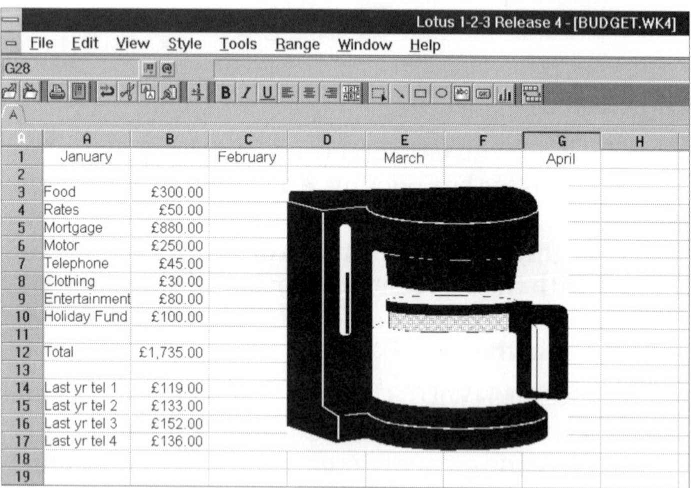

Summary

This has given you a taste of some of the things you can do with a spreadsheet program. There are more than 300 pages in the Lotus manual, explaining the finer points in much greater detail.

Also there are training courses, both commercial and those run as evening classes.

A further insight into some of the techniques available in *1-2-3* is given in the animated introduction which comes with the program. A little man in a black tail coat runs, jumps and flies around sample worksheets in a highly instructive and entertaining way.

CHAPTER 11

Desktop publishing

This is the next step after word processing; or if you were really ambitious, you could skip wp altogether and produce all your work in a DTP program.

The uses of DTP are described, to give you access to programs with every imaginable way of dealing with words and pictures to make them look their best.

11

Desktop publishing

The next step after word processing

The line between word processing and desktop publishing is becoming harder to draw. There was a time when word processors could be used for words alone; they allowed you to write letters and reports; they had mail-merge, which enabled the same letter to be sent to many different people but with their individual names and addresses added automatically.

Word processors had spell-checking and the search and replace facility, so that every occurrence of, say, 'colour blind' could be changed to 'chromatically challenged' throughout a document.

Nowadays word processors can put pictures into a report, split the text into multiple columns and provide headers and footers whose contents are derived automatically from headings and sub-headings.

Perhaps the main differences are negative ones: DTP (desktop publishing) programs don't usually have mail-merge and WP (word processor or word processing) doesn't generally have the full DTP facilities of indexing, cross-referencing (for example 'see page 27'), table of contents generation, frame anchoring (keeping pictures with their associated text), conditional text, or table formatting. Even some DTP programs don't have all of these, by the way.

The DTP program that was used to create this book is *FrameMaker*, which has everything, including the former WP preserves of spell-checking and search & replace. About the only thing it doesn't have, because it doesn't need it, is mail-merge.

A further advantage of *FrameMaker* is that it is 'multi-platform', in other words the work it produces can be transferred between different operating systems: DOS, Mac and UNIX.

Multi-platform

There are three main 'platforms': DOS, Mac and UNIX, of which by far the most popular is DOS. Whatever anyone does in this life, someone else always thinks they can do it better. This applies in computing probably more strongly than in any other area of enterprise.

For this reason we have different operating systems (platforms) which tackle the job in different ways. File handling is different, the commands are different and the programs, though achieving the same ends, have to be tailored for compatibility with their particular platform.

A multi-platform (or cross-platform) program will have been written differently for the different platforms, but its files will be able to be created in, say DOS, and then used on a Mac and *vice versa*. FrameMaker files are interchangeable between all three of these platforms.

The uses of DTP

DTP is used in the production of correspondence, leaflets, brochures, magazines, company reports, books. Letters, simple leaflets and material for internal consumption can be printed out, nominally on the top of the same desk as the computer, and are then ready for distribution.

Beyond the desktop

For higher quality work, and for larger quantities, we have to make use of more specialised machinery that wouldn't fit on the average desk. Suppose we are producing the company report and accounts. These are intended to impress the shareholders, so a few sheets of

A4, printed on the office laser printer at 300 dots per inch (dpi) and stapled together, just wouldn't do. In order to look really crisp, the pages should be printed at a much higher resolution: between four and eight times higher. The text will then be sharper, the illustrations clearer.

For higher quality work like this, the desktop laser printer would still come in handy, but only as far as providing proofs for checking before going on to the next stage.

Lithography and photolithography

We must now re-enter the world of printing as it was immediately before the advent of DTP. An image of our work has to be transferred to a flexible metal plate which can be wrapped around a drum in a rotary printing press. Oil-based ink will be applied to the plate, sticking to the image (which is slightly greasy) and being transferred from there to the paper. A thin film of water prevents the ink from getting onto the areas of the printing plate where there is no image, so that we don't get totally black pages.

This process is called photolithography. Many years ago there was lithographic printing, in which images were drawn on to a flat stone (Greek: lithos = stone; graphē = writing). The ink was applied, followed by a film of water, then one sheet of paper at a time was pressed down onto the stone and came away with the image.

The author was once taken on a tour of Waterlow's, the printers, and watched in amazement as an artist transferred one of Terence Cuneo's railway engine pictures to stones. He had the original in front of him and, using only a grey crayon and his eyes, was splitting the painting into its component colours and transferring each one to a separate stone. The painting was to be reproduced in something like 14 colours, each of which had to be separated visually. The stones would then have had their individual ink colours applied, and each print would have visited each of the 14 stones one after the other as the colours were built up to give a perfect full-colour reproduction of the original. As if that were not enough, it all had to be done back to front so the picture came out the right way round.

Today we would point a process camera at the painting and press a button, which is far less interesting, but more politically correct because it gives everyone an equal chance of achieving the same results without standing out from the crowd!

To get our image on to the printing plate photographically, it has to be put onto film. It is the production of this film that is the next stage, once we have gone as far as we can go with our work on the desktop.

Our files will be sent to a photosetting bureau who will put the pages onto film. Photosetting, or filmsetting machines have lasers in them which 'write with light' on photographic film. The principle is broadly similar to the desktop laser printer, but achieves a higher resolution by virtue of the difference in size between the particles of toner used by laser printers and the much finer grain size of photographic film.

The film goes to the plate-maker who transfers the image to a litho plate, which can then be used for printing multiple copies.

As well as producing black and white pages, many DTP programs have colour separation facilities. This enables them to take in scanned images in full colour, separate them into their four components, cyan, magenta, yellow and black (CMYK), which leads to the production of four black images, each of which will cause the correct amount of the colour it represents to be deposited onto the paper.

Horses for courses

Some DTP programs tend to provide specialist facilities: *QuarkXPress*, for example, is ideal for magazine production because its typographical controls are well developed and it will 'flow' an article from the bottom of one page to halfway down a column three pages further forward. On the other hand, it doesn't support running headers and footers (apart from page numbering), neither can it generate an index nor do cross-referencing.

Running headers & footers

Headers are the words appearing above the general run of text, indicating what is going on on that page. Footers do the same thing at the bottom of the page, and usually include the page number.

Running headers and footers are 'alive'. They repeat a chosen part of the text and will change themselves if that text is changed. Also if that text is moved on to another page, say by the addition of a few paragraphs on a previous page, a running header (or footer) will reflect the change, moving with it to the new position.

On this page the left header is the chapter title, Desktop publishing, and the right header has been set to repeat the first occurrence of the second level of sub-head, in this case 'The facilities'. The footer shows the first level of sub-head, 'The next step after word processing', and the page number.

The facilities

Paragraph formatting

Every press of the Return key creates a new paragraph. It might be a paragraph with several lines of text, it could be a single word, or it could be just the paragraph marker itself.

Each paragraph should be given a 'format', 'style' or 'tag' (the word used depends on which program you're using). This means giving it a name, such as Body Text or Sub-head 2 or Caption, and choosing a typeface and point size for it.

When you have created a tag, you can apply it to other selected paragraphs so that they immediately take on all the same characteristics. For example you might want all your sub-heads to be in Helvetica Bold 12pt.

Rather than having to address each one individually and set up the face and size each time, you would select the sub-head, go into the Paragraph Catalogue and choose the appropriate tag.

The face and size settings for your paragraph are only the beginning. You can also choose any or all of the following:

ALIGNMENT

Whether the text is justified (straight edges on both sides), ranged left (straight left hand edge, ragged right), centred on the page, or ranged right (straight right hand edge, ragged left).

INDENTS

The text might start 'full out', that is with no indent. You might want an indent for the first line only, or perhaps for the entire block of text. The right hand edge could also be indented so that the text was set to a narrower width than the rest of the document.

LEADING (INTER-LINE SPACING)

Lines of type usually have added space between them: normally between one and two points (this paragraph is leaded one and a half points).

In the days of metal type, the spacing between lines was increased either by adding lead in the form of cast strips or by using a font with a deeper body. From this we get the word 'leading' which can also be called inter-line spacing (meaning the distance between the bottom of one line and the top of the next, not the pitch).

PARAGRAPH SPACING

Sets the spacing above and below the paragraph. See, for example, how the sub-heading '**WEIGHT**' is closer to its own text than it is to the last line of this paragraph.

WEIGHT

A choice of medium or bold. Some typefaces, though, have more weights, including light and semi-bold.

ANGLE

Text is almost always set in roman, or upright, but you can set the odd paragraph in italics (sometimes called *oblique*) if you have a good reason for it.

TAB SETTING

You can set up paragraphs for columns of figures, or text, with left, right, centre and decimal tabs. Some DTP programs won't let you use tabs if the text is justified.

KEEP WITH NEXT

Choosing this parameter for a heading makes sure that it will always stay with its following text, and not be left isolated on the bottom of the previous page.

START AT TOP OF PAGE

If you have really major headings, like chapter titles, you'll want them to lead off on a page of their own, and probably to start on a right hand page as well. These requirements can be set into the paragraph tag.

OTHER ATTRIBUTES

These are normally applied to single characters, words or phrases: Underline, Overline, Strikethrough (for legal work), Superscript, Subscript (examples shown overleaf).

WIDOWS AND ORPHANS

You can set the minimum number of lines before and after a page or column break, so avoiding the single line at the head of a page (widow) or at the foot (orphan).

Text formatting

Text formatting is a way of applying local changes to your copy, such as putting a word into italics. If, for example, your paragraph is set in Garamond Condensed 11 pt and you change one of its words to italic, then that word will be put into Garamond Condensed 11 pt Italic, if that font exists. Should the face have no related italic, it will remain in roman. No attempt is made to substitute a similar italic, though there's nothing to prevent you from doing so.

In desktop publishing, the different characteristics that you can apply to letters, words, phrases, even entire paragraphs, are called 'attributes'. Drag the cursor over the area of copy whose attributes you wish to change, so that it shows on the screen in reverse video, then help yourself from the following selection.

TEXT ATTRIBUTES

roman	*italic*	**bold**
bold italic	underline	overline
superscript	~~strike through~~	subscript

KERNING

This is a way of varying the space between any two characters.

The pair: AV, has normal kerning; while this one: AV, has been kerned together more tightly. When you come to do a headline in, say, 24pt, you can improve the look of it tremendously by the judicious use of kerning. Some pairs may need to be brought closer together, others moved further apart.

TRACKING

Similar to kerning, but applied to a whole word or line of type, even a complete paragraph. You may find yourself with a 'loose line', where a long word in a justified paragraph has gone over to the next line, leaving behind a great deal of air between words and letters. The best way of dealing with this is to re-write the passage, but if the author is not available you might be able to tighten up the tracking and pull that long word back into the previous line to improve the look of it. Another possibility is to hyphenate the troublesome word.

HYPHENATION

You can turn automatic hyphenation on or off, and you can choose how many hyphenated words to allow. Too many and the right hand edge of your page will start to look like a nail brush, making reading unnecessarily difficult.

Words are checked automatically against a built-in hyphenation dictionary to see where they should be broken.

General features

SEARCH AND REPLACE

(Also called Find & Change.)

The more advanced Search & Replace utilities can find a dozen or more different features: paragraph tags, markers, cross-references, and let you decide whether or not to change the one currently found and displayed in context.

SPELL CHECKING

We all need to have our spelling checked; even the most erudite can make typing errors or have blind spots with 'ie' and 'ei'. There used only to be 'American English' spell-checkers which would want to change 'colour' to 'color', but now most programs have 'English English'. (And this one has just queried the spelling of 'color'!)

As with Search & Replace, you are shown the word that the checker has picked up, together with at least a few words on either side. You then have the option of making the recommended change, allowing the word through (it might be someone's surname) or adding it to the built-in dictionary so that it will be accepted next time round.

CHANGING CAPITALISATION

To save retyping a heading or phrase, you can highlight it with the text cursor then choose from a menu whether to have it all in capitals, all in lower case or with initial caps.

AUTOMATIC SAVING

Saving your work to disk

A choice of saving your work to disk at regular intervals, say every five minutes. You may select the time interval and whether or not to use the facility at all. But think hard before you spurn the offer! If your DTP program doesn't have this facility you should develop the 'Control S Twitch'. This causes the little finger to hold down the Ctrl Key while the forefinger presses the S. It's a popular short-cut way to save.

HEADERS & FOOTERS

(Sometimes called 'Running Headers & Footers'.) For this book we are using three variable (or 'running') headers, two variable footers and a fixed one. Headers and Footers can derive their information from many sources, but we have chosen the paragraph tag called 'Head 2' to display at the top left of all left hand pages and at the top right of all right hand pages.

At the top right of the left hand page the header is the chapter number, while the chapter title appears at the top left of the facing page.

The footers show the page numbers on the outside edges, the book's title bottom right of the left hand page and the current main heading (Head 1) bottom left of the right hand page.

All of this is set up in different ways according to the program you're using, but it is perfectly straight-forward. The idea, of course, is to make it easy to find things as you flip through the pages.

CROSS-REFERENCE MARKERS

It is useful to be able to say "see page 86" with the confidence that the subject will still be on that page when the document is finished. With DTP's ability to move chunks of text about, it's quite possible that you should have said "see page 93".

However, you can attach an invisible marker to the item currently on page 86, so that its presence will be known, wherever it ends up. Now you say "see page " and the program adds a cross-reference code so that it will always point to the correct place.

INDEX MARKERS

Indexing is pure magic. You put invisible (non-printing) markers against the words, tell the program how you want each word to appear in the index, press the metaphorical button and you have an alphabetical index. You can create an index across a single chapter or a complete document.

TABLE OF CONTENTS

The Table of Contents is usually based on selected paragraph tags, in a similar way to Headers & Footers. You specify which tags are to be used, and the order of priority. The program displays the text that has been given those tags, in the form of a contents list.

UNDO and REDO

If you've deleted something accidentally, or made an awful mistake of one kind or another, you can Undo it. This facility is usually in the Edit Menu. There is one rather important proviso: it must be the last thing you did. If you make a mistake, then you make another, you can only undo the later one. Undo can only be applied to the most recent mouse or keyboard operation. There are programs with up to 99 levels of Undo, but these are the exception.

Some programs also have a Redo, so that you can put back something that you have undone.

REVERT TO PREVIOUS (ABANDON)

This, too, is a way of recovering from disaster, or possibly a chapter of disasters. You can choose to abandon all the work you have done *since you last saved*, and revert to the previous version.

Automatic backups don't count as the last saved version; they are normally saved using a slightly modified file name.

If you are of a nervous or pessimistic disposition you could use the 'Save As ...' option and save your work each time under a different name, for example LIFEWRKA.DOC, LIFEWRKB.DOC etc. The use of letters is recommended, rather than numbers, since there are 26 of them; that should be enough for wearers of even the greyest-coloured glasses.

ANCHORED FRAMES

When you draw a frame, to contain pictures or words, it is drawn onto the page itself, and the text flows round it. If copy is added before the frame, it will push the following text further on, maybe to the next page. So your picture, illustrating a particular point in the text, could be left high and dry, surrounded by alien words.

Anchoring the frame to the text makes sure that it moves with its associated paragraph. It will hold its original horizontal position relative to the page, say 10mm to the right of the main column, but is free to move vertically.

TABLES

Instead of having to draw tables by hand, you can use the Table Editor. This gives you a choice of line weights and the ability to put tints on individual cells, columns or rows. A great benefit is that columns will grow as you add more text. There is a small table (showing text attributes) on page 216.

VARIABLES IN PLACE OF TEXT

You are preparing a leaflet on a new product, only they haven't decided what to call it yet. There will be many occasions when you need to use its name in the text. You could put in 'Widget' throughout and then use Search & Replace to find 'Widget' and replace it with the new name. Or you could use a *variable*.

Variables (in the context of DTP) are placeholders for text that you can change manually, like our Widget, or text to be updated automatically, like a date or a page number.

CONDITIONAL TEXT & GRAPHICS

This is a speciality of *FrameMaker*. Suppose you are preparing a set of manuals to cover the different versions of a new car. There will be different engine sizes and alternative trims, but much of the information will apply throughout the range. You can prepare just one manual and assign condition tags to the parts that will vary from one model to another.

TEMPLATES

The whole idea of DTP is to make a graphic designer's life simpler. This applies whether you *are* a designer, whether you are going through the protracted business of becoming one, or even if this will be the first time you have ever sharpened a pencil.

Templates are a major step in the simplification process. For a start, many DTP programs supply you with ready-made layouts, or templates, for a variety of documents. You may use these or not; they have been prepared for users with no previous experience.

The big thing about templates, which can include paragraph tags, is that they save you doing the same thing over and over again. Once you have designed your newsletter, or left and right manual pages, you can save the layout as a template and re-use it as often as you like. As well as being a labour-saving idea it also ensures that the second and subsequent editions have the same house style as the first.

Words & pictures from other programs

Most, if not all, of your illustrations will be coming in from outside the DTP program. This process is called 'importing'. The corollary is that when you have produced a picture in a drawing program for use elsewhere, it is called 'exporting'.

Exporting and importing

The export command prepares a graphic file for import by other programs. It has to be converted from the format in which, say, *CorelDRAW!* works, into one that will be acceptable to your DTP program. You choose a file name for it, a directory for it to be stored in, and the graphic format in which it will be exported.

There are lots of graphic formats about, but they divide into two main types: bitmapped graphics and vector graphics.

Graphic files

A bitmapped picture is composed entirely of dots. The position of each dot is put into a 'map' in the file when it is saved in a drawing program, or as a scanned image. The map is used to put all the dots back on screen (or on the printed page) when the file is called up again.

Vector (or vectored) graphics are stored as a series of mathematical formulae, rather than the 'map' of a series of dots held in a bitmapped graphic file. Vectored graphics are based on work done by Monsieur Bézier, who developed the idea of converting drawings into mathematical expressions. The files produced in this way are much more compact than bitmaps and can give drawings to any degree of enlargement without loss of quality. This is in marked contrast to bitmaps, in which anything other than a horizontal or vertical line becomes more and more obviously jagged as it is enlarged.

As yet, no-one has devised a satisfactory way of converting bitmaps to vectors. There's your chance to make a fortune!

The format of a graphic file is shown by its suffix (the dot and three letters following the file name), such as '.PCX' for bitmaps and '.WMF' for vectors. So you might have a bitmapped file called JAGGEDY.PCX and a vector graphics drawing stored as PURELINE.WMF. Many programs will ask you what sort of file you wish to import, and from which directory; they then give you an alphabetical list of all the files with that extension so that you can make your choice.

The frame

While some programs will allow you to import text straight onto the page, graphics must always be put into a container called a 'frame'.

Some programs have dual-purpose frames, others have one sort for graphics and another for text. The standard way of putting in a frame is to click on a Frame Icon, put your cursor at the top left of the place you want the frame to be, then drag the cursor downwards and to the right until the dotted box is the correct size. If you let go the left mouse button too soon, don't worry; you can adjust the size using the frame's handles.

Importing text

Just as pictures can be imported from drawing and scanning programs, so can text be imported from word processors and text editors, into frames or onto a page.

DTP programs try to cope with text from popular word processors, and many of them have long lists of the WP formats they can handle. Don't worry too much about whether your WP is listed; as long as it can convert the text to plain ASCII you will be able to import it. You'll lose any text attributes, but they can be restored by hand if you have the original material.

LOW ASCII (PLAIN & LEGIBLE)

ASCII is the simplest text format. It stands for the American Standard Code for Information Interchange, and is pronounced 'Askey'. Plain ASCII files contain only the characters used for reading and writing: the letters of the alphabet, numbers, punctuation marks and so on. If you display a plain ASCII file to the screen, using the DOS 'TYPE' command, every character can be understood.

The ASCII Code (see also Appendix B) uses numbers, which the computer understands, to represent the signs that we can decipher. It also contains many symbols that form no part of normal literary intercourse. There are 256 of them altogether, but plain ASCII files (should) use only the legible ones which, for the standard unaccented English characters, lie in the range 32 (the space character) to 122 (the lower case z). You don't have to memorise these codes, by the way, just type away at the keyboard and your computer will do all the work of translating your key strokes into binary arithmetic.

HIGH ANSI (FOREIGN ACCENTS & SYMBOLS)

Some high ANSI characters (see Appendix A for the full ANSI character set) are used by word processors as codes within a code, to give the text formatting instructions (attributes). If your program lists a WP as acceptable, it means that it can understand the codes in same way that the WP does. Each software house has its own idea of the best character to use for, say, switching text to italic, hence the need for the universally understood language of low ASCII.

CHAPTER 12

Multimedia

Multimedia is, as yet, not developed to the stage where it is living up to the hype that surrounds it. The idea of having music and animation on a computer screen is great, but it is not new.

The CD-ROM is perhaps the most worthwhile advance in this field. It can hold up to 650 megabytes of programs and/or data; more than many a hard disk.

When the CD can be written to and read from as economically as our existing floppy disk, then things really will be looking up.

12

Multimedia

Films and encyclopaedias on your screen

Multimedia combines the medium of sound with the medium of vision. To justify being 'multimedia' instead of the less exotic sounding but more accurate 'duomedia', these have been subdivided into speech and music, words and pictures, static and moving.

The multimedia 'revolution' is based on the compact disk, already popular as a clean and crisp source of sound. It didn't take the computer industry long to realise that if CDs could hold digitally encoded sound, they could cope easily with simple binary code.

It was a short step from there to adapting audio CD players to connect with computers, so that the enormous capacity of the compact disk (about 650Mb) could be used for program files as well as music.

The interactive medium?

It all depends on what you mean by 'interactive'. Many years ago a program called 'Eliza' was all the rage. It asked you personal questions and latched on to key words in your responses. The first question was so worded that your reply inevitably included the word 'mother' or 'father'. It then asked further pseudo-psychological questions which suggested that you were either father-fixated or struggling along with an Oedipus complex. This was all very 'interactive' and amusing, and might almost have won the prize for passing the 'Turing test'.

Alan Turing: born 1912, died 1954, was a pioneer of computing as long ago as 1937. He also worked on Enigma, the code-breaking computer, during World War 2. To pass the Turing test, a computer had to respond in such a way that you couldn't tell whether a machine or a person was putting replies onto the screen.

However, 99.99% of programs written for the PC are already interactive: you tell them something and they respond as they have been programmed to do.

Who's a pretty boy then?

If you are looking for open-ended interaction, talk to your budgerigar; at least he might do something unexpected. The information on CD-ROM is presented in absolutely predictable ways: click on *this* icon and *that* will happen. If you click on the same button in the same circumstances tomorrow, exactly the same thing will happen again.

There are 'interactive' games and films, but nothing can happen that has not been recorded on the CD and written into the program. Forget the hype; multimedia is about as interactive as your bathroom light switch.

The equipment you need

You have two choices: buy a new multimedia PC with all the gear on board, or buy the bits and pieces and fit them to your existing machine. Either way, the emphasis is on *buy*. The cynical view might be that all the hardware and software manufacturers get together once a year to work out ways of separating us from our money. They're on to a real winner with this one.

The extra bits:

Double speed CD-ROM drive
Sound card
Pair of speakers

A mouse is also essential, but most computer manufacturers supply one with each new machine.

Minimum computer specification

The absolute minimum comes out as a 386SX with 4 Mbytes of RAM. Naturally enough, the more memory and the faster the machine the better it will be.

The monitor has to be good enough to show all those marvellous images. It should be at least a 14 inch Super VGA. The graphics card has to be fast enough to build the pictures quickly.

Try before you buy

Whichever way you do it, be sure to see your chosen set-up in action before placing the order. Direct sales outlets should be able to give you the name of someone nearby who would be only too pleased to show you their new toy.

What multimedia can do

The lighter side

Encarta *'s opening screen. This appears in full colour on a Super VGA monitor, together with background speech and music.*

All the Encarta *pictures used in this chapter are acknowledged to be the work of the Microsoft Corporation.*

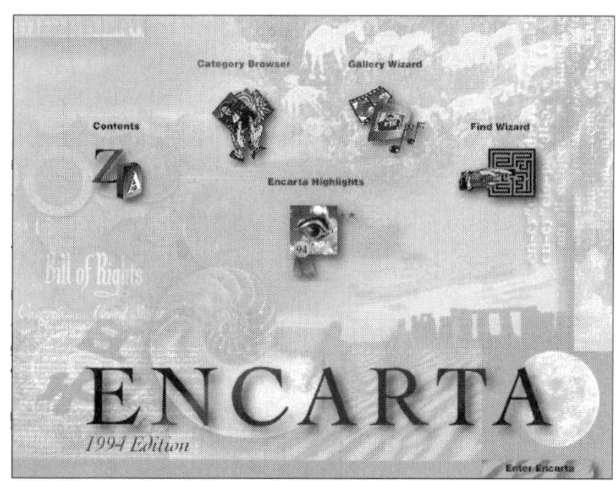

This, and the next two pictures are from Microsoft *Encarta*, an encylopaedia with sound and pictures, some of which are animated. The opening screen has 'hot spots' around the five icons; clicking on them brings up the chosen area of interest.

What we shall be looking at here is one small part of one aspect of the encyclopaedia. Like conventionally printed versions, this one has more information than you'll probably ever find time to look at.

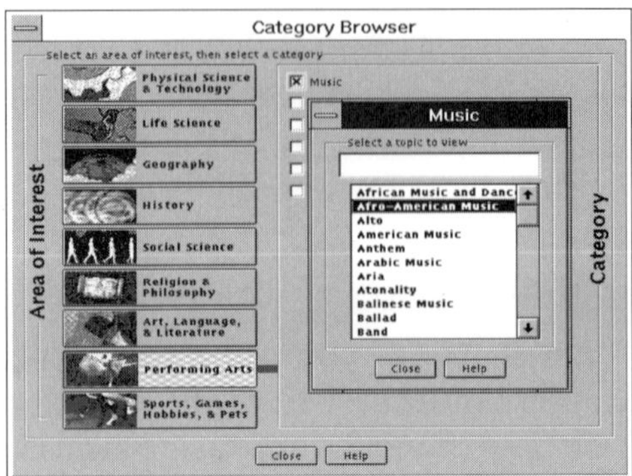

After clicking on the Category Browser icon, this window appears. A click on Performing Arts brings up six selection boxes from which music was chosen. Afro-American music was selected in the Music window.

The CD case for *Encarta* says 'Microsoft Home' in the top left corner. Whatever you do, don't take a copy to work, or you'll get nothing done for days. It is fascinating to browse through, and listening to the music is enthralling (three plays of Leadbelly singing a snatch of *Goodnight Irene* accompanied the screen capturing process!).

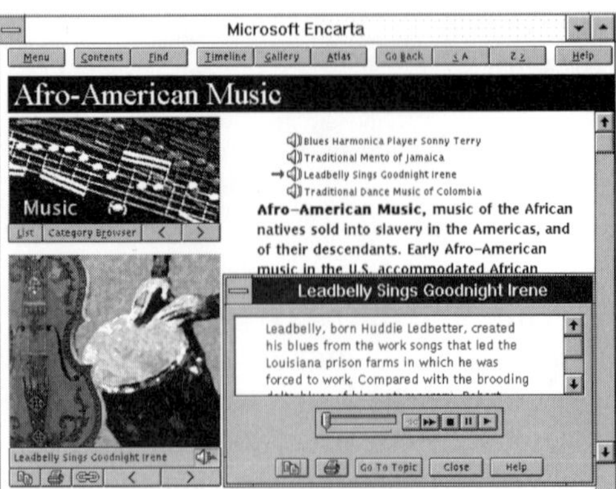

Choose the sample you'd like to hear, by clicking on it, then click on the loudspeaker icon below the lower right-hand corner of the picture. The CD track can be set back to the beginning, paused, stopped or wound forward by clicking on the control buttons.

While the music is playing, you can scroll through a brief biography of the artist. At the end of the text there are references to the source of the music so you can go out and buy the vinyl or audio CD.

Games

The quality of games on CD-ROM has not, as you might have expected, taken a quantum leap forward. The sound quality of the introductions can be enhanced, but once the game is running, the CD tracks can't be accessed quickly enough to accompany other things happening randomly on the screen.

Light with a serious purpose

For the children there are disks that combine education with entertainment (spawning a dreadful new word 'edutainment' in the process). The production of these animated books and games is a worthwhile idea as long as they are being taught the right things in the right way. There is always the danger that the chance of turning a quick penny will attract people with more interest in making money than building young minds.

In the meantime, it should be a great help to be able to read along while the text is highlighted in time with the spoken word (though nothing beats the personal attention of the parents when teaching a child to read).

Video and 'films'

As yet it doesn't make sense to buy an extra card to enable you to see poor quality video on a part of your computer screen. Later the cost might be justified, if you wanted to access the alternative stories that 'interactive video' could provide. Just now it is better to watch them on your television set.

The more serious side

Program installation from CD

The CD-ROM, essential for multimedia, has had a useful spin-off. Instead of the half dozen or more floppy disks that were needed to install a new piece of software, we are seeing more and more CDs with all the program files on them. An added benefit for the user is that as the capacity of the CD is so vast, the software houses are filling them up with all sorts of extras.

CorelDRAW!, for example, has used the space to give us hundreds of clip-art pictures and many more fonts than were on the floppy disk set.

Some software houses no longer supply floppies, and have gone over exclusively to CD-ROM, making the drive an essential piece of equipment.

The Oxford English Dictionary

Imagine *the* dictionary on CD. It will find a word far more quickly and with less physical effort than the printed version. It will carry out custom searches, including a search for the occurrence of any word, or group of words, throughout all 21 volumes. It is also a quarter of the price.

Summary

Looking at multimedia from the touchline, it doesn't seem that there is any great improvement over what we had already. The exceptions to this are in the presentation of reference works and educational material; good quality sound does, literally, give an added dimension. Otherwise it will only be when it becomes cheaper to record, and if necessary re-record, on CD-ROM, that multimedia may be classed as a major step forward.

Music

Using MIDI (Musical Instrument Digital Interface), it is possible to write (or rather, assemble) and play music on a PC, even to see 'the dots' as the music plays. But does it go any further than equipment that has been on the market for years?

Presentations

Some of these work very well on ordinary PCs already.

Games

Coping with random events and trying to keep pace with them using sound effects or music from different CD-ROM tracks is well nigh impossible. Might as well stick with the present system.

Reference works

Encyclopaedias, dictionaries and other sources of reference are ideal for multimedia. The Oxford Companion to Music, as well as The Oxford Companion to the Theatre would go extremely well with sound and vision.

Teaching aids

Another great possibility. Already going well, bound to get even better. Lotus' *ScreenCam* will capture the moving equivalent of the screen shot. All your mouse movements, screen changes, menus dropping down or popping up can be recorded together with a running commentary if you like. When the editing facility comes along it will be even better. At present if you fluff your lines you have to go back to the beginning and start again. But recordings go onto the hard disk (no CD-ROM necessary), so non-multimedia PCs are all you need for that.

Multimedia for its own sake

This is probably what it's best at. Being set up and played about with. Seeing if you can get anything constructive out of it.

CHAPTER 13

Programming

If you've a mind for it, programming is more fun than computer games, even 'interactive' ones. It is more satisfying and can be considerably more productive.

When you have finished a program, you have a 'soft machine' that will run for ever. It will perform perfectly (assuming, of course, that you have taken all the bugs and syntax errors out of it), and will show no sign of the metaphorical bits of Sellotape and Blue Tack that you may have used to get it running.

This chapter shows you how to get started on your first program.

13

Programming

Writing cheap and cheerful programs

There are two types of programmer: the person who knocks something up to do a particular job and the full-time programmer who spends most of the day churning out hundreds of lines of code in a serious programming language.

You will be shown the fun part. No mention will be made of object-oriented programming, nor of the Common Business Oriented Language (COBOL).

We'll be looking at *QuickBASIC*, which has five great advantages over some of the others:

1 It uses mostly plain English
2 It can run extremely quickly
3 You can draw and paint with it (if you try)
4 It's not so powerful that it might upset things
5 It's on your hard disk now, ready to use

High and low level languages

QuickBASIC is a high level language, machine code is at the lowest level. The 'level' of a language is inversely proportional to the amount of skill and experience needed to use it. Very, very few people write directly in machine code; a select few write in Assembler, which uses three-letter abbreviations for its instructions and is marginally less specialised than machine code. More write in C and C++, while many use one called

FORTRAN (FORmula TRANslation) language for scientific and mathematical use. Lots of people use COBOL (COmmon Business Oriented Language). Anybody capable of logical thought can see what's going on in *QuickBASIC* without too many problems.

Don't worry about the names of all these languages. They're quoted just to let you know that there are lots of them about. We'll stick with *QuickBASIC*.

'What's in a name': a sample *QuickBASIC* program

You'll find you can make sense of most of this straight away. Full explanation follows on page 240ff.

```
'WHATNAME.BAS

'Clear the screen for a clean start
    CLS

'Give maximum likely lengths of names in arrays
    DIM FirstNameArray$(25)
    DIM SurnameArray$(25)

'Ask for name
    PRINT "What is your first name, please? ";
    INPUT "",FirstName$
    PRINT "And your surname? "
    INPUT "",Surname$

'Clear the screen again to make room for very long names
    CLS

'Print line space and acknowledge
    PRINT
    PRINT "Thank you, "; FirstName$; ", ";

'Calculate and print length of names
'Find length of the longer of the two names
    IF LEN(FirstName$) > LEN(Surname$) THEN
        MaxNameLength = LEN(FirstName$)
        PRINT "both names are"; MaxNameLength;
        PRINT "characters long."
```

```
    ELSE
        IF LEN(FirstName$) > LEN(Surname$) THEN
            MaxNameLength = LEN(FirstName$)
        ELSE
            MaxNameLength = LEN(surname$)
        END IF
        PRINT "your first name is"; LEN(FirstName$);
        PRINT "characters long"
        PRINT "and your surname is"; LEN(Surname$);
        PRINT "characters."
    END IF
    PRINT

'Put characters of first name into an array
    FOR j = 1 to LEN(FirstName$)
        FirstNameArray$(j) = MID$(FirstName$, j, 1)
    NEXT

'Put characters of surname into an array
    FOR j = 1 to LEN(Surname$)
        SurnameArray$(j) = MID$(Surname$, j, 1)
    NEXT

'Show ASCII code numbers of characters used in full name
    PRINT "The ASCII code numbers ";
    PRINT "for the letters of your name are:"
    FOR j = 1 to MaxNameLength
        'Start printing characters of first name
        'at row 7, column 5
        LOCATE j + 6, 5
        'Don't try to print non-existent characters
        IF FirstNameArray$(j) <> "" THEN
            PRINT FirstNameArray$(j); "=";
            PRINT USING "###"; ASC(FirstNameArray$(j));
        END IF
        'Start printing characters of surname
        'at row 7, column 14
        LOCATE j + 6, 14
        'Don't try to print non-existent characters
        IF SurnameArray$(j) <> "" THEN
            PRINT SurnameArray$(j); "=";
            PRINT USING "###"; ASC(SurnameArray$(j));
        END IF
    NEXT
```

The whys and wherefores of 'What's in a name'

This program asks the user to type in a name; it then tells them how many letters are in the name and gives them the ASCII code numbers of those letters. Not astonishingly useful in itself, but it will show you how to lay out a program and introduce you to some of the more important concepts and commands (statements) used in *QuickBASIC* programming.

To get it to run on your machine, type C:\DOS\QBASIC at the command prompt (C:\), then press Return. Press the Esc key to clear *QuickBASIC*'s opening message, then type in the listing starting on page 238. Copy it *precisely* or it won't work properly. Computers are very fussy about syntax (the grammatical structure and punctuation of instructions given to them). They will fail to carry out exactly what you are trying to tell them if you have put so much as a semicolon out of place.

'WHATNAME.BAS

Starting from the top, the single quotation mark, "'", lets the program know that what follows is not to be acted upon: it is not an instruction. It has the same effect as **REM**, short for 'remark', which you might also see used in CONFIG.SYS and AUTOEXEC.BAT when a line is put out of commission temporarily.

It is good practice to have the name of the program at the beginning so that when you come across a print-out, or *listing*, you know at once which program it is. Another standard practice is to have the programmer's name and the date, followed by the dates and details of any subsequent revisions to the program.

CLS

Clear screen command. Everything on the screen disappears and new text starts at the top. This also works on the DOS ***command line***.

DIM

Short for 'dimension'. As most languages need to know the size of arrays (explained over the page) before they are used; it is sensible to put the **DIM** command at the beginning of the program.

Variables

Variables

A variable as used in a computer language is similar to the variables you find in a formula. The E and m in $E=mc^2$ are variables (c, the speed of light, is a constant), but while formula variables represent only values, computer variables can also contain letters and words.

The first variable we come across is **FirstName$**, which is a *string variable* as shown by the dollar sign at the end. String variables can be used to hold anything from a single character to many words, while a *numeric variable* can hold only a numeric value. There is a subtle difference here: a string variable *can* hold a number, but only as a 'picture' of that number, not its value. We shall find out later (page 244) how to convert this back to a number, using the VAL function.

The contents of a *variable* can change according to the circumstances. Something you have defined as a *constant* stays as it is: Pi will always be 3.14159. For example, the first time you run this program, the variable **FirstName$** might be "George", the second time it might be "Frederika".

Variable names are given by you, the programmer. You can call a variable anything you like, so long as you use only letters of the alphabet, numbers or the decimal point. The name can be up to 40 characters long so, space permitting, you might as well use as many as you need to give the variable a usefully descriptive name. There was a time when you could use only one character; coming back to the program a month later it was almost impossible to remember what information each variable held.

There is one limiting factor in giving names to variables: you can't have words used by *QuickBASIC* itself. These are called *reserved words*. However if you add other letters then *QuickBASIC* doesn't recognise the word and all is well. For example, 'name' is a reserved word, but using it in **FirstName$** is OK.

Some examples of string variables:

FirstName$ = "Fred"
FirstCharacter$ = "F"
SocialSecurityNum$ = "LT444223B"
BookInfo$ = "Oliver Twist, Dickens, £14.99".

Some examples of numeric variables

BookCost = 12.95

TownPopulation% = 5638 (% signifies an integer)

ChinaPopulation& = 1114237369
(& signifies a long integer)

CloseNumber! = 6.9999999
(! signifies a single precision number, 7 decimal places)

VeryCloseNumber#=14.9999999999999999
(# signifies double precision, accurate to 15 dec places)

j = 1

That last numeric variable is an example of the one time when you *should* use a single character, in this case **j**. It is especially useful in **For ... Next** loops (page 249) and is infinitely preferable to the use of capital **I** which is easily mistaken for the figure one: **I** versus **1**, especially when looking for a bug somewhere amongst several pages of code!

Array variables

An array is a store of string or numeric variables. The advantage of using arrays for variables which hold related information is that you can list, or process, parts of the array.

Suppose you are starting up as a book seller. You have five books in stock:

Chambers Dictionary, Ed Catherine Schwarz, 22.50
Oxford Companion to the Mind, Ed Richard Gregory, 25.00
The Complete Typographer, Christopher Perfect, 25.00
Noddy goes to Toytown, Enid Blyton, 4.50
Radio 1, its impact on British culture, Fred Harebrain, 1.50

This information can go into a two-dimensional array which we shall call `BookStock$()`.

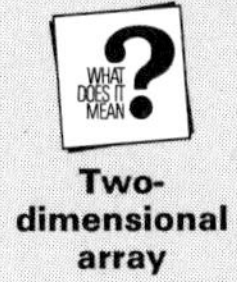

Two-dimensional array

As we have five books and three headings (title, author, price), the two dimensions will be 5 and 3, to contain the 5 books, each of which has 3 elements.

We'll dimension it like this at the head of the program:

```
DIM BookStock$(5, 3)
```

We would have used a one-dimensional array if we had only been interested in storing the titles, or if we did not foresee any need to process the elements separately, and were going to store them as a single element in one unbroken line: Book$(1) = "Chambers Dictionary, Ed Catherine Schwarz, 22.50".

These are the elements of our two-dimensional array:

BookStock$(1,1) = "Chambers Dictionary"
BookStock$(1,2) = "Ed Catherine Schwarz"
BookStock$(1,3) = "22.50"
BookStock$(2,1) = "Oxford Companion to the Mind"
BookStock$(2,2) = "Ed Richard Gregory"
BookStock$(2,3) = "25.00"
BookStock$(3,1) = "The Complete Typographer"
BookStock$(3,2) = "Christopher Perfect"
BookStock$(3,3) = "25.00"
BookStock$(4,1) = "Noddy goes to Toytown"
BookStock$(4,2) = "Enid Blyton"
BookStock$(4,3) = "4.50)
BookStock$(5,1) = "Radio 1, its impact on British culture"
BookStock$(5,2) = "Fred Harebrain"
BookStock$(5,3) = "1.50"

The information has to be put into the array. This program snippet shows how you might do it:

```
FOR j = 1 to 5'              We've only got 5 books so far
    PRINT "Key in Title, Author, Price"
    PRINT "Press return after each one"
    FOR k = 1 to 3'       We have 3 headings
        INPUT "", BookStock$(j, k)
    NEXT k
NEXT j
```

Now we can start to use the array as a miniature database. We can print it all:

```
FOR j = 1 TO 5
    FOR k = 1 to 3
        PRINT BookStock$(j, k),
    NEXT k
    PRINT
NEXT j
```

Or we could print just the titles:

```
FOR j = 1 TO 5
    PRINT BookStock$(j, 1)
NEXT j
```

Or we could find the value of our stock:

```
StockValue = 0

FOR j = 1 TO 5
    StockValue = StockValue + VAL(BookStock$(j, 3))
NEXT j
```

When the shop really gets going, we shall probably have lost count of how many books we have. However, provided we have kept our records up to date it is easy enough to find out the total:

```
BookTotal = 0

DO
    j = j + 1
LOOP UNTIL BookStock$(j, 1) = ""

BookTotal = j - 1
PRINT "Total number of books ="; BookTotal
```

It would be a good idea to store all the information on a file so that we didn't have to go through the entire shop and enter all the details every time.

PRINT Statement

`PRINT` puts things on the screen, while `LPRINT` sends them to the printer to give you a 'hard copy'. The first use of this command is in the line:

```
PRINT "What is your first name, please? ";
```

It is fairly evident that the words to be printed are enclosed in double quotation marks, but notice the semicolon at the end of the line. This is an instruction that we don't want a line break. In this case we get:

```
What is your first name, please?
```

and the cursor is positioned after the space to the right of the question mark, waiting for the user to type in a name. Without the semicolon the cursor would be at the start of the next line.

The word `PRINT` on its own prints a line space.

PRINT USING Statement

This gives a tidy appearance to your printing on the screen; similarly `LPRINT USING` formats the output to the printer.

In 'What's in a name' the statement:

```
PRINT USING "###"; ASC(FirstNameArray$(j));
```

caused the ASCII code numbers of the letters of the first name to line up one above the other, ranging from the *right*, whether the code number was two or three digits:

```
F =  70
r = 114
a =  97
n = 110
c =  99
e = 101
s = 115
```

Had the PRINT USING statement not been in there, the digits would all have started from the *left*:

```
F = 70
r = 114
a = 97
n = 110
c = 99
e = 101
s = 115
```

The hash characters may also have a decimal point, "#####.##" which, as well as aligning everything on the decimal point, will round off any extra digits. For example, 983.665 would be rounded to 983.67.

There are other formatting characters besides the hash, including the facility to format letters as well as numbers. All of these are in the manual.

IF ... THEN ... ELSE Statement

This conditional statement is extremely valuable in programming. It is used in exactly the same way that you might use it in English (except you would probably say 'otherwise' rather than 'else').

For the sake of these examples we shall take it that the numeric variable **Funds** has been established earlier in the program, perhaps by reading bank statement details from a database or spreadsheet.

```
IF Funds >= 180000 THEN
    CouldBuyABentleyMulsanneTurbo = 1
ELSE
    CouldBuyABentleyMulsanneTurbo = 0
    CouldBuyARelantRobin = 1
END IF
```

It can also be more subtle than this, allowing for more than one logical condition:

```
IF Funds >= 180000 THEN
    CouldBuyABentleyMulsanneTurbo = 1
ELSEIF Funds >= 50000 THEN
    CouldBuyABentleyMulsanneTurbo = 0
    CouldBuyAnAudiS2Coupé = 1
ELSEIF Funds >= 10000 THEN
    CouldBuyABentleyMulsanneTurbo = 0
    CouldBuyAnAudiS2Coupé = 0
    CouldBuyASmallVolvo = 1
ELSE
    CouldBuyABentleyMulsanneTurbo = 0
    CouldBuyAnAudiS2Coupé = 0
    CouldBuyASmallVolvo = 0
    CouldBuyARelantRobin = 1
END IF
```

A brief digression follows, to look at a more elegant way of dealing with several conditions.

SELECT CASE Statement

This doesn't appear in the 'What's in a name' program, but is a neat way of handling larger numbers of conditions. For this example we'll assume, again, that the variable **Funds** has a value that has been determined earlier in the program.

```
SELECT CASE Funds
    CASE >= 180000
        CouldBuyABentleyMulsanneTurbo = 1
    CASE >= 50000
        CouldBuyAnAudiS2Coupé = 1
    CASE >= 10000
        CouldBuyASmallVolvo = 1
    CASE ELSE
        CouldBuyARelantRobin = 1
END SELECT
```

Food for thought: if your bank statement showed £180,000 or more and you had put the cars in reverse order, you would have had a positive answer for all four cars from the 'which one can I afford?' question. That would be a typical example of *'what you thought you had said'* as against *'what you actually said'*; a common cause of premature hair loss and nervous indigestion.

LEN Function

LEN is one of several string handling functions. It is used here first to compare the length of the word contained in the variable **FirstName$** with the length of the word in **Surname$**. In the next line it puts the number of characters from the string in **FirstName$** into the numeric variable **MaxNameLength**.

MID$ Function

MID$** is one of the trio of functions: **LEFT$, **MID$**, **RIGHT$**, which 'return a substring of a string'. This means that you can take strings apart and see what's in them without altering the original string (unless you want to).

If **FirstName$** was "**Jonathan**" then
LEFT$(FirstName$, 3) would be "**Jon**",
MID$(FirstName$, 3, 3) would be "**nat**" and
RIGHT$(FirstName$, 6) would be "**nathan**".

MID$ has three 'arguments':

1. A string expression either as the word itself, in this case 'Jonathan', or as a string variable such as FirstName$ containing the characters.

2. The start position, in this case at the third character.

3. The number of characters to extract.

As it is possible to specify any character or group of characters, **MID$** is useful for extracting one character at a time from a string expression. It was used as shown below, under FOR ... NEXT loop, to copy the characters into **FirstNameArray$**.

FOR ... NEXT loop

This enables you to carry out an operation as many times as you need, or until a certain condition is met. It 'loops' round, operating on as many lines as there are between **FOR** and **NEXT**, returning to the first line when it reaches **NEXT** and adding one to the variable (in this case j), each time:

```
FOR j = 1 to LEN(FirstName$)
    FirstNameArray$(j) = MID$(FirstName$, j, 1)
NEXT
```

If we had known how many characters were going to be in the first name, say 8, then we could have written:

```
FOR j = 1 to 8
    FirstNameArray$(j) = MID$(FirstName$, j, 1)
NEXT
```

It would loop 8 times and then go on to the next stage.

But the program must be able to cope with anything from 'Jo' to 'Mangosuthu', so **LEN** is used to find the number of characters in the current first name.

We'll assume the name to be Henry, so **FirstName$** will be 'Henry'. Applying the **MID$** function to 'Henry' we get:

```
MID$(FirstName$, 1, 1) = "H"
MID$(FirstName$, 2, 1) = "e"
MID$(FirstName$, 3, 1) = "n"
MID$(FirstName$, 4, 1) = "r"
MID$(FirstName$, 5, 1) = "y"
```

On the first pass `j = 1`, so:

```
FirstNameArray$(1) = MID$(FirstName$, 1, 1)' = "H"
```

On the second pass, `j` is incremented by one, so `j = 2`:

```
FirstNameArray$(2) = MID$(FirstName$, 2, 1)' = "e"
```

On the third pass, `j` is incremented again, so `j = 3`:

```
FirstNameArray$(3) = MID$(FirstName$, 3, 1)' = "n"
```

and so on.

LOCATE

The computer screen is 25 rows high and 80 columns wide (in its standard set-up). Using **LOCATE** you can specify exactly where something should be shown.

```
'Print "Hello" on row 7, starting at column 5
LOCATE 7, 5
PRINT "Hello"
```

As you see from page 239, you can use *variables* as arguments in the **LOCATE** statement, for example the `j` in `LOCATE j + 6, 5`. This lets you place the next character in the following row directly beneath the previous one.

Testing and running programs

Once the program has been written, it can be run from within *QuickBASIC* to make sure that it produces the correct results and doesn't 'fall over' with a syntax error.

To run your program, either hold down a Shift key and press the function key F5 or go into the Run menu and click on Start. If the program runs successfully first time and produces the correct result straight away, telephone the *Guinness Book of Records*.

If it runs, but produces unexpected results, check through and look for errors in applied logic (what you *actually* said as against what you *thought* you had said). Fear not for your sanity; everybody does it.

If you have made a typing error, however slight, it will almost always lead to a syntax error. Good old QB stops at the error, highlights the offending line and gives you its interpretation of the error. *Interpretation* is the key word here, because there is a limited selection of error messages and there isn't always one to describe exactly what has gone wrong.

If you find you are enjoying programming, buy a full copy of *QuickBASIC* complete with the manuals. They are packed with further functions and commands (which are known as 'statements') as well as heaps of general information to make life easier for you.

Once you have the *full version* and the program is working to your complete satisfaction, you can compile it into an EXE file which can be run from the DOS prompt or from within *Windows*. You can then also distribute the EXE version to your friends. Just go into the Run menu and click on Make EXE.

Programming is enormous fun, and can be extremely interesting (in the Chinese sense!).

Epilogue

Go forth, and let the computer do the multiplying

Well, here we are at the end of the book; your general education in computing complete. The aim has been to introduce you to some of the techniques available for making it easier to write, draw and calculate.

Now, at least, when you pick up a new instruction manual, you won't be dismayed to discover that they don't tell you what the program is *for*, or *why* you might need it; you'll know already.

Be sure that 'new' means 'better'

The world of computing is fascinating and ever-changing. Although the underlying principles remain the same, the applications are constantly being modified. These changes are usually for the better, though sometimes newer and subtler bugs are introduced with the upgrades.

Make sure, too, that your hardware won't be left behind by these latest developments. This could be because more memory is needed, or maybe that it needs a faster machine than your present model. The latest software may need more hard disk space than you can spare, though the way prices of hard disks have been falling, this is much les of a problem than it used to be.

Check with the computer press

Computer magazines will usually have advance copies of new software releases, and will report the pros and cons. If the cons outweigh the pros, hold off getting the new version until everything has been fixed. After all, if you liked the earlier one you can stay with it for a little while longer.

The same applies to hardware. Magazine publishers carry out extensive testing of new products, often printed in the form of comparative reviews. They are there for your benefit; do study them before buying.

No-one will ever know it all

Perhaps the greatest thing about computing is that there is no chance whatever of becoming bored! Even if you know your favourite program inside out, it's bound to be changed soon to keep up with the competition.

The discipline of computing is stimulating and challenging; this, it can be guaranteed, will last you for life.

GLOSSARY

Every trade and calling has its jargon, from the saggar-maker's bottom-knocker in the pottery industry to random access memory in this one. These special words and phrases often seem impenetrable on first acquaintance but you'll soon find yourself rattling off computing terms and buzz words with the best of them.

The only reason for their existence should be that they save time and space by condensing many words into few. If they don't achieve that object then the originators and users of the jargon are being deliberately cryptic and unhelpful, for which there is no excuse.

Glossary

386 enhanced mode

See Enhanced mode.

8086, 8088, 80286, 80386, 286, 386, i486

See CPU

8087, 80287, 80387, i487SX

See maths coprocessor.

access time

Used in connection with storage devices such as memory and hard disks. Refers to the average time taken to begin delivering stored information from the point at which it was requested. On a hard disk this would be the time taken for the drive mechanism to find and open a file, and begin to deliver information to the PC. The lower this time the higher the speed. See also transfer rate.

adaptor

Normally refers to the circuit, usually in the form of an expansion card, that connects to the monitor to generate the video display. See MDA, Hercules, CGA, EGA, VGA, SVGA.

ANSI

American National Standards Institute. One of the ANSI codes is a numbered list of all the European characters available on computers, which is given in full in Appendix A. See also the ASCII code, Appendix B.

ANSI.SYS

One of the many standards defined by ANSI is a system of codes that can be used to control aspects of the screen such as the colours of the text and its background. The codes are contained in the text and, instead of being printed, are acted upon by the terminal/screen. A terminal that obeys these commands is known as an ANSI terminal. ANSI.SYS is a program supplied with all versions of DOS that, once installed, remains in memory. It intercepts text on its way to the screen, looking for and obeying ANSI codes – making the PC emulate an ANSI terminal, in effect. Once you know how to output ANSI codes to the screen, you can control colours, cursor position and so on. You can also modify the operation of the keyboard.

Apple Macintosh

A desktop computer that doesn't run the same programs as IBM-compatible PCs, and doesn't normally run MS-DOS. Instead it runs an operating system that looks similar to *Windows*, the latest version of which is called System 7. Macs are used a lot in the world of DTP and graphic design.

application

A program or collection of programs that makes the PC carry out a specific job such as being a word processor or a database system.

archiving

Storing old files which can't be discarded but are taking up valuable room on your hard disk. You may archive (copy) them to floppy disk or tape, for example. The term archiving may also be applied to the act of using a file compression utility, since one would often be used when making archives. However, an archive doesn't necessarily involve compression, and a compressor isn't only used for archiving.

ASCII

American Standard Code for Information Interchange. Pronounced 'Askey'. Computers only deal with numbers (see byte and bit), so each character of text must be represented by a numeric code. Capital A is 65, B is 66 and so on. ASCII is a widely used list specifying which numbers represent which characters. See Appendix B; see also ANSI and Appendix A.

assembler

A language where the programmer is working directly with the CPU. Long-winded and hard to write, but the only way to extract maximum performance when it matters. Other languages trade off ease of use for slower execution speed and larger program files. See machine code.

AT

Advanced Technology. An IBM model designation for its first PC with an 80286 CPU. Now often applied to machines with 80386 and i486 CPUs.

AUTOEXEC.BAT

A text file full of DOS commands, most of which you would normally have to type in every time you started up the PC. Instead, as soon as DOS has loaded and before it presents you with the command line, it automatically reads the file and executes the commands it finds there, just as if you were typing them in. See CONFIG.SYS and batch file.

back up

The process of copying data from one storage medium, for instance a hard disk, to another such as one or more floppy disks or a tape streamer. The back-up copy can be used if the original is accidentally destroyed.

BASIC

Beginner's All purpose Symbolic Instruction Code. One of the easiest languages for writing programs. Many PCs come supplied with a version of BASIC.

batch files

Text files whose name ends in .BAT. They mostly contains instructions that could have been typed at the DOS command line. When you type the name of a batch file (without the .BAT) at the command line, the instructions in it are read and acted upon, just as if you were typing them in. Batch files save you time and effort if you run the same sets of instructions repeatedly. See AUTOEXEC.BAT.

baud

A measure of the speed at which a modem can transfer data over the telephone line. It is commonly taken to mean bits per second, but is in fact a measure of the number of signal changes per second on the line. At one time they were the same, but data compression techniques now mean that the number of bits being transferred per second can be higher than the baud rate. See V22 and comms.

BBS (Bulletin Board System)

A computer attached to a modem and running special BBS software. People with modems and comms software can dial the BBS so that the computers are linked via the phone line. You can then leave messages for other users, retrieve (download) files left by other people (shareware programs, interesting pictures and sound files for example) or copy files to it (upload) for other people to download.

benchmark

A test of the performance (usually the speed of a piece of software or hardware). In the case of hardware, a special benchmark program runs the tests and displays the results.

Bernoulli drive

A type of disk drive that uses large removable cartridges up to 90Mb capacity. The name derives from a phenomenon known as the Bernoulli effect.

It concerns the way the edge of a spinning flexible disk is sucked towards, but never touches, a stationary surface. In the drive this is arranged so that the disk gets sucked from a sagging position into a horizontal one. The read/write head pokes through the surface.

BIOS

Usually refers to programs permanently recorded in a chip (a read-only memory, or ROM chip) fitted to the PC. DOS and applications can use them to perform basic input and output operations like screen printing, hence the name Basic Input/Output System.

binary

Numbers written in base 2 where a digit can only be 0 or 1. Decimal 1, 2, 3, 4, 5 translate as 1, 10, 11, 100, 101. See page 6.

bit

A byte is divided into eight bits Each bit can represent the digits 1 or 0. Eight digits in binary notation can form numbers whose decimal values are between 0 and 255. In a memory chip, a bit is really a tiny electronic switch that can only be either on or off. See page 8.

bitmap

A bitmapped picture, as opposed to a vectored graphic, is composed entirely of dots. The position of each dot is held in a 'map' in the file. These files have the extension .PCX, .TIF, .GIF, .BMP among others.

boot

The process the PC goes through when it starts up, it checks itself, then loads the operating system from disk. Re-boot means to force the PC to go through its start-up sequence again.

BubbleJet

Canon's proprietary name for its ink jet printers.

bus

A circuit that carries data between different parts of the computer, the data transport equivalent of a motorway.

byte

A unit of storage capacity in a computer, a memory cell. It will hold a number between 0 and 255. These numbers can be used as codes to represent text characters, see ASCII, and other data. They can also represent instructions to the CPU. See bit and machine code.

C

A powerful, and not particularly easy language.

C++

An even more powerful, and even less easy language.

cache (disk)

An area of memory used to store a copy of data recently read from or written to a hard disk. When a program requests data from the disk, if it is in the cache it can be supplied a lot more quickly than bringing the disk mechanism into play.

The result is to speed up operation of the program. The more memory allocated to the cache, the more chance there is of the required data being in there. A disk cache is usually set up by a special utility. See memory cache.

CAD

Computer aided design or computer assisted drafting, depending on who you listen to. An application program that turns the PC into the equivalent of a draftsman's drawing board and instruments. See pen plotter.

CD-ROM

Compact disc read-only memory. Like an audio CD but used as a storage medium for programs and data. Very high capacity but the PC cannot save information on it, only read from it. Used to distribute a large quantity of material that doesn't need to be changed.

cell

See spreadsheet.

Centronics

See parallel port.

CGA

Colour Graphics adaptor. IBM's first attempt at a colour display adaptor. Chunky characters and graphics coupled with limited colours make it seem crude by today's standards. See MDA, EGA.

character

A letter, numeral, punctuation mark or special symbol that can be displayed on the screen or printer. See ASCII.

chip

A complex electronic circuit formed in a one-piece silicon wafer. It is housed in a thin rectangular block (usually black) which has external metal contacts. Often known as an integrated circuit (IC) which originally meant miniaturised conventional components on a circuit board housed in a larger package.

clipboard

The clipboard is a *Windows* accessory on to which text and graphics may be 'pasted'. The pasted text or graphics are actually stored in memory, and you can get them out at any time. A double click on the clipboard icon will show you if there's anything in there:

Windows takes care of accessing the clipboard to put things in and take them out. All you have to do is either cut or copy something from the program you're working in; it finds its own way to the clipboard.

The single limitation of the clipboard prior to Microsoft *Windows for WorkGroups* version 3.11, is that there can only be one thing in there at a time. In other words, as soon as you do another 'cut' or 'copy' you will lose (or *overwrite*, as it's known) anything already in there.

Windows for WorkGroups has a ClipBook; you can now paste things into it from the clipboard, and back out again.

A useful feature is that you can 'paste' from the Clipboard as often as you like and the original will still be there. This is of more use in graphics applications than for text. Although the term 'paste' is used, they are not glued to the spot but can be moved to different positions in the drawing.

clock speed

A measure of the performance of the computer based on the frequency of the crystal. Not an absolute indicator, because there are other factors to take into account.

clone

A PC not made by IBM but which will run the same software and use the same hardware add-ons as a genuine IBM machine.

CMOS

Complementary metal oxide semiconductor. Used to make chips that have low power requirements. The CMOS RAM in an AT-class machine is a small area of battery-powered memory used to store certain settings while the PC is switched off, such as the type of hard disk fitted and the current time.

COM file

See EXE file.

compatible

Used in many contexts, such as IBM-compatible, LaserJet-compatible or SoundBlaster-compatible. The IBM PC, Hewlett Packard LaserJet printer and the SoundBlaster sound card were all products that became so popular they dominated their markets. Much software has therefore been written to work with them.

CONFIG.SYS

A text file containing commands. It is read by DOS as it loads itself, and the commands acted upon. It differs from AUTOEXEC.BAT in two ways. Firstly, it is read earlier in the boot sequence before DOS has fully loaded, and deals with more fundamental configuration options. Secondly, the instructions in it would not be recognised by the DOS command line interpreter as the type it could deal with.

controller

In the context of disks it means an electronic circuit that acts as an interface between the software and the drive. Programs needing to read from or write to the disk say what they require, and the controller is responsible for operating the mechanism.

colour palettes

The PC can only display a finite number of colours on the screen at any one time, the exact number depending on the video adaptor you have fitted. For example, in some cases only 16 colours may be permitted. Some adaptors have the facility to choose each colour from a wider selection called the palette, so it might be a case of any 16 from a palette of 64. However, the term palette is sometimes applied to the 16 colours rather than the 64, so you have to look at the context to decide exactly what is meant.

command line

When you are in DOS and see the C:\ prompt (also called the command prompt), you are 'on the command line'. Anything you enter, by typing and then pressing Return, will be treated as a command. If you type in gibberish, or make a slight mistake in the name of a command, you will get the error message "`Bad command or file name`". When you get it right, whatever you have asked to happen will happen.

comms

Short for communications. The act of exchanging data between computers, often via the telephone system using a modem.

contiguous file

One in which the data is unfragmented; it is in a continuous stream.

conventional memory

The standard memory supplied with all computers, usually 640K (the present upper usable limit), for use by DOS, device drivers and programs.

coprocessor

See CPU. A coprocessor has processing power in the same way that a CPU does, but it specialises in one type of task and works alongside the main processor. The idea is that it takes over time-consuming operations from the CPU, letting it get on with other things and thus speeding up the computer's overall performance. Typical applications would be a maths coprocessor or the coprocessor on a graphics accelerator video card.

CPU

Central processing unit, the chip with ultimate control of your PC's hardware. It is told what to do by programs. The CPU chips used in PCs were designed by Intel and given an identifying number: 8088, 8086, 80286, 80386 and i486, in increasing order of power and capability. From the 80286 onwards, the '80' is often omitted, these chips being referred to as 286, 386 and so on. See also V20/V30 and SX chips.

crash

A serious program malfunction which has unpredictable results. Often the PC locks up entirely, and you have to re-boot.

cursor

The cursor takes different forms, depending on where you are and what you are doing. The commonest form is the vertical hairline of the text cursor. The cursor can be moved around the screen by moving the mouse when you are in *Windows*, or by using the cursor keys (those with arrows pointing up, down, left or right) if you are in a program that doesn't support the use of a mouse.

cut and Paste

Windows allows you not only to cut or copy something out of a document and paste it somewhere else in the same piece, but also to cut or copy from one application and paste into another. This is one of the reasons that computers need a lot of memory. When anything is 'cut' from its current position it is immediately 'pasted' onto the *Windows Clipboard* for safe keeping.

The 'pasted' text or graphics are actually stored in memory, and you can get them out at any time. A double click on the Clipboard icon will show you if there's anything in there.

The process is fully automatic; *Windows* takes care of accessing the Clipboard to put things in and take them out.

daisywheel printer

A printer where characters are mounted on a 'daisywheel' and used with a technique similar to that used by typewriters. The characters are mounted radially on the daisywheel (or printwheel), where they form the tips of the petals of the 'daisy'. The daisywheel is rotated to bring the correct character into line. This is struck smartly from behind and goes forward to make an impression on the paper. Daisywheel printers are incapable of reproducing graphics and are extremely noisy. There aren't many of them about these days.

DAT

Digital audio tape

data

Information in a computer system being processed by a program, for example names in a database or figures in a spreadsheet. Confusingly, the data being processed may be another program, for instance in the context of a disk cache, 'data' may include program files.

database

A program that stores information, for example a list of names and addresses or a book catalogue, in such a way that it can easily be retrieved by use of searching and sorting facilities. The information is typically stored in records, each record corresponding to a card in a conventional index.

Within each record are one or more fields. If the database contained a list of names and addresses, for example, each person would have their own record within which their name, the lines of their address, and the telephone number would have their own fields.

default

The value which the computer will use unless you have advised it to the contrary. For example the Timeout settings (page 160) are given default values at the time of the original installation of *Windows*, but these can be changed to suit the circumstances.

The default printer is the one you have chosen from your list of printers (page 157). If you have only one printer in the list then that will be the default.

Default can be used as a noun: 'the *default* has been set to 45 seconds'; as a verb: 'Device not selected *defaults* to 90 seconds', and as an adjective: 'the *default* printer is the NEC Pinwriter P7'.

device driver

A piece of software that loads into memory when the PC starts up, and stays there until it is switched off. In this sense it is like a TSR, but it usually loads earlier in the boot-up process by being named in CONFIG.SYS. A device driver becomes an extension to DOS, and is therefore more tightly integrated with the system than an ordinary TSR. It has the special purpose of enabling other programs (including DOS itself) to make use of devices they wouldn't otherwise know existed or how to control. A mouse driver is a good example. A device driver may alternatively enhance the use of a device the system already knows about. ANSI.SYS is one example, disk space doublers like Stacker are another.

digitiser pad

A pad and input device which either looks like a mouse with an integral cross-hair, or a stylus. It is used for accurate positioning of an on-screen pointer. The stylus or mouse-like component (puck) is used in conjunction with the special pad, allowing software to determine its location in relation to a coordinate system. This contrasts with a mouse where only its motion relative to its last position can be determined.

Dingbat

See Zapf Dingbats.

DIP

Dual in-line package, a chip where the connectors form two lines, one down each long side. You will also read about DIP switches, which are tiny blocks of switches mounted directly on a circuit board and used to set up particular options (such as skipping the perforation on a dot matrix printer). These often also appear on motherboards and expansion cards.

directory

A self-contained area of a disk (hard or floppy) in which related files are stored. Chapter 5 deals entirely with the relationship between files and directories.

disk

General term covering various types of media used to store program and data files. In most cases they can be both read from and written to by the PC. See drive, hard disk, floppy disk and CD-ROM.

Many types (though not all of them, see optical drive) rely on a magnetic coating similar to that used on audio tapes. Before information can be saved on such a disk, it must be formatted with a pattern of concentric rings (tracks) which are subdivided into sectors.

disk cache

See Cache (disk)

disk doublers / compressors

Programs (usually in the form of a device driver) that use file compression algorithms to compress and decompress information going to and from a disk. The disk thereby appears to be approximately twice its nominal size. Can be used on floppy as well as hard disks.

DOS

Disk operating system. See also MS-DOS and DR DOS.

dot matrix

A printer where the characters and graphics are formed from a grid of dots (matrix) produced by wire pins. They come in two widths: 80 column and 132 column. The standard 80-column dot matrix printer is adequate for most purposes, the 132-column being used for accounts and spreadsheets.

download

See BBS.

DPI

Dots per inch. Used as a measure of resolution, usually applied to laser printers. Typically 300 dpi or 600 dpi, though this figure is rising steadily. A similar unit is LPI, lines per inch, more often used higher up the scale for imagesetters, which can be in the order of 1270 lpi, 2540 lpi and above.

DR DOS

Digital Research Disk Operating System. A competitor to MS-DOS that will run the same software and obey the same or similar commands.

drive

In the context of a disk it is the mechanism that holds the storage medium and reads and writes the information.

driver

A piece of software that enables DOS and/or application programs to access particular pieces of hardware and make use of their facilities. An example would be a new printer with facilities unavailable in other models. A driver would be written to allow popular existing programs (*Windows*, for example) to use the new features.

DTP

Desktop publishing. An application program for designing pages of graphics and text as found in books, magazines, newsletters, adverts and the like.

EGA

Enhanced graphics adaptor. A step up from CGA offering a sharper image by virtue of there being more dots on the screen, plus more colours. See also VGA

EISA

Extended industry standard architecture. A non-IBM design of PC more advanced than AT and XT machines. It is a competitor to MCA. See also ISA.

E-mail

An electronic postal system that stores messages on a central computer, usually in the form of text files, although programs and other data can be handled too. Messages are sent via a PC and a modem link or network.

EMS (expanded memory)

See expanded memory.

enhanced mode

Windows can run in either of two modes: standard or, if your hardware supports it, 386 enhanced mode. Enhanced mode gives access to virtual memory.

environment

A set of programs designed to work together, giving seamless and transparent access to many interlinked facilities. *Windows* is an environment, as is DOS and as was GEM.

EXE file

Files whose names end in .COM or .EXE are programs. Internally the two types are structured slightly differently. COM files are an older specification and limited to 64K in size. The EXE file structure was developed to overcome this and other limitations. See also batch file.

expanded / extended memory

Different ways of adding memory beyond the basic 640K. Expanded memory, also known as LIM EMS (Lotus Intel Microsoft Expanded Memory Specification) can be fitted to all PCs. Hardware restrictions dictate that it works differently to normal memory, and programs have to be specially designed to use it. Expanded memory acts like a notebook which applications can employ for additional data storage capacity, flipping back and forth between pages as required. This is useful, but less flexible than the 'continuous stationery' of conventional memory.

Design limitations in the 8088 and 8086 CPU chips meant that PCs fitted with them could not have extended memory; you needed an 80286 or better.

Extended memory simply adds more RAM on top of the basic 640K which is normally supplied with these PCs and accessed by MS-DOS based programs. MS-DOS and most programs run from it cannot normally use extended memory, or at least can only do so in a very limited way. However, *Windows 3* and OS/2 can take full advantage of extended memory, and by extension so can applications specially written to run in these environments.

expanded memory manager

Makes extended memory mimic expanded memory. If you have a 386 or above, you can make more conventional memory available for running programs by using an expanded memory manager such as EMM386 (a device driver which comes with MS-DOS) or QEMM (a 'third party' product), Both of these use extended memory to simulate expanded memory, and provide access to the upper memory area,

expansion bus

See Bus. The PC has what is known as 'open architecture', meaning that companies other than the original designer (IBM) have free access to technical information. This enables them to build extra circuit boards (known as expansion boards or expansion cards, or just cards) that can be plugged into multi-way connectors (expansion slots) provided for the purpose.

These boards add capabilities not found on the motherboard. For example, in many cases the video and disk controller circuits are on expansion cards. In traditional PC design, the expansion slots all sit on a circuit board (called the motherboard) that acts as a communication highway between the CPU and the cards. Imagine the CPU as the city at the end of a motorway, with the expansion slots being junctions. Unlike a motorway, however, communication along the expansion bus is slower than in the core circuitry (the city streets), so any feature provided on a card will operate more slowly than if it had been part of the core design.

expansion card

A circuit board that fits into an expansion slot. Typically a sound card or one to drive a scanner, printer or monitor.

expansion slots

Printed circuit connectors inside the PC into which can be plugged circuit boards that add extra capabilities to the machine.

extended memory (XMS)

See Expanded / extended memory.

extended memory manager

HIMEM.SYS is an extended memory manager which conforms to the XMS (Lotus/Intel/Microsoft/AST eXtended Memory Specification), which specifies a standard way for programs to use it cooperatively.

The aim of the extended memory manager is to provide access to extended memory and ensure that no two programs try to use the same part of extended memory at the same time.

New versions of *Windows* and DOS both include revised versions of HIMEM.SYS that leap-frog each other. Use whichever version is the more recent.

FDD

Floppy disk drive.

field

See database.

file

A self-contained body of information stored on disk that can be retrieved at a later date. It can be a program, a document from a word processor, an address list from a database, a year's sales figures from a spreadsheet, even a picture. The file is given a name so that you can refer to it.

file compression

It is often possible to reduce the size of a file by re-arranging the data it contains into a more compact format. For instance one area of the file may be identical to another. These duplicate areas can be eliminated, and small markers left in their place. When the file is expanded (de-compressed) back into a usable state, these markers will indicate how to reconstitute it.

This is just one of many ways data can be compacted. Some files are automatically compressed/decompressed by the application that writes and reads them. For example PCX files incorporate a simple compression technique.

Utility programs such as PKzip and LHA also exist which will compress one or more files and combine them into a single storage (or archive) file. The utility will also de-compress the files when they are needed.

filmsetting

See Photosetting

floppy disk

A flexible disk, although it may be contained in a rigid case, that is removable from the drive. Two sizes are available for the PC: 5.25-inch and 3.5-inch. Each size comes in two or more capacities. Floppies have less storage space, are slower and, in the long run, less reliable than other types of disk.

font

Strictly speaking, a particular size and style of a typeface, for example 14pt Times Italic. Times is the design (the typeface), Italic is its style (oblique), and 14pt (14 point) is a measure of the height of the characters. In computing, the term font is often used to mean typeface.

format

Used mainly in two contexts. To format a disk means to lay down a structure of tracks and sectors ready to receive programs and data.

A file format is a set of rules governing the way information is structured inside a file. Any program that knows the rules can read or write files that conform to them.

For example, graphics files are often in a format known as PCX. In theory, a painting, DTP or word processor program that understands the rules governing PCX can make sense of PCX files produced by other software. In practice, the PCX format has been 'tweaked' into several different versions, some of which are no longer universally recognisable.

graphics

Any screen or hard copy output where pictures are constructed from tiny dots allowing almost anything to be drawn. See MDA and Hercules.

graphics accelerator

A special type of video card with circuits designed to speed up screen operations involving graphics, by taking over a lot of the work normally performed by the CPU. *Windows* and *Windows* applications benefit particularly, since screen operations are often a significant bottleneck on performance. An accelerator card only improves applications for which special drivers are supplied, probably with the card itself. With other applications it behaves like an ordinary VGA or SVGA card.

graphics tablet

Used instead of a mouse. A stylus is connected to a port on the computer, in a similar way to the mouse. You draw on the tablet with the stylus; the movements are transmitted to the application you're working on.

GUI

Graphical user interface. Another name for WIMP.

hard disk

A combined disk and drive mechanism usually permanently fixed inside the PC, though removable and portable external versions exist. Much faster and far higher capacity than a floppy disk, so they are normally used for primary day-to-day storage.

hardware

The electronic and mechanical units that make up the computer and its peripherals.

HDD

Hard disk drive.

Hercules

A company which produces a mono display adaptor combining MDA-standard text-only output with a special graphics mode. Hercules produces other products, including top-end colour adaptors, but its name is often used to refer to this old widely-adopted mono standard.

hexadecimal

Often shortened to 'hex' and meaning numbers to the base 16. The decimal (base 10) numbers 1 to 15 are represented as 1, 2, 3, 4, 5, 6, 7, 8, 9, A, B, C, D, E, F. Decimal 16 becomes hexadecimal 10, and so on. Mainly of interest to programmers.

high memory

The first 64K of expanded memory. It is given this special name because, owing to a design quirk in 286 and later CPU chips, more recent versions of DOS can make use of it even though it should in theory be inaccessible. Making use of high memory enables DOS to leave more of the basic 640K free for application programs.

HMA (High Memory Area)

The high memory area. Different from upper memory.

IBM

International Business Machines, the company that designed the original PC and is still a leading manufacturer. See also clone.

IC

Integrated circuit, see chip.

icon

A small pictorial representation of a program or facility. One of the more obvious features of *Windows* is its Graphical User Interface (GUI). It is so simple to have representations of all the programs you might ever want to use spread before you in the form of little pictures which can be double-clicked on to cause any of them to run.

In contrast, to run a program from DOS it is necessary (a) to know the precise name of the executable file with its full path and (b) to enter them on the command line (which is all covered in Chapter 4).

As well as being double-clicked on to run their program, icons can be dragged into new positions in their own window, or even to a different window.

You can see which program any selected icon will launch, and which directory it is in, by clicking on the Program Manager **File** menu and choosing **Properties...**, which will put up the **Program Item Properties** window.

IDE

Integrated drive electronics. Refers to a hard disk drive where much of the circuitry that used to be on the hard disk controller card is fitted to the drive unit. See also interface.

ink-jet

A printer where characters and graphics are formed from a grid of dots (a matrix) produced by fine ink nozzles. See BubbleJet.

integer

A whole number. Integer division discards any remainder, so that, for example, 7 divided by 2 becomes 3 (the remainder disappears).

integrated package

A minimum of word processor, spreadsheet and database bundled together. Other programs may be included, such as graphics and comms. They may be parts of a single program, or a collection of individual programs loaded from a menu system. Integrated packages tend to be cheaper and less fully-featured than their individual components when bought separately.

interface

Software or hardware that sits between two other pieces of software or hardware and acts as a go-between. Without the interface they cannot communicate with each other. An example would be a hard disk controller which allows the PC to control the mechanism to save and retrieve files.

interleave factor

Usually mentioned in connection with hard disks. It describes one aspect of the way information is arranged on the disk. The lower the ratio stated, the faster data can be transferred, with 1:1 being the optimum.

ISA

Industry standard architecture, the design of PC usually classed as an AT. See EISA and MCA.

K

Kilobyte (1,024 bytes).

LAN

Local area network. A network on one site where all devices on the network are directly connected together. See also WAN.

language

A way of writing programs. Different languages have different ways of telling the PC what to do, some being better than others for particular types of task. DOS and all your .EXE and .COM files were written with a programming language. See machine code.

laser printer

A printer which uses photocopier technology to output high-quality pages of text and graphics.

LIM EMS

See Expanded memory.

local bus

The problem with the expansion bus is that, compared with the rest of the PC, it transfers data slowly. This inhibits the performance of some devices that operate via the expansion bus: principally video cards (slow screen update) and hard disk controllers (slow loading and saving of files).

Local bus is, in effect, an additional expansion bus of more modern design that gives greatly increased data transfer rates. It was originally intended for video cards – hence VESA having defined one of the competing standards (VL-Bus) – but hard disk and other cards where speed is important are being produced to fit local bus slots. Cards must be specially designed not only to run in local bus slots, but for a particular standard of local bus.

Beware of PCs advertised as having a couple of VL-Bus slots, but being supplied with an ordinary video card fitted in the conventional expansion bus. You will see no benefit from local bus unless the PC has the special video and/or hard disk card to fit it.

Macintosh, Mac

See Apple Macintosh.

machine code

Numeric instruction codes understood by the CPU. Languages except assembler generate several machine code instructions for each command. In assembler, one command translates to one instruction.

macro

A stored sequence of keystrokes that can be replayed by pressing just one or two keys or by entering a short command. It's a short-cut to save typing.

mail merge

The process whereby, for example, multiple copies of a letter created with a word processor can have names and addresses read in from a database and inserted at designated points to form personalised correspondence.

maths coprocessor

A chip inside a PC that speeds up programs which do a lot of calculations using floating point numbers, numbers with a fractional part. Programs must be specially written to take advantage of the chip if it is fitted.

Common maths coprocessors can be numbered 8087, 80287, 80387SX, 80387DX or i487SX depending on the type of CPU they are designed to work with. The i486DX has a coprocessor built in, but the i486SX does not.

Mbyte

Megabyte (1,024K, therefore 1,048,576 bytes).

MCA

Microchannel architecture. IBM's design of PC intended to supersede machines based on the XT and AT standards. See EISA. It hasn't really caught on, despite some real advantages.

MDA

Mono Display Adaptor. IBM's original screen display standard. It could only generate text, and so was unsuitable for the construction of pictures from individual dots. See Hercules, CGA.

memory

Electronic circuits that store programs and data when they are active. See RAM and ROM.

memory cache

A small area of fast memory (it can be written to or read from more quickly than most memory chips) separate from the PC's main memory pool. It is used to store the most frequently accessed sections of the currently running program. Consequently programs run more quickly. Fast memory tends to be expensive, hence its use in a cache rather than for all the RAM in the machine. See disk cache.

MFM

Modified frequency modulation, a common method of storing information on the surface of a hard disk. See RLL.

MIDI

Musical Instrument Digital Interface. A standard connector and communications technique that allows suitably equipped computers and musical instruments to control each other to greatly expand their musical processing abilities.

modem

MOdulator/ DEModulator, a hardware device that connects to the PC and allows it to communicate worldwide with other computers via the telephone system. A modem translates the 1s and 0s of computer data into a rapid sequence of high and low tones. See comms.

motherboard

The main circuit board in your PC which carries the components forming the heart of the computer. Built on to it are the expansion slots (printed circuit connectors) into which expansion cards are plugged.

mouse

A device that can be pushed around your desk to control an on-screen pointer. A mouse can move the cursor around the screen much more smoothly and quickly than the four cursor keys; that is its *raison d'être*. Most mouse activities are performed by moving the cursor to a particular button or area of the screen and clicking with the left mouse button. In this book 'click on' this button or that will mean with the *left* mouse button unless specified as the right.

The 'double click' is two left button clicks made very quickly (to differentiate between a click made now and another made a second or two later). You can change the expected time interval between clicks by going into the Program Manager.

As well as mouse *clicks*, we also have mouse *drags*. For example, to move either scroll button you would put the cursor on it, hold down the left mouse button, drag the scroll button to the required position then release your pressure on the mouse.

Connects either to a serial port or mouse socket. See also WIMP.

MPC

Multimedia PC. A minimum specification, defined by Microsoft, for PCs intended to run multimedia applications: a 386SX processor, CD-ROM drive, MIDI and digitised sound, *Windows*, multimedia extensions.

MS-DOS

Microsoft Disk Operating System. See operating system.

multitasking

Running more than one program or doing more than one job simultaneously.

multimedia

Using the PC to blend motion and still video, hi-fi sound, computer-generated text and graphics to present information such as a training course or a catalogue of animals.

network

A way of linking several PCs together so that they can swap files and share resources such as printers and hard disks. Printing across a network means outputting to a printer on the network rather than one attached to your own printer port. See also LAN and WAN.

operating system

A program which is automatically loaded into your PC when it is switched on and provides the A:>, B:> or C:> prompt. When you type a command it either acts on it if it is built in, COPY, for example, or looks for a program of that name on the disk and runs it.

optical character recognition (OCR)

The process of turning a graphical image of text, such as a fax or a page from a magazine, into ASCII text understood by word processors.

optical disk

A form of disk drive that involves the use of laser light as part of the recording/retrieval process. There are several competing types, not all of which are commercially available. Some drives mix magnetic and optical techniques (referred to as magneto-optical drives).

OS/2

A multi-tasking, WIMP-based operating system devised by IBM and Microsoft, intended as the successor to MS-DOS. It does, however, have rivals in *Windows NT*, and to a lesser extent Unix, with other competitors on the horizon. Its ultimate success is not yet clear. Microsoft has pulled out, leaving development of OS/2 in the hands of IBM.

parallel port

A socket on the back of your PC that can be used to exchange information with other devices that also have a parallel port fitted. It is usually used with a printer and often known as a Centronics port. It employs a faster technique than that used by the serial port.

partition

A sub-division of a hard disk made at a much more fundamental level than a directory. Partitions and directories are related in a similar way to continents and countries (sub directories would be cities and towns; files would be people). Different partitions can contain different operating systems with their programs and files. Partitions are usually made to behave as if they were different hard disks, so on a machine with a single drive split into three partitions, DOS would recognise the partitions as drives C:, D: and E:. These are known as logical drives. A useful tip if you have multiple drives is to include the line `LASTDRIVE = Z` in your CONFIG.SYS file,

Pascal

A language, used a lot in education, that is powerful enough to be used in commercial programming projects.

path

A list of directories and sub-directories, usually written into the AUTOEXEC.BAT file, through which DOS will search for a program you have just asked it to run, if it isn't in the current directory. The PATH command can also be run from DOS: the word on its own will print the current path setup to the screen; PATH followed by one or more directory names will supersede the existing setup.

PC

The IBM Personal Computer, its clones and successors.

PCW

A computer made by Amstrad based on earlier technology than that employed in the PC. It is mainly used for word processing and cannot be used to run MS-DOS or other PC programs.

PCX

A bitmapped graphics file format.

pen plotter

Akin to a printer, but works by moving pens over the surface of the paper. Often used in conjunction with CAD software to produce engineering drawings, for example.

Pentium

Currently the fastest CPU.

peripheral

Strictly speaking any device connected to the core computing circuitry of CPU and memory, for example the disk drives. Usually taken to mean items outside the case, such as printers.

photosetting

Also known as filmsetting. Producing printed material of a very high quality for subsequent reproduction in quantity. Photosetting machines produce their output on film or bromide, to resolutions of 1270, 2540 and more lines per inch.

pick list

List of items from which you make your choice by clicking on it. Long pick lists only display part of their list at any one time, and have a scroll bar on the right hand side so that you can move to items that are at present out of sight.

pipe

See Redirecting command input and output

pixel

Each dot (picture element) on the screen. Every character, line or filled area you see is built from pixels, rather like colouring in squares on graph paper.

plotter

See pen plotter.

port

Round the back of the system unit are the connectors (or 'ports'). They're not called sockets because some of them are male connectors, with pins sticking out. These connectors are bolted to the ends of 'cards' (printed circuit boards with resistors, capacitors and yet more chips attached to them) which are tucked away out of sight inside the system unit, where they are plugged in to the 'Motherboard'.

Each of the peripheral devices: the screen, the printer and so on (see page 24), is attached to the computer via a connector to its own special card.

Most PCs have at least one serial port and one parallel port. The mouse will usually be plugged in to its own port or a serial port, the printer into a parallel port and the screen into the video port.

portable PC

A small PC designed to be carried around. Some models have batteries so they can be used on the move.

PostScript

A type of computer programming language which is understood by some laser printers. Commands in PostScript do such things as print text, draw lines and fill areas. A PostScript file is a complete set of instructions that tells the printer how to draw one or more pages.

printer

A piece of hardware that the PC uses to print text and graphics on paper. See daisywheel, dot matrix, ink jet, and laser.

print to a file

Instead of printing onto paper in the usual way, it sometimes happens that you need your work to be printed by a type of printer that you yourself don't possess, for example a PostScript printer or a photosetter. In this case you prepare the page(s) as normal, but use the *Windows* Printers setup to choose the required printer and, instead of connecting it to a port, use 'print to file'. Either print directly to a floppy disk or copy the file on to a floppy. The information on this disk can now be used on another printer.

program

A sequence of instructions that tell the CPU what to do. Since the CPU controls the rest of the machine, a program can access all the available facilities, memory, screen, keyboard, mouse, disk drives and so on. By executing programs the PC's hardware is made to act as a word processor, spreadsheet, database and so on. A programmer is either a person who writes programs, or a device for putting programs into ROMs.

RAM

Random access memory, where a program loaded from disk is stored while it is being executed by the CPU. RAM is also used by the program as a storage area for its data. When the power is removed from RAM, its contents are lost. See ROM.

real time

An expression used especially in process control applications where data is fed to the computer, which instantly determines an appropriate course of action, presenting it on screen and often driving servomotors to close valves or take some other physical course of action to keep the process running smoothly. In such cases the program is said to be running in real time.

re-boot

See boot.

record

See database.

redirecting command input and output

Information is generally *input* to the computer from the keyboard, and *output* to the screen. It is possible, though, that you may want a text file to be 'redirected' to the printer, or a directory listing to be printed (copied) to a file.

To display the contents of an ASCII file (eg AUTOEXEC.BAT or CONFIG.SYS) on screen, you would enter:
TYPE AUTOEXEC.BAT
whereas to send it to the printer, you would enter:
TYPE AUTOEXEC.BAT>PRN
Full details are given in the DOS manual.

resolution

A computer display is composed of rows and columns of dots from which all characters, lines and filled areas are built. Resolution is a measure of the number of rows and columns.

On the screen, for example, 320 by 256 means 320 dots across and 256 high. Printers measure resolution slightly differently. Instead of the total number of dots, it is the number of dots per inch, or dpi. The more dots in an area, the higher the resolution and the crisper the display.

RISC

Reduced instruction set computer. Refers to a type of CPU that is simpler but faster than conventional designs as used in PCs.

RLL

Run length limited, a method of storing information on a hard disk in which data is compressed, compared to MFM, to give around 50 per cent extra capacity and faster data transfer rate.

ROM

Read-only memory. Cannot be written to by the CPU but it does not lose data when the power is switched off. Used by hardware manufacturers to incorporate programs and data that must be permanently available. See also RAM.

root directory

The directory from which all others spring. Usually C:\ on computers with a single hard disk (and A:\ for the floppy).

RS232

The name of an international standard governing the way a serial port works.

'RS232' is often used instead of 'serial port'.

scanner

A device which scans photographs or other illustrations to create either grey scale or colour images for re-use in DTP and graphics programs.

screen mode

Usually given in terms of pixel count horizontally and vertically, for example 640 by 480, 1024 by 768, 1280 by 1024. The PC's display is composed of a fine grid of dots (pixels), each of which may be set to one of a finite number of colours. The more pixels there are on the screen, the higher the resolution. Similarly the greater the range of colours available, the more realistic the image. The drawback is that higher resolutions and greater colour ranges require more memory to accommodate the PC's internal representation of what it is putting on the screen. And because more information is being stored, it takes longer to update the screen.

The number of screen modes available depends on the video card. The fastest option is text mode. This is a special mode in which the smallest thing that can be changed on the screen is an entire character. Here the characters are represented in memory by two numbers: one to indicate the character and other its colour. Whereas in graphics modes each pixel has its own number, and dozens of them are used to 'paint' each character on the screen.

screen saver

The facility is built into *Windows* (accessed via the Control Panel icon, then the DeskTop icon) to switch the screen off if nobody's used the keyboard or mouse for a while. This is to prevent the current picture from being burnt into the screen if it should be left on for an extended period. You can choose how long a delay there should be before it is switched off. Also you can choose from a growing number of screen saver graphics images to take the place of the original matter on the screen. The essence of screen saving is that nothing should stay in one place on the screen for any length of time, so you can have goldfish swimming around, firework displays, the old flying toasters, almost anything as long as it moves.

screen shots

Screen shots, sometimes called 'screen grabs' are most useful for demonstrating what should be visible on the screen at any particular time (this book is peppered with them).

They are also useful when something appears on your screen that either shouldn't be there or doesn't seem to make sense. They provide a record that can be sent away to the tech support people who should be able to explain what has gone wrong with the system. It will also confirm that you didn't imagine or fabricate the incident.

A screen shot is a bitmapped image (a photograph) of the screen which can be saved and printed. There are special programs such as the excellent *Paint Shop Pro*, which have all sorts of facilities for taking and manipulating screen shots as well as saving them in a variety of graphic formats. *Windows* itself provides elementary screen shooting facilities.

scroll bars

Scroll bars are used for moving to areas which are at present out of sight. They can move lists up and down, they can also move the entire contents of windows up and down.

There is a 'worked example' of the use of scroll bars in *Windows Write* on page 141.

SCSI

Small Computer Systems Interface. A general-purpose high-speed multitasking electronic interface used to connect a computer to peripheral devices such as suitably equipped printers and disk drives. Up to seven devices can be joined to one SCSI port.

sector

See disk.

segmented hypergraphics

The 'hot spots' on a screen picture that you click on to take you to another part of the program. A snazzier way than using menus.

serial port

A socket on the back of your PC that can be used to connect it to a computer or other device such as a mouse, modem or pen plotter that also has a serial port. It is used to send and receive information. Also known as RS232. See also parallel port.

shadow RAM

Also known as shadow memory. Usually refers to RAM in the upper memory area being put to a particular use. In this area live programs that are etched into ROM chips, because they have to be permanently available whether or not there is a disk drive to load them into memory. The main example is the BIOS. ROM chips are inherently slow to yield their information, meaning that a program stored in ROM runs more slowly than the same thing stored in RAM.

Shadow memory is a system whereby a chunk of RAM is re-located to the same addresses that are occupied by the ROM, the contents are copied into RAM, and the ROM switched off. The result is that the formerly ROM-based programs can now run from RAM, and so execute much more quickly.

It is the two blocks of memory existing at the same addresses, one obscuring the other, that give rise to the term 'shadow memory'.

short-cut keys

Short-cuts are sometimes useful, sometimes a longer way round if it means letting go of the mouse to use your hand on the keyboard.

The short-cut to any *Windows* menu item is to hold down the Alt Key (or Alt Gr if there's one on your keyboard) and type the underlined character of the menu name, then type the underlined character of the menu item you require.

There is one important reservation about the use of short-cut keys: different software houses often use different key combinations. Sometimes the same software house will use different short-cuts in different programs.

If you are using one program all the time it's easy enough. If using several it might be better to use the mouse to select from the menus; at least you'll be sure of getting what you want

SIM/SIMM

Single in-line memory module, very like a SIP except there are no legs. Instead there are metal strips on the edge of the device which fit into a socket. See also DIP.

SIP

Single in-line package, a chip, or set of chips mounted on a miniature circuit board, with connector legs in one line along an edge. See SIM and DIP.

software

Programs and data stored in the computer or on media such as disks.

sound card

An expansion card which, used in conjunction with external speakers, greatly improves the PC's dismal sound capabilities. Essential for multimedia, games and music software, and increasingly being used for serious digitised speech applications.

spreadsheet

A program used to store and perform calculations on figures. It is based on a grid of cells corresponding to the squares on a piece of ruled paper. Each cell can contain explanatory text, a number, or a formula that acts upon the contents of other cells.

SVGA

Super VGA: VGA with extra facilities, worth having if your software supports them. Not an IBM standard, but one devised by third-party video adaptor manufacturers. See XGA.

swap file

An area of the hard disk to and from which information in memory is swapped, to free that memory for more immediate use. Also known as virtual memory. You can choose to have a permanent swap file if you have plenty of disk space; second best is a temporary swap file.

SX chips

The 386SX is a version of the 386 CPU. It does almost everything a 386 (or 80386DX, to give it its full name) can do, but fits circuit boards using components intended to work with the older 80286 CPU. The result is a cheaper PC which has a 386 PC's special capabilities but runs more slowly. The 486SX is a version of the 486 CPU (now known as the i486DX). It lacks the 486's on-board maths coprocessor, but retains other improvements of the 486 over the 386. A 487SX maths coprocessor is available.

system disk

A floppy disk that contains copies of essential operating system (DOS) files from which a boot can be performed. System disks are created by adding the /S switch to the FORMAT command: **`FORMAT A:/S`** to copy the system files and make the disk in drive A: into a freshly-formatted system disk.

system files

The files, normally hidden from the DIR command, that contain the operating system. The PC finds and loads them when it starts up.

system unit

The box that houses the CPU, the motherboard, expansion slots, hard disk(s), floppy disk(s), everything except the keyboard, screen and printer.

tape streamer

A device used to keep a copy of files from a hard disk. These back-up files are stored on a tape cartridge which is removed and kept somewhere safe. In the event of files being accidentally lost from the hard drive they can easily be restored.

text attributes

'Text attributes' is computer-speak for the things you can do to a character to change the way it looks:

1. Normal (also called Regular or Medium)
2. *Italic*
3. **Bold**
4. Underline
5. Superscript
6. Subscript
7. ~~strikethrough~~
8. overline
9. SMALL CAPS
10. Text colour

and their possible combinations

text mode

See screen mode.

third party product

Hardware or software supplied by a company other than the original computer manufacturer or software supplier. Third party products are intended to improve on the original specification.

toner

Powder pigment used by laser printers to make an image on paper or overhead film.

toolkit

Applicable to specialist areas such as programmers' toolkits, but in general meaning a collection of programs that perform maintenance, repair and other routine tasks. For example a toolkit may be able to revive deleted files, fix corrupted disks and make disk copying easier. The list of functions varies from one package to another.

track

See disk.

tracker ball

Rather like a mouse on its back, the device remains stationary and you rotate the ball to move an on-screen pointer.

transfer rate

Usually mentioned in connection with hard disks. Refers to the rate at which data is transferred from the drive to the PC's memory. The larger the number, the faster the drive. This figure is more important than access time.

TSR (Terminate and Stay Resident program)

Programs are usually started up, do whatever they are designed to do and then, when you've finished using them, you close them. TSRs, on the other hand, are started (mostly automatically, by being included in AUTOEXEC.BAT) and then left to run alongside other programs, providing additional facilities for the computer user. One such is *SideKick*, which has been on the market for many years. This provided all sorts of useful and, as it pre-dated *Windows*, otherwise unavailable goodies, such as a calculator, diary, notepad, dialler, ASCII table. You used the 'hot key' combination Ctrl + Alt, and up it popped so that you could, for example, do some calculations while writing a letter and then paste the result into the letter.

typeface

See font.

typesetting

Producing printed material of a high quality for subsequent reproduction in quantity. This used to be the preserve of typesetting bureaux, using very expensive photosetting machines giving resolutions of 1270, 2540 and more lines per inch. Nowadays, with laser printers giving resolutions up to 1800 dots per inch, a great deal of work is produced 'in house' at considerably less cost. There is, however, an upper limit to the fineness of line that the laser printer toner can hold. Therefore for high quality work, especially when involving illustrations, photosetting is still the answer.

upload

See BBS

upper memory

Between conventional memory (the first 640K) and extended memory is a 384K gap. Parts of it are occupied by hardware such as the BIOS and the video adapter, but there is unused space that is not fitted with memory chips. A memory manager can take advantage of the special capabilities of the 386 and 486 CPUs to relocate some extended memory in this space, where it becomes upper memory.

V20/V30

CPU chips made by NEC. Equivalent to Intel's 8088/ 8086 chips but working up to 30 per cent faster.

V22, V23 etc

These are the names of internationally agreed standards applying to modems and refer to the speed at which they can operate. A modem will probably be able to operate at more than one speed. Common V numbers are:

V21	300/300
V23	1200/75
V22	1200/1200
V22bis	2400/2400
V32	9600/9600
V32bis	14400/14400

The pairs of figures on the right are the rates at which the modem can receive and transmit data, measured in bits per second.

V is short for vitesse, the French for 'quickness' or 'speed'. The standards were set by the CCITT, an international telecoms body. See also baud and comms.

VDU

Visual display unit, the monitor or screen.

vector graphics

A picture stored as a series of mathematical formulae, rather than the 'map' of a series of dots held in a bitmapped graphic file. Vector (also, more correctly, 'vectored') graphics are based on work done by Bézier, who developed the idea of converting drawings into mathematical expressions. The files produced in this way are much more compact than bitmaps and can give drawings to any degree of enlargement without loss of quality. This is in marked contrast to bitmaps, in which anything other than a horizontal or vertical line becomes more and more obviously jagged as it is enlarged.

VESA

Video Electronics Standards Association. A group of companies with an interest in the PC's video display (screen). VESA aims to define standards where none existed before, and which were causing problems for programmers and users.

virtual memory

See Swap file

VGA

Video Graphics Array. IBM's third stab at a mass-market colour video adaptor. Still more colours and higher resolution than EGA. Until recently the most popular standard on new machines, though SVGA has probably overtaken it now.

video card

See adaptor.

virus

A program that secretly installs itself in a PC and tampers with the system so that it runs automatically. The virus makes copies of itself and thereby spreads to other PCs, normally via floppy disks. Some viruses have no bad effects while others wipe data from disks or do something else destructive. They are produced by 'viropaths': an odd group of people with just enough knowledge but not enough sense.

Because of media hype they are often blamed for trouble they don't cause, though the threat they present demands that suitable precautions be taken to protect against the possibility of infection.

WAN

Wide area network, a network that spreads over several sites. Each site will have a local network system (LAN), and talk to the other systems by means of modem or radio link.

wild cards

Wild cards come in useful when dealing with several files at a time, perhaps searching for them in a directory, or copying, renaming or deleting them.

Rather than handling each one individually, it helps to use the wild cards: '*' and '?', to take the place of parts of the file names. For example, to delete all the files with the extension '.DAT' from a directory, you would use:

```
DEL C:\DIRNAME\*.DAT
```

The asterisk, or 'star' as it's usually called in this context, stands for as many characters in the file name as you want. It takes effect from where it is placed in the name, and goes on up to the full stop. The file extension is not affected by a star in the name itself:

DEL C:\PICTURES\FRED*.PCX

would delete **FRED0001.PCX, FRED0002.PCX** etc, but not **FRED0001.BMP, FRED0001.WMF** etc.

while, with a star in the extension

DEL C:\PICTURES\FRED0001.*

would knock out **FRED0001.PCX, FRED0001.BMP** and **FRED0001.WMF**. So, before you use a command with wild cards, it is always a good idea to test with DIR to see what would be deleted when you used DEL.

The question mark character, '?', stands for only one character at a time. This would make it useful for deleting all the PCX files starting with FRED that were in single figures:

DEL C:\PICTURES\FRED000?.PCX

it wouldn't touch **FRED0010.PCX** and above.

A final example, with both wild cards in action, used here to delete all *Windows* bitmaps (extension .BMP) and *Windows* Metafiles (extension .WMF) from a directory:

DEL C:\PICTURES*.?M?

as recommended before, test this command with:

DIR C:\PICTURES*.?M?

before applying it.

WIMP

Acronym for windows, icons, menus, pointer (or windows, icons, mouse, pull-down menus depending on who you listen to).

It's the general name for easy-to-use systems like *Windows* and GEM where the PC's screen imitates a desktop on which there are folders and pieces of paper.

Items are represented graphically and selected by moving the pointer and clicking the mouse button. Actions are invoked from menus pulled down from a bar at the top of the screen.

Modern WIMPs rarely have the mouse as the sole means of control, but they are generally easier to use with one.

WIN.INI

A file in the WINDOWS directory, set up by *Windows* when it is installed. WIN.INI is a text file, which means that it can be changed using a text editor, such as *Windows* Notepad or DOS Edit. It contains a list of all the fonts you are using in *Windows*, and a great deal more besides. It will do no harm to load it into Notepad to see what's there, but don't change anything unless you know exactly what you're doing!

Winchester

Another name (slang) for a hard disk, named after the Winchester 30-30 rifle. An early IBM hard disk was known as the 30-30 drive because it had 30Mbyte of permanent storage and 30Mbyte of removable storage.

Windows

A program written by Microsoft that runs in concert with MS-DOS to provide a WIMP method of control. It overcomes many of the limitations of MS-DOS.

Windows swap file

See Swap file

word processor

A program used instead of a typewriter, with extra features such as the ability to delete and undelete text, move blocks of it around the document and check the spelling. Only when you're completely happy with your work need you put it on paper with a printer.

WORM

Write Once, Read Many (times). Describes storage devices that the user can record information on but cannot erase or overwrite.

WYSIWYG

Pronounced 'wizzy-wig'. An acronym for 'what you see is what you get'. Refers to programs that accurately represent on the screen the appearance of the final printed output. Most DTP programs as well as a smaller number of word processors are WYSIWYG.

XGA

Extended Graphics Array. IBM's newest video adaptor, intended to supersede VGA, but yet to find its way into the mass clone market. See also SVGA.

XMS

Extended memory. See Expanded / extended Memory.

XT

Extra technology, an IBM model designation now generally accepted to mean any PC with an 8088 or 8086 CPU.

Zapf Dingbats

A typeface, designed by Hermann Zapf, that is composed of symbols such as arrows, stars, ticks and crosses. See also font.

zp file

A file generated by the utility program PKzip. See file compression.

APPENDIX

A

ANSI Codes for use in *Windows*

There will come a time when you need to use characters beyond those shown on the 'QWERTY' key caps: the 'é' possibly, or maybe the 'ö' or 'ü'.

All the available characters are listed here with the American National Standards Institute code numbers that make them accessible from the keyboard. This is done by setting Num Lock on, holding down the Alt key, typing the corresponding code number on the key pad then releasing the Alt key (type the whole number, including leading zeros).

Characters 000 to 031 do not print.

By the way, the characters have all been given one-word names. So when you see the ™ symbol described as 'trademarkserif', it's not a typographical error!

ANSI code	Character	Name	ANSI code	Character	Name
000		null	032		space
001		soh	033	!	exclam
002		stx	034	"	quotedbl
003		etx	035	#	numbersign
004		eot	036	$	dollar
005		enq	037	%	percent
006		ack	038	&	ampersand
007		bell (beep)	039	'	quotesingle
008		backspace	040	(	parenleft
009		tab	041	)	parenright
010		line feed	042	*	asterisk
011		home	043	+	plus
012		form feed	044	,	comma
013		carriage return (enter)	045	-	hyphen
014		so	046	.	period
015		si	047	/	slash
016		dle	048	0	zero
017		dc1	049	1	one
018		dc2	050	2	two
019		dc3	051	3	three
020		dc4	052	4	four
021		nak	053	5	five
022		syn	054	6	six
023		etb	055	7	seven
024		can	056	8	eight
025		em	057	9	nine
026		sub	058	:	colon
027		escape	059	;	semicolon
028		cursor right	060	<	less
029		cursor left	061	=	equal
030		cursor up	062	>	more
031		cursor down	063	?	question

ANSI code	Character	Name	ANSI code	Character	Name
064	@	at	096	`	grave
065	A	A	097	a	a
066	B	B	098	b	b
067	C	C	099	c	c
068	D	D	0100	d	d
069	E	E	0101	e	e
070	F	F	0102	f	f
071	G	G	0103	g	g
072	H	H	0104	h	h
073	I	I	0105	i	i
074	J	J	0106	j	j
075	K	K	0107	k	k
076	L	L	0108	l	l
077	M	M	0109	m	m
078	N	N	0110	n	n
079	O	O	0111	o	o
080	P	P	0112	p	p
081	Q	Q	0113	q	q
082	R	R	0114	r	r
083	S	S	0115	s	s
084	T	T	0116	t	t
085	U	U	0117	u	u
086	V	V	0118	v	v
087	W	W	0119	w	w
088	X	X	0120	x	x
089	Y	Y	0121	y	y
090	Z	Z	0122	z	z
091	[	bracketleft	0123	{	braceleft
092	\	backslash	0124	|	bar
093	]	bracketright	0125	}	braceright
094	^	asciicircum	0126	~	asciitilde
095	_	underscore	0127		not used by *Windows*

ANSI code	Character	Name	ANSI code	Character	Name
0128		not used by *Windows*	0160		not used by *Windows*
0129		not used by *Windows*	0161	¡	exclamdown
0130	‚	quotesinglbase	0162	¢	cent
0131	ƒ	florin	0163	£	sterling
0132	„	quotedblbase	0164	¤	currency
0133	…	ellipsis	0165	¥	yen
0134	†	dagger	0166	¦	pipe
0135	‡	daggerdbl	0167	§	section
0136	ˆ	circumflex	0168	¨	dieresis
0137	‰	perthousand	0169	©	copyrightserif
0138	Š	Scaron	0170	ª	ordfeminine
0139	‹	guilsingleft	0171	«	guillemotleft
0140	Œ	OE (diphthong)	0172	¬	logicalnot
0141		not used by *Windows*	0173	-	minus
0142		not used by *Windows*	0174	®	registerserif
0143		not used by *Windows*	0175	¯	macron
0144		not used by *Windows*	0176	°	ring
0145	‘	quoteleft	0177	±	plusminus
0146	’	quoteright	0178	²	(superior 2)
0147	“	quotedblleft	0179	³	(superior 3)
0148	”	quotedblright	0180	´	acute
0149	•	bullet	0181	µ	mu
0150	–	endash	0182	¶	paragraph
0151	—	emdash	0183	·	periodcentred
0152	˜	tilde	0184	¸	cedilla
0153	™	trademarkserif	0185	¹	(superior 1)
0154	š	scaron	0186	º	ordmasculine
0155	›	guilsingright	0187	»	guillemotright
0156	œ	oe (diphthong)	0188	¼	(quarter)
0157		not used by *Windows*	0189	½	(half)
0158		not used by *Windows*	0190	¾	(three-quarters)
0159	Ÿ	Ydieresis	0191	¿	questiondown

ANSI code	Character	Name	ANSI code	Character	Name
0192	À	Agrave	0224	à	agrave
0193	Á	Aacute	0225	á	agrave
0194	Â	Acircumflex	0226	â	acircumflex
0195	Ã	Atilde	0227	ã	atilde
0196	Ä	Adieresis	0228	ä	adieresis
0197	Å	Aring	0229	å	aring
0198	Æ	AE (diphthong)	0230	æ	ae (diphthong)
0199	Ç	Ccedilla	0231	ç	ccedilla
0200	È	Egrave	0232	è	egrave
0201	É	Eacute	0233	é	eacute
0202	Ê	Ecircumflex	0234	ê	ecircumflex
0203	Ë	Edieresis	0235	ë	edieresis
0204	Ì	Igrave	0236	ì	igrave
0205	Í	Iacute	0237	í	iacute
0206	Î	Icircumflex	0238	î	icircumflex
0207	Ï	Idieresis	0239	ï	idieresis
0208	Đ	Eth	0240	ð	eth
0209	Ñ	Ntilde	0241	ñ	ntilde
0210	Ò	Ograve	0242	ò	ograve
0211	Ó	Oacute	0243	ó	oacute
0212	Ô	Ocircumflex	0244	ô	ocircumflex
0213	Õ	Otilde	0245	õ	otilde
0214	Ö	Odieresis	0246	ö	odieresis
0215	×	(multiply)	0247	÷	(divide)
0216	Ø	Oslash	0248	ø	oslash
0217	Ù	Ugrave	0249	ù	ugrave
0218	Ú	Uacute	0250	ú	uacute
0219	Û	Ucircumflex	0251	û	ucircumflex
0220	Ü	Udieresis	0252	ü	udieresis
0221	Ý	Ygrave	0253	ý	yacute
0222	Þ	Thorn	0254	þ	thorn
0223	ß	germandbls	0255	ÿ	ydieresis

APPENDIX

B

ASCII Codes for use in DOS

(See Appendix A for* ANSI *Codes for use in Windows)

Characters 179 to 218 are used for drawing single and double line boxes to accompany DOS text, see page 303 for examples.

All the available characters are listed here with the American Standard Code for Information Interchange (ASCII) code numbers that make them accessible from the keyboard. This is done by holding down the Alt key, typing the correspon-ding code number on the key pad then releasing the Alt key.

Characters 000 to 031 do not print.

ASCII code	Character	Name	ASCII code	Character	Name
000		null	032		space
001		soh	033	!	exclam
002		stx	034	"	quotedbl
003		etx	035	#	numbersign
004		eot	036	$	dollar
005		enq	037	%	percent
006		ack	038	&	ampersand
007		bell (beep)	039	'	quotesingle
008		backspace	040	(	parenleft
009		tab	041	)	parenright
010		line feed	042	*	asterisk
011		home	043	+	plus
012		form feed	044	,	comma
013		carriage return (enter)	045	-	hyphen
014		so	046	.	period
015		si	047	/	slash
016		dle	048	0	zero
017		dc1	049	1	one
018		dc2	050	2	two
019		dc3	051	3	three
020		dc4	052	4	four
021		nak	053	5	five
022		syn	054	6	six
023		etb	055	7	seven
024		can	056	8	eight
025		em	057	9	nine
026		sub	058	:	colon
027		escape	059	;	semicolon
028		cursor right	060	<	less
029		cursor left	061	=	equal
030		cursor up	062	>	more
031		cursor down	063	?	question

ASCII code	Char-acter	Name	ASCII code	Char-acter	Name
064	@	at	096	'	grave
065	A	A	097	a	a
066	B	B	098	b	b
067	C	C	099	c	c
068	D	D	100	d	d
069	E	E	101	e	e
070	F	F	102	f	f
071	G	G	103	g	g
072	H	H	104	h	h
073	I	I	105	i	i
074	J	J	106	j	j
075	K	K	107	k	k
076	L	L	108	l	l
077	M	M	109	m	m
078	N	N	110	n	n
079	O	O	111	o	o
080	P	P	112	p	p
081	Q	Q	113	q	q
082	R	R	114	r	r
083	S	S	115	s	s
084	T	T	116	t	t
085	U	U	117	u	u
086	V	V	118	v	v
087	W	W	119	w	w
088	X	X	120	x	x
089	Y	Y	121	y	y
090	Z	Z	122	z	z
091	[	bracketleft	123	{	braceleft
092	\	backslash	124	|	bar
093	]	bracketright	125	}	braceright
094	^	asciicircum	126	~	asciitilde
095	_	underscore	127	,	quotesinglbase

ASCII code	Character	Name	ASCII code	Character	Name
128	Ç	Ccedilla	160	á	aacute
129	ü	udieresis	161	í	iacute
130	é	eacute	162	ó	oacute
131	â	acircumflex	163	ú	uacute
132	ä	adieresis	164	ñ	ntilde
133	à	agrave	165	Ñ	Ntilde
134	å	aring	166	ª	ordfeminine
135	ç	ccedilla	167	º	ordmasculine
136	ê	ecircumflex	168	¿	questiondown
137	ë	edieresis	169	⌐	
138	è	egrave	170	¬	logicalnot
139	ï	idieresis	171	½	(half)
140	î	icircumflex	172	¼	(quarter)
141	ì	igrave	173	¡	exclamdown
142	Ä	Adieresis	174	«	guillemotleft
143	Å	Aring	175	»	guillemotright
144	É	Eacute	176	░	
145	æ	ae (diphthong)	177	▒	
146	Æ	AE (diphthong)	178	▓	
147	ô	ocircumflex	179	│	
148	ö	odieresis	180	┤	
149	ò	ograve	181	╡	
150	û	ucircumflex	182	╢	
151	ù	ugrave	183	╖	
152	ÿ	ydieresis	184	╕	
153	Ö	Odieresis	185	╣	
154	Ü	Udieresis	186	║	
155	¢	cent	187	╗	
156	£	sterling	188	╝	
157	¥	yen	189	╜	
158	Pt	peseta	190	╛	
159	ƒ	florin	191	┐	

ASCII code	Char-acter	Name	ASCII code	Char-acter	Name
192	└		224	α	alpha
193	┴		225	β	beta
194	┬		226	Γ	Gamma
195	├		227	π	pi
196	─		228	Σ	Sigma
197	┼		229	σ	sigma
198	╞		230	μ	mu
199	╟		231	τ	tau
200	╚		232	Φ	Phi
201	╔		233	θ	theta
202	╩		234	Ω	Omega
203	╦		235	δ	delta
204	╠		236	∝	infinity
205	═		237	Ø	Oslash
206	╬		238	∈	element
207	╧		239	∩	intersection
208	╨		240	≡	equivalence
209	╤		241	±	plusminus
210	╥		242	≥	greaterequal
211	╙		243	≤	lessequal
212	╘		244	⌠	integraltp
213	╒		245	⌡	integralbt
214	╓		246	÷	divide
215	╫		247	≈	(approximately equal)
216	╪		248	°	ring
217	┘		249	•	bullet
218	┌		250	·	periodcentred, dotmath
219	█		251	√	radical
220	▄		252	η	eta
221	▌		253	^{2}	(superior 2)
222	▐		254	■	(square bullet)
223	▀		255		(blank)

Using the ASCII code to draw boxes

There could come a time when you needed to revert to the pre-*Windows* era and create boxes for use on the DOS screen. A typical application would be a box with the word 'MENU' typed in the centre, and a list of selections underneath it.

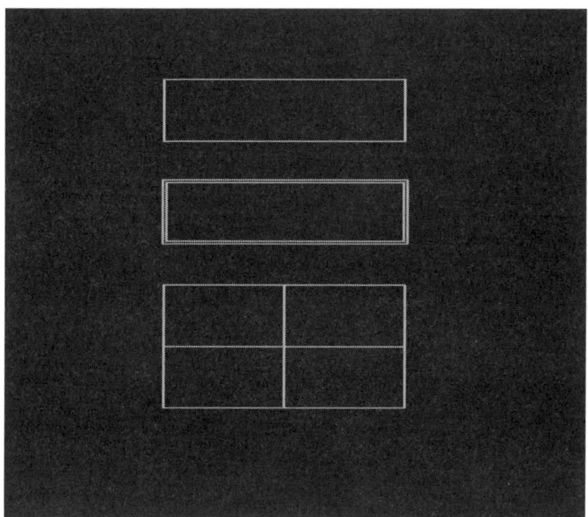

Drawing the boxes with a batch file

The three different types of box in the screen shot above were 'drawn' using ASCII characters. They were typed in a batch file that was created in the DOS Edit utility by typing **`EDIT DOSBOXES.BAT`** at the DOS prompt, and pressing Return. When completed, it was run by typing DOSBOXES and pressing return

The first line of the file should be **`@ECHO OFF`**, so that the instructions themselves are not printed. Each subsequent line of the batch file starts with the word **`ECHO`** (meaning 'print'), followed by a number of spaces so that the boxes go to the centre of the screen. Then, the crucial bit, each character is keyed in by holding down Alt, typing the ASCII code number on the keypad, then releasing the Alt key.

Here follow the character codes for every conceivable single and double line box that can be created in DOS.

ASCII Characters for a single line box

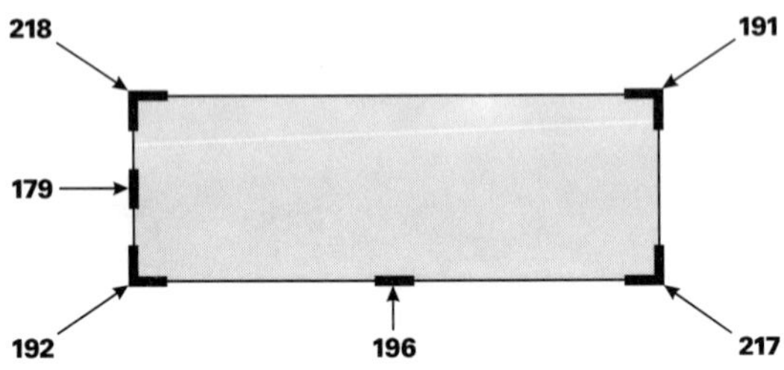

ASCII Characters for a double line box

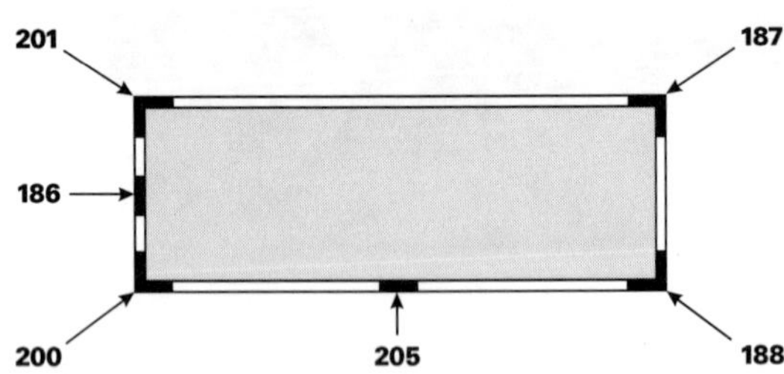

ASCII Characters for multiple single line boxes

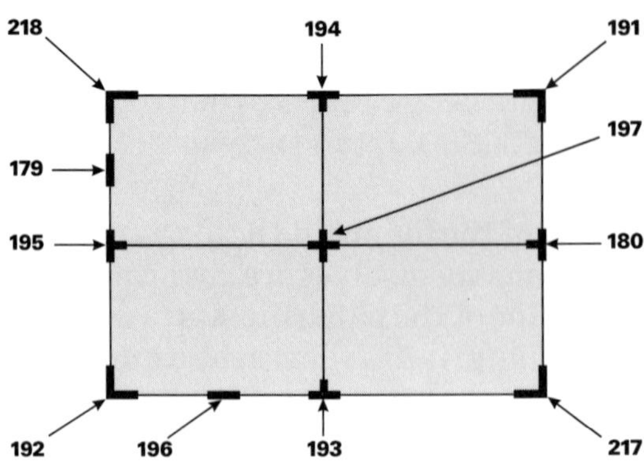

ASCII Characters for multiple double line boxes

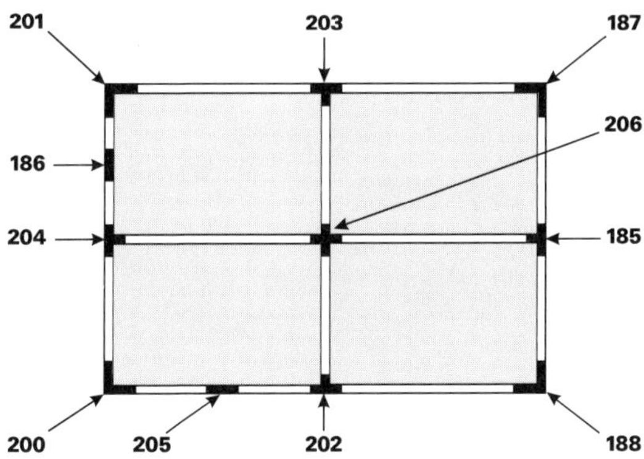

ASCII Characters for combined multiple single and double line boxes

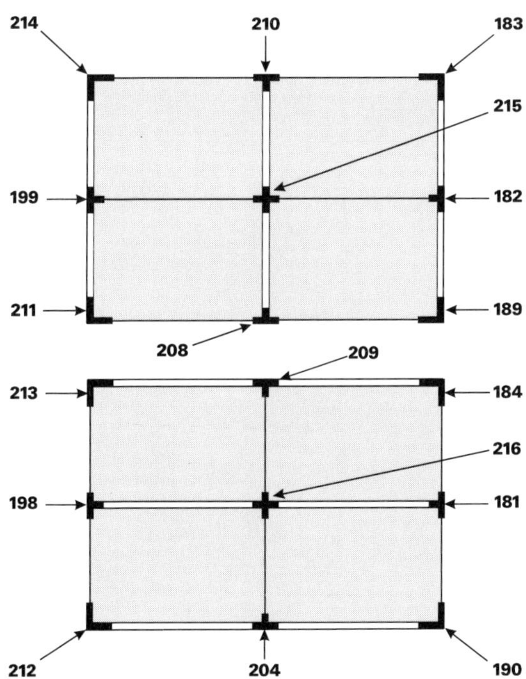

INDEX

Indexed words and phrases will normally lead to some form of enlightenment, rather than just an occurrence of the word or phrase.

Subjects that have been covered more fully have their page numbers shown in **bold**.

Index

@echo off ... 69
386 enhanced mode ... 87, 257
80286, 286 ... 257
80386, 386 ... 257
8086, 8088 ... 257
8087, 80287, 80387, i487SX ... 257

A

abandon ... 219
accented characters ... 120, 123
access time ... 257
adaptor ... 257
adding pictures to Cardfile ... 176
alignment ... 214
alphanumeric ... 174
anchored frames ... 220
ANSI ... 257
ANSI code ... **291–296**
ANSI.SYS ... 257
Apple Macintosh ... 257
application ... 258
archive file attribute ... 68
archiving ... 258
arguments ... 248, 250
array variables ... 242
ASCII ... 223, 258
ASCII code ... 4, **297–305**
assembler ... 258
AT ... 258
attributes ... 215, 216
attributes, file ... **68**
attributes, text ... 216, 224
AUTOEXEC.BAT ... 66, 117, 258

B

back up ... 258
backslash ... 95, 112
BASIC ... 259
batch files ... 67, 259
baud ... 259
BBS (Bulletin Board System) ... 259
benchmark ... 259
Bernoulli drive ... 259
binary arithmetic ... **6–8**
BIOS ... 259
bit ... 8
bitmap ... 260
bitmapped graphics ... 222
bold ... 216
bold italic ... 216
Boolean Logic ... 189
boot ... 260
booting ... 79
bottom up ... 175
browse ... 182
BubbleJet ... 260
budgeting ... 199–202
bureau ... 212
bus ... 260
byte ... 8, 260

C

cache (disk) ... 260
CAD ... 261
calculations ... 198
calculator ... 42
calendar ... 42
capitalisation ... 217
card index system ... 175
Cardfile
- adding pictures ... 176
- alphanumeric order ... 181
- bringing a card to the front ... 181
- browsing ... 182
- duplicating cards ... 178
- Edit menu ... 180
- extracting information ... 182
- finding records ... 176

index field ... 174, 182
index line ... 180
Index window ... 180
listing records ... 182
records ... 174
saving the file ... 178
searching ... 177, 182
setting up ... 177
short-cut keys ... 179
sorted records ... 175

carriage return / line feed ... 108
CD-ROM ... 261
cell ... 261
cell contents ... 199
centred text ... 214
Centronics ... 261
CGA ... 261
character ... 261
character map ... 121–122
character menu ... 134
character sets ... 125
chip ... 261
clear screen command (CLS) ... 240
clip-art ... 206
clipboard ... 261
clock ... 38
clock speed ... 262
clone ... 262
CMOS ... 262
code pages ... 125
coffee machine ... 189
colour palettes ... 263
colour separation ... 212
column width ... 203
COM file ... 262
command line ... 263
command switch ... 55
comms ... 263
compatible ... 262
compile ... 251
computer users
designers ... 14
professional firms ... 16
retired people ... 15
school teachers ... 15
small businesses ... 14
students ... 15
writers ... 14

conditional statement ... 246
conditional text and graphics ... 221
CONFIG.SYS ... 66, 117, 262
contents list ... 219
contiguous file ... 263
Control panel ... 36
controller ... 262
conventional memory ... 85, 263
coprocessor ... 263
CorelDRAW! ... 176, 222
country setting for UK ... 117
CPU ... 263
crash ... 264
cross references ... 218
Ctrl + Alt + Del ... 114
Ctrl + C ... 113
cursor ... 264
cut and paste ... 264

D

daisywheel printer ... 264
DAT ... 264
data ... 264
database ... 265
Between ... 190
browse ... 185
BROWSE NOMODIFY ... 194
dBase language ... 184
DISTINCT ... 193
Do Query ... 191
Exactly Like ... 189
field name ... 188
fields ... 183
FROM ... 193
In ... 190
index field ... 174, 183
INTO CURSOR QUERY ... 193
Less Than ... 189
Like ... 189
More Than ... 189
program code sample ... 192
programming ... 192

- programs 184
- queries 183
- Query window 192
- record 174
- RQBE (Relational Query By Example) 186
- RQBE window 187
- Rushmore 191
- SELECT 193
- selected output 188
- selecting a database 187
- setting up a query **186–191**
- SQL (Structured Query Language) 184
- view SQL 192
- WHERE 193

databases **171–194**
date formats 204
dBase language 184
default 265
delete right to left 102
desktop publishing **209–224**
device driver 265
digitiser pad 265
dimensioning arrays (DIM) 241
Dingbat 265
DIP 266
directories
- directories described **75–79**
- root directory 79
- tree 79

directory 266
disk 266
disk cache 266
disk doubler 266
DOS 266
DOS commands
- BACKUP 49
- CD (change directory) 51
- CLS (clear screen) 52
- COPY 52
- DATE 54
- DEL (delete) 55
- DIR (directory) 55
- DISKCOPY 56
- DOSKEY 56
- EDIT 57
- FIND 58
- FORMAT 58
- MD (make directory) 60
- PATH 61
- PROMPT 62
- RD (remove directory) 63
- RENAME 63
- RESTORE 63
- TIME 64
- TYPE 64

DOS, the operating system **47–71**
dot matrix 266
download 266
DPI 266
DR DOS 267
drive 267
driver 267
DTP **209-224**, 267

E

echo 70
EGA 267
EISA 267
E-mail 267
EMS (expanded memory) 91, 267
enhanced mode 257, 267
environment 268
EXE file 268
expanded memory (EMS) 86, 91, 268
expanded memory manager 268
expansion bus 268
expansion card 269
expansion slots 269
expressions, building 199
extended memory (XMS) 90, 268, 269
extended memory manager 269

F

FDD 269
field 269
file 269
file attributes **68**
file compression 270

File Manager ... 35, 75, 77
files
  extensions ... 77
  file names ... 78
  files described ... **75–79**
  saving ... 78
  suffixes ... 77
  Windows File Manager ... 75, 77
filmsetting ... 270
filmsetting bureau ... 212
find and change ... 217
finding records ... 176
floppy disk ... 11, 270
floppy disk drive ... 23
font ... 270
font angle ... 215
font weight ... 214
footers ... 218
FOR ... NEXT loop ... 249
foreign languages ... 119, 124
format ... 270
formatting characters ... 246
forward slash ... 95
frame anchoring ... 220
FrameMaker ... 210, 221
frames ... 223
full out ... 214

G

graphic formats ... 222
Graphical User Interface (GUI) ... 272
graphics ... 271
graphics accelerator ... 271
graphics tablet ... 271
graphics, importing ... **221–223**
GUI ... 271

H

hard disk ... 11, 271
hardware ... **21–28**, 271
HDD ... 271
headers and footers ... 218
Hercules ... 271
hexadecimal ... 271
hidden cells ... 203
hidden file attribute ... 68
hiding data ... 205
high level language ... 237
high memory ... 85, 272
HIMEM.SYS ... 85
HMA (High Memory Area) ... 85, 272
hyphenation ... 217
hyphenation dictionary ... 217

I

i486 ... 257
IBM ... 272
IC ... 272
icon ... **272**
IDE ... 272
IF ... THEN ... ELSE Statement ... 246
importing graphics ... **221–223**
importing text ... **223–224**
indents ... 214
index field ... 174
indexing ... 219
indicator lights ... 99
ink-jet ... 272
integer ... 272
integrated package ... 273
interactivity ... 227
interface ... 273
interleave factor ... 273
inter-line spacing ... 214
International icon ... 116
interrupts ... 70
ISA ... 273
italics ... 215, 216

J

justified ... 214

K

keep with next 215
kerning 216
key caps 115
keyboard **95–127**
keyboard setting for UK 117
keyboard, logical 115
keyboard, physical 115
keys
  Alt (Alternative) keys 114
  Asterisk 100
  Backslash 111
  Backspace (delete right to left) 102
  Break 98
  Caps lock 110
  Circumflex 100
  Ctrl (Control) keys 113
  Cursor keys 114
  Delete (left to right) 108
  End 109
  Escape 96
  Function keys 96
  Greater Than 113
  Less Than 112
  Logical Not / Grave Accent / Bar 99
  Page down 109
  Pause 98
  Pipe (broken bar) 111
  Print Screen 97
  Scroll Lock 98
  Shift keys 110
  System Request 97
  Underline 101
Kilobyte 9

L

LAN 273
language 273
laser printer 273
leading 214
LEFT$ function 248
LEN function 248
LIM EMS 273
local bus 273
LOCATE statement 250
logical keyboard 115
loose line 216
Lotus *1-2-3* **197–206**
low ASCII 224
low level language 237
LPRINT statement 245

M

machine code 274
Macintosh 257
macro 274
macro recorder 43
mail merge 274
maths coprocessor 274
MCA 275
MDA 275
Megabyte 9
memory **83–91**, 275
  computer vs calculator 3
  random access 86
  volatile 10
memory cache 275
memory manager 85
MFM 275
MID$ Function 248
MIDI 275
modem 27, 275
monitor 10
motherboard 17, 87, 275
mouse 276
MPC 276
MS-DOS 276
multimedia **227–233**, 276
multimedia equipment 228
multitasking 276
music 232

N

network 276
non-printing keys 95
notepad 43

number formats 203
numeric variables 241, 242
nybble 9

O

oblique (italic) 215
OCR (Optical Character Recognition) 25
operating system 276
optical character recognition (OCR) 25, 277
optical disk 277
OS/2 277
overline 216

P

page numbers 218
Paintbrush 40
paragraph catalogue 214
paragraph formatting 213
paragraph spacing 214
paragraph style 213
paragraph tag 213, 221
parallel port 17, 277
partition 277
Pascal 277
path 277
PC 278
PCW 278
PCX 278
pen plotter 278
Pentium 278
performance processing 198
peripheral 278
peripheral devices 17
permanent swap file 88
photosetting 278
physical keyboard 115
pick list 278
pipe 111, 278
pixel 278
plain ASCII 223
planning 198
plotter 278
port 279
  parallel 17
  serial 17
  video 17
portable PC 279
PostScript 279
Print manager 38
PRINT statement 245
print to a file 279
PRINT USING statement 245
printers 24, 279
program 279
programming **237–251**
programming languages 237
programs & data **12–13**
projections 198

Q

QFIND 55
QuarkXPress 212
QuickBASIC **237–251**
QWERTY keys 95

R

RAM 280
random access file 90
random access memory **86–89**
ranged left 214
ranged right 214
readability 217
read-only file attribute 68
read-only memory **89**
real time 280
re-boot 280
record 174, 280
redirecting command input & output 280
reference works 233
reserved words 242
resolution 280
revert to previous 219
RIGHT$ function 248
RISC 280
RLL 281
ROM (Read-Only Memory) 89, 281

ROM BIOS 84, 89
roman 216
roman font 215
root directory 79, 281
row height 203
RQBE (Relational Query By Example) 186
RS232 281
RTFM 71
running headers and footers 218

S

saving files **78**
saving your work 218
scanner 25, 281
screen 10
screen mode 281
screen saver 281
screen shots 282
scroll 98
scroll bars 282
SCSI 282
search and replace 217
searching 177
sector 282
segmented hypergraphics 282
SELECT CASE statement 247
sequential file 90
serial port 17, 283
setting up a Cardfile 177
setting up the computer 65
shadow RAM 283
shift lock 110
short-cut keys 179, 283
SIM/SIMM 283
SIP 283
software 284
sorting records 175
sound card 284
spell checking 217
spreadsheets **197–206**, 284
SQL (Structured Query Language) 184
start at top of page 215
strike-through 216
string variables 241, 242
subscript 216
superscript 216
SVGA 284
swap files 87, 284
switch 55
SX chips 284
system disk 284
system file attribute 68
system files 284
system unit 285

T

tab setting 215
table of contents 219
tables 220
tape streamer 26, 285
teaching aids 233
templates 221
temporary swap file 88
Terminal 41
text
    attributes 203, 215, 216
    centred 214
    conditional 221
    editor 223
    formatting 215–217, 224
    full out 214
    markers 219
    ranged right 214
text attributes 285
text mode 285
third party product 285
time formats 204
toner 285
toolkit 286
top down 175
track 286
tracker ball 286
tracking 216
transfer rate 286
TSR 286
Turing, Alan 228
typeface 286
typesetting 286

U

UK, US and other keyboards 115
underlining 101, 216
undo 144
undo and redo 219
uninterruptible power supply 26
upload 287
upper memory 287
UPS 26

V

V20/V30 287
V22, V23 etc 287
VAL function 244
variables 220, 241
VDU 287
vector graphics 222, 287
VESA 288
VGA 288
video card 288
video port 17
virtual memory 87, 288
virus 288
visual display unit 10

W

WAN 288
what if 198
wild card 288
WIMP 289
WIN.INI 289
Winchester 290
Windows **31–43**, 290
- Calculator 42
- Calendar 42
- Cardfile 43
- Character map 40
- Clock 38
- Control panel 36
- File Manager 35, 75, 77
- Macro recorder 43
- Notepad 43
- Paintbrush 40
- Print manager 38
- saving files **78**
- Terminal 41
- Write 40

Windows Cardfile **173–182**
Windows swap file 290
word breaks 217
word processing **131–167**
- adding pictures 145
- changing the typeface 133
- cut and paste 142
- editing text 139
- embedded graphics 146
- importing graphics 145
- linked graphics 148
- paragraph formatting 152
- paragraph menu 154
- paragraph styles 163
- printer timeout 160
- printing 156
- saving your work 137
- scroll bars 141
- selecting text 133
- setting up the printer 156
- short cut keys 136
- wipe and type 139

word processor 223, 224, 290
worksheet 197, 198
WORM 290
WYSIWYG 290

X

XGA 290
XMS (extended memory) 90, 290
XT 290

Z

Zapf Dingbats 290
zip file 290

Other titles from FUTURE PUBLISHING

Copies of the following books are available direct from

Future Publishing Limited,
Freepost (BS4900)
Somerton,
Somerset, TA11 6BR.

Alternatively they are available in all good bookshops. Retailers can order copies from our distributors, Computer Bookshops, on 021 706 1250

Books currently in print from Future, Computing Books

All you need to know imprint

The overall aim of the imprint is to cover the software features most users use most of the time, enabling the reader to get up and running as quickly as possible.

The books assume a familiarity with the *Windows* environment, and all are written with a series of helpful icons highlighting important information. They are written with a walk-through tutorial style, and make extensive use of illustrations and screen grabs.

All books will be suitable for Beginners and Intermediate users

☐ **All you Need to Know about WordPerfect 6.0a for Windows**
by Stephen Copestake
ISBN 1 85870 056 6
Pages 320
Publication Date November 1994
Ord no FBB 0566

Covers version 6.0 with the added refinements included in the interim release 6.0a. As well as providing a complete insight into WordPerfect 6.0 for Windows, the book provides a quick check list of all the new features for those upgrading from previous versions.

☐ **All you Need to Know about Excel 5.0 for Windows**
by Stephen Copestake
ISBN 1 85870 057 4
Pages 320
Publication Date November 1994
Ord no FBB 0574

This book takes a jargon-free look at Excel 5.0 for Windows – it covers the features which most users use, most of the time. Icons draw your attention to useful hints, tips and key techniques, while the tutorial style and liberal use of illustrations lets you gain a thorough understanding of the software in the shortest possible time.

☐ **All you Need to Know about Lotus 1-2-3 (versions 4.0 & 5.0) for Windows**
by Ian Sinclair
ISBN 1 85870 058 2
Pages 300
Publication Date October 1994
Ord no 0582

The book covers all the main elements of this leading spreadsheet package including its often unexploited data handling capabilities. In order to keep you up to date with all the latest developments the book includes all the refinements of the latest release, version 5.0.

☐ **All you Need to Know about CD-ROM**
by Damien Noonan
ISBN 1 85870 059 0
Dimensions 235mm x 185mm
Pages 320
Publication Date November 1994
Ord no FBB 0590

From the publishers of CD-ROM Today magazine, written by the launch editor, Damien Noonan. CD ROM has finally emerged as the way forward for computing, this book provides a comprehensive insight into the technology and its applications.

☐ **All you Need to Know about the INTERNET**
by Davey Winder
ISBN 1 85870 064 7
Pages 320
Publication Date October 1994
Ord no FBB 0647

A comprehensive guide to exploring the network written by the UK's leading communications expert Davey Winder. Whether you are a beginner or one of the original netsurfers this book will unlock the 'information super-highway'.

Money Management imprint -

☐ **Money Management with Quicken 6.0 for DOS**
by Jean Miles
ISBN 1 85870 012 4
Trim 205mm x 120mm
Price £8.95
Pages 230
Ord no. FBB0124

Now into its third print run the book has enjoyed success exceeded only by the software sales!! and is every bit a best seller. It serves as a comprehensive guide to all the facilities of Intuit's DOS version of this leading finance package.

☐ **Money Management with Quicken 3.0 for Windows**
by Jean Miles (May 1994)
ISBN 1 85870 017 5
Trim 220mm x 150mm
Price £12.95
Pages 280
Ord no FBB0175

The second Quicken book from the pen of Jean Miles, this book has the Official backing of the software publishers, Intuit Software. A comprehensive look at this latest release of Quicken. This book is already established on the path to best seller status.

☐ **Money Management with Sage Moneywise 2.0 for Windows**
by Jean Miles (October 1994)
ISBN 1 85870 043 4
Trim 220mm x 150mm
Price £12.95
Pages 250
Ord no FBB 0434

The third Money Management book. Covers all the features of SageSoft's entry level package Moneywise. As with all the Money Management books it has the full endorsement of the software developers.

☐ **Money Management with Microsoft Money 3.0 for Windows**
by Andrew Marlow (October 1994)
ISBN 1 85870 044 2
Trim 220mm x 150mm
Price £12.95
Pages 280
Ord no FBB 0442

The fourth book of the imprint, written for Microsoft's latest version of their personal accounting package, Money 3.0.

Professional imprint -

☐ **The Complete Desktop Publishing Guidebook**
by Simon Williams & Geoffrey Oakshott (October 1994)
ISBN 1 85870 003 5
Trim 235mm x 185mm
Price £24.95
Pages 470
Ord no. FBB 0035

A thorough insight into desktop publishing and design. This book provides all the advise and guidance on how to use dtp as an effective business tool. From the Publishers of PC Plus magazine.

☐ **Successful Business Accounting with Sage Sterling +2 Version 2**
by Andrew Marlow (June 1994)
ISBN 1 85870 013 2
Trim 235mm x 185mm
Price £24.95
Pages 300
Ord no FBB0132

A comprehensive look at the Sage +2 range of business products, comes with a free copy of the Bank Interest Calculator software direct from Sage UK, and over 20 business templates produced by the Author.

☐ **The Complete Access Workbook**
by Arthur Tennick (May 1994)
ISBN 1 85870 011 6
Trim 223mm x 190mm
Price £17.95
Pages 250
Ord no FBB 0116

A comprehensive database package requires something similar from a book. The Complete Access Workbook provides something for every type of user whether an absolute beginner or a professional programmer. It will guide you through the process of designing your database.

☐ **The Modem and Communications Guidebook**
by Sue Schofield
(November 1993)
ISBN 1 85870 000 0
Trim 235mm x 185mm
Price £19.95
Pages 350
Ord no. FBB0000

Written and researched in the UK, this book makes communications easy to learn, productive and trouble-free. Clear explanations of all the basic ideas without the unnecessary jargon, make the process of going on-line painless and straightforward. This book has very quickly established itself as a best seller. Book includes free comms software and CIX subscription.

☐ **Windows 3.1 HelpScreen**
by Arthur Tennick (November 1993)
ISBN 1 85870 001 9
Trim 223mm x 190mm
Price £19.95
Pages 350
Ord no. FBB0019

Provides the straight forward answers to all the questions you might have about Windows - this book is for those with a basic familiarity with Windows but who wish to progress and quickly build their expertise. With a wealth of Windows books available it is reassuring to know you have the hallmark of authority from the UK's leading PC magazine PC Plus.

☐ **The PC Plus HelpScreen Collection**
by Barry Thomas (October 1993)
ISBN 1 85870 002 7
Trim 240mm x 205mm
Price £14.95 (includes disk)
Pages 150
Ord no FBB 0027

A compilation of the last two years of HelpScreen pages within PC Plus. All material has been edited and rewritten to provide accessible time saving information.

☐ **The Software Guide (March 1994)**
Trim 240mm x170mm
Price £24.95
Pages 450
Ord no PSG003

The authoritative new directory of IBM-compatible PC software, this book comes to you from the publishers of the Britain's best selling PC magazine, PC Plus. It provides details of more than 3000 software products including hardware requirements, price and feature analysis.

Cheques and Postal orders should be made payable to Future Publishing Limited and sent with a copy of any of these coupons to -

Future Publishing Limited,
Freepost (BS4900)
Somerton,
Somerset,
TA11 6BR.

Please note that all prices for published books and pre-publication orders are list price but as a service to our current readers are fully inclusive of all postage and packing.